"There are no big words, just small words strung together from roots!"

According to the *New York Times*, your chances for success are directly related to the size of your vocabulary. *Vocabulary Dynamics* enables you to radically increase your vocabulary skills, doubling or tripling your word power in 30 to 60 days. This is the only book that explores word roots and word history as a basis for connecting word meanings to life experience.

"For the well-educated, this book's 'why' explanations make fascinating reading. For those who need more help, the book will solve a multitude of problems—from poor spelling to mispronunciation. I can't imagine an English teacher anywhere who wouldn't keep this book handy for students with language difficulties and questions."
—**Dianna Booher, communications consultant, author of *Clean Up Your Act: Effective Ways to Organize Paperwork—and Get It Out of Your Life, The Confident Communicator,* and many other books**

"*Vocabulary Dynamics* turns the task of learning words into pure fun. Read this book and not only will you learn thousands of useful words: you'll never forget them. Gwen Harrison skillfully uses word-roots and word histories to etch whole families of words into the reader's mind. The result is a delightful method to expand one's vocabulary."
—**Irwin Berent and Rod Evans, authors of *The Right Words***

VOCABULARY
DYNAMICS

GWEN HARRISON

WARNER BOOKS

A Time Warner Company

WARNER BOOKS EDITION

Copyright © 1992 by Gwen Harrison
All rights reserved.

Cover design by Don Puckey

Warner Books, Inc.
1271 Avenue of the Americas
New York, NY 10020
Visit our web site at
http://pathfinder.com/twep

W A Time Warner Company

Printed in the United States of America

First Printing: October, 1992

10 9 8 7 6 5

To

the memory of my son Tony, whose love for
the written word helped shape his beautiful spirit

my daughter Glenda for uncounted hours
so generously contributed to careful typing
of the manuscript

my daughter Susan for her gentle
understanding and loving encouragement

my son Tim for his inspiring example of
stubborn persistence in reaching his goals

my mother Helen, whose life defines *Love*,
for her influence on all of us

and

the staffs of Foster Youth Services and
Jane Lathrop School, who provided not only the
warmth of their support, but my first vocabulary
students—Joseph, Jennifer, Shawn, Shane,
Sandy, and Jose.

Contents

Introduction
Becoming Word-Wise

Words give you power. They are the tools with which you think, communicate, and learn. The more words you know, the better you think, communicate, and absorb knowledge—not just about English, but about everything that is important to you.

Words enhance your ability to survive. If you found yourself in a foreign country with no knowledge of the language and could not make yourself understood, survival would be difficult. But as you learned more of that language, living there would become easier. The same is true of living in your own country. The more limited your vocabulary is, the harder survival is. And certainly you want more than just to survive. You want to succeed at your goals. It is an indisputable fact that your chances for success increase with the size of your vocabulary.

Building a large vocabulary doesn't require you to spend tedious hours memorizing definitions. It does require that you become word-conscious, that you have curiosity about words, not only about their meanings but about their origins. The study of word origins is called etymology (et-a-MOL-a-jee). Etymology is a method of learning words by associating them with their histories. When you learn the story that goes with a word, it is almost impossible to forget the word's definition.

Etymology also teaches the origins of word parts—roots, prefixes, and suffixes—so that long words that seem hard to understand can be easily learned or figured out. For example, the word *philology* (fil-OL-o-jee) comes from two Greek words, *philos*, which means "loving," and *logos*, meaning "word." The basic definition of *philology*, then, is "loving words." From that simple definition it is easy to remember its broader definition, which is the scientific study of the development of words and languages.

Language began with the need to communicate such basic human needs and activities as hunting, eating, sleeping, coming and going, leading and following, pushing and pulling. The majority of modern English words—even long words with very abstract meanings—were derived from small Latin or Greek words that indicated the most ordinary activities, objects, and experiences. These small words became the roots of larger, more complex words. This book shows you how simple it is to learn big words by knowing their roots, and that learning one root can be the key that unlocks the meaning of many words. This method not only will greatly expand your vocabulary, but your spelling will improve. As you learn words by their parts—roots, prefixes, and suffixes—you will find how easy each part is to spell, so that long words will be no more difficult than short ones.

Chapter 20 is devoted to the study of words that came from Greek and Roman mythology. These words are presented along with the myths with which they are associated. Reading the stories will help fix their definitions in your mind. Another lesson teaches words that came from ancient philosophies. From that, you will learn some words that describe people today—how they think, how they view life—even though the words originated thousands of years ago.

Each chapter will involve you in practicing certain words—pronouncing them, writing them, and placing them where they belong in the exercises. To make new words a permanent part of your vocabulary, it's important to do the exercises. You must say the words, write them, and practice using them in their proper context if they are to become truly your possessions.

This book is actually intended to do more than help you increase your vocabulary. Its overall purpose is to make you, in a sense, a philologist in your own right, to promote your love of words, because words convey all the knowledge that's ever been discovered, all the exciting ideas ever pondered, and all the great thoughts ever expressed. Words teach you about everything that lies outside your own experience. Acquire a full, rich vocabulary, and you will gain entrance into a wider, more exciting world.

Perhaps the most basic ingredient for effective vocabulary building is abundant curiosity. We need to see words as more than combinations of letters to be defined and memorized.

Note that not every word in each list will be used in the exercises.

1

How Words Work

The purpose of this book is not only to teach you hundreds of words but to show you how words work. In this lesson, you will begin to analyze words—that is, break them down into their elements of roots, prefixes, and suffixes. Roots are the basic building blocks of words; they are the keys that unlock the basic definitions. Prefixes give further clues to definitions. Suffixes tell you mainly whether the words are nouns, verbs, adjectives, or adverbs. With knowledge of how words are built, you can quickly master new words.

It must be emphasized that for vocabulary building, no method can substitute for reading. Reading is extremely important, and many words can be figured out by their connection to the subject. But readers lose interest when they are confronted with long, unfamiliar words that require them to stop to find their meanings in a dictionary in order to make sense of what is being read. This is as frustrating as traveling a muddy road and getting stuck every few feet.

Big words don't have to be roadblocks to reading. When you learn words by their parts—prefixes, roots, and suffixes—you soon realize that there is no such thing as a "big" word. What seems a big word is only a combination of small words with simple meanings.

This method of vocabulary building is called etymology

(et-a-MOL-a-jee). The word *etymology* looks like a big word, but it is actually based on the simple Greek root *etymon*, which means "word origin" or "word root." The suffix *-logy*, or *-ology*, means "knowledge, science or study of." Etymology is the knowledge or study of word roots.

Here is how etymology works: The Latin root *port*, for example, means "carry" or "bear." By combining *port* with prefixes, we get words with various definitions, but each relates in some way to *carry* or *bear*.

Prefix	Root	Word	Basic Meaning
im- in	+ port	= import	carry in
ex- out	+ port	= export	carry out
de- away	+ port	= deport	carry out
trans- across	+ port	= transport	carry across

Suffixes help determine the functions of words—that is, their parts of speech. The suffix *-er*, meaning "one who" (or sometimes "that which"), when added to *port* produces the noun *porter*, meaning "one who carries baggage." The addition of the suffix *-able* forms the adjective *portable*, which describes something that is able to be carried easily. A common suffix that means "the act of" is *-ion* and its other forms *-tion* and *-ation*. This suffix serves to change verbs into nouns, as in *deportation*—the act of deporting.

The chart at right shows an analysis of words based on the root *lev* or its stem *levi*. (A word stem is a root with an added vowel.) This root means "raise," "lift," and also "light" in the sense of weight.

Word	Prefix	Root	Suffix	Definition
lever		*lev-* raise +	*-er*, that which	that which raises; a device for lifting weight
alleviate	*al-* to	+ *levi* light +	*-ate*, make	to make light; lighten a burden; relieve pain or distress
levity		*levi* light +	*-ty*, the quality of	the quality of being light; lack of seriousness
elevate	*e-* outward	+ *lev*, raise +	*-ate*, cause	cause to raise, lift to a higher rank or station
elevator	*e-* up	+ *lev-* raise +	*-at(e)*, cause + *-or*, that which	that which causes something to be raised; a lift or hoist
levitate		*levi* raise +	*(t)ate*, cause	cause to rise; make objects or bodies float in air by supernatural means

Exercise 1.1

Try building some words. Using the list below, combine elements into words that match the definitions that are given. Write the words in the blank spaces on the left. (Answers to all the exercises throughout this book can be found after the last chapter, beginning on p. 357.)

Prefix	Root	Suffix
peri-, around	*bio* life	*-ion*
sym-, together with, same	*graph,* write; draw, *gram* record	*-y*
tele-, far; from a distance	*meter* measure	*-logy,* study, knowledge science of
	micro very small	
	phon, sound *phono* *phone*	
	photo light	
	scope instrument for seeing	
	vis see, sight	

Word	Basic Meaning	Broader Definition
Example:		
phonograph	recorded sound	a device for reproducing recorded sounds
1. _____	sounds made together	a large orchestra; a musical composition for a large orchestra

Word	Basic Meaning	Broader Definition
2. _____	sound from afar	device for transmitting speech or sound from a distance through wire or other channels
3. _____	measure around	the distance around something; outer boundary
4. _____	recorded in light	a picture made by the chemical action of light on film
5. _____	write from afar	device for sending messages from a distance through wire or other channels; also, a message so sent
6. _____	see from afar	transmission of pictures from a distance by means of radio waves
7. _____	instrument for seeing afar	an instrument for making distant objects appear closer
8. _____	instrument for seeing small objects	an instrument for enlarging objects too small to be seen with normal vision

Word	Basic Meaning	Broader Definition
9. _____	instrument for seeing around	an instrument used in submarines or trenches to see objects on the surface

Learning words by their parts not only makes definitions easier to learn, but spelling becomes easier, too. Here are a group of words based on the Greek root **onym**, which means "name." First, practice pronouncing each word before going on to its definition.

You may be surprised at how easy these words are to understand and spell after you analyze them.

synonym, synonymous
(SIN-a-nim, sin-NON-a-mus)

The prefix *syn-* means "same"; the root **onym** means "name." Literally, **synonym** means "same name." Actually, **synonyms** are different words whose meanings are much the same, as in these words: *sick, ill; quick, fast, rapid; little, small.*

Synonymous is an adjective meaning "having the same definition; meaning the same; similar in meaning."

To spell **synonym**, simply join the prefix *syn-* to the root **onym**. The suffix *-ous* is a common suffix used to form adjectives. Added to **synonym**, it forms the adjective **synonymous**.

antonym (ANT-a-nim)

The prefix *ant-* is a shortened form of *anti-*, which means "against; opposite." An **antonym** is the name of an opposite thing, or a word that means the opposite of another word. These word pairs are examples of **antonyms**: *day, night; happy, sad; asleep, awake.*

To spell **antonym**, just join the prefix *ant-* to the root **onym**.

anonym, anonymous
(AN-a-nim, a-NON-a-mus)

The prefix *an-* means "without." **Anonym** means "without name." This word is not as common, however, as its adjective form, **anonymous**, which means "of unknown name; bearing no name." Spell *anonymous* by joining *an-* to **onym** and adding *-ous*.

acronym (AK-ra-nim)

This word comes from the roots **acro**, meaning "high," and **onym**, meaning "name." **Acronyms** are words made by combining the initial letters of a series of words into a word. SALT, for example, is an **acronym** that stands for Strategic Arms Limitation Treaty. **Acronyms** are usually (but not always) formed from capital letters—that is, letters in the upper or higher case. Thus, an **acronym** is, literally, a name made from "high letters."

For this spelling, obviously you must drop one of the *o*'s when joining the two elements.

homonym (HOM-a-nim)

A combination of the prefix *homo-*, meaning "same," and *onym*, **homonym**, like *synonym*, literally means "same name." Its precise meaning, however, is "a word that is identical to another in spelling and pronunciation, but different in meaning, as *ball*, a sphere, and *ball*, a dance." Words that are pronounced the same but spelled differently, such as led and lead (the metal), are sometimes called homonyms, but the more precise term for these is *homophones*.

A second meaning of **homonym** is "a namesake; one who has the same name as another."

pseudonym (SUE-da-nim)

The word *pseudo* means "false." Its prefix form is *pseudo*. A **pseudonym** is a false name.

Unlike most roots, **pseudo** is *unphonetic*, which means that it isn't spelled the way it sounds. The *p* in *pseudo* is silent, as is the *e*. Word parts that are not phonetic have to be memorized.

patronymic (pat-row-NIM-ik)

Pater is a Latin word that means "father." The first defini-tion of the noun **patronymic** is "a family name; last name, or surname." The second and more interesting meaning of **patronymic** is "a name formed from the name of a father or male ancestor." Example: *Johnson*, son of John; *MacDonald*, son of Donald; *Fitzpatrick*, son of Patrick.

In the spelling of **patronymic**, *pater* is contracted to *patr* and joined to **onym**, which is followed by the suffix *-ic*.

metonymy (me-TAHN-a-mee)

Derived from the prefix *meta-* meaning "changed" and **onym**, meaning "name," a **metonym** is literally a changed name. **Metonymy** is the substitution of a closely associated word or phrase for the name itself. Examples are *White House* to mean "the President," *the crown* to mean "the king." A **metonym** is one of the words used in **metonymy**.

Exercise 1.2

Match the words you have just studied to their definitions, making sure that you spell them correctly. Remember that the base **onym** must appear in each word.

Example:

pseudonym   false name

1. _____   name taken from a father

2. _____   literally, "no name"

3. _____   bearing no name; of unknown name

4. _____   word that means the opposite of another

5. _____   word that means the same as another

6. _____   meaning the same; similar in meaning

7. _____   a figure of speech used to represent the person or thing with which it is associated

8. _____ word that is spelled and pronounced the same as another

9. _____ word made from initial letters of words in a series

Exercise 1.3

Test your understanding of the *onym* words by using the appropriate ones in the sentences below.

1. An _____ letter is one that is unsigned.

2. A SWAT team is a police unit. SWAT means "Special Weapons and Tactics." This kind of word is an _____.

3. The word *wicked* is a _____ for *evil*.

4. *Good* and *evil* are _____s.

5. The word *brag* is _____ with the word *boast*.

6. Some examples of _____ are *the crown decreed . . . , the White House said . . . , hardhats at work*.

7. In the nineteenth century, women authors often used men's names to get their books published. Charlotte Brontë, for example, used the pen name Currer Bell. This pen name was a _____.

8. The surname Robertson is a _____.

9. These words are _____s: *loaf (of bread)* and *loaf*, *meaning loiter*.

One of the interesting things about learning word roots is the way in which the study of one word-group leads to knowledge of another group. For instance, the word *acronym* from the *onym* group contains the root **acro**, which forms the base of *acrobat*, meaning "a high-wire or trapeze performer," and *acrophobia*, meaning "extreme fear of heights." Dozens of words are formed with *phobia*, which, as you probably know, means "intense fear of certain objects or situations." *Claus-*

trophobia is one of the most common phobias. People who have it feel panicky when they are confined in closed places. The Latin word *claustrum* means "closed place"; *claudere* means "to close." From these words come the roots **clud** and **clus**, meaning "close, shut."

The following are English words based on **clud** and **clus**.

include, inclusion, inclusive
(in-KLOOD, in-KLOO-zhun, in-KLOO-siv)

Include means "to enclose with; to have or take in as part of something": *Include your check with the order. The price includes tax.*

Inclusion is the act of including: *the inclusion of drug education in the curriculum.*

Inclusive means "covering, or including all": *an inclusive volume of Shakespeare's plays; an inclusive list of items bought last month.*

exclude, exclusion, exclusive
(ex-KLOOD, ex-KLOO-zhun, ex-KLOO-siv)

The prefix *ex-* means "out." *Exclude* means "to shut out": *These invitations exclude children from the party.*

Exclusion is the act of shutting out, or excluding: *the exclusion of women from higher-paying jobs.*

Exclusive means (1) shutting out, or excluding all but a select group: *an exclusive restaurant*; (2) belonging to one, not shared: *an exclusive news story*

conclude, conclusion, conclusive
(cun-KLOOD, cun-KLOO-zhun, cun-KLOO-siv)

One definition of the prefix *con-* is "thoroughly." *Conclude* means "close thoroughly" in the sense of ending something: *The principal concluded the meeting.*

The second definition of *conclude* is "thoroughly closed" in the sense of settling or ending doubt about a question or matter: *Scientific studies concluded that smoking is a major cause of lung cancer.*

A **conclusion** is (1) the close or end of something: *the* *conclusion of the story*, (2) the settling of a matter; a decision: *the jury's conclusion*.

Conclusive means "convincing; ending doubt": *conclusive evidence of guilt*.

seclude, seclusion (si-KLOOD, si-KLOO-zhun)

The prefix *se-* means "apart" or "away." **Seclude** means "shut away; remove from the society of others; isolate; hide from view": *He secluded himself in his cabin. The cabin was secluded in the dense woods*.

Seclusion is the state of being shut away, secluded: *He enjoyed the quiet seclusion of the woods*.

preclude, preclusion
(pree-KLOOD, pree-KLOO-zhun)

The prefix *pre-* means "before." **Preclude** means "to exclude, or shut out beforehand; to prevent because of preexisting condition or prior action": *Failure to pay his debts precluded him from receiving another loan*.

Preclusion means "hindrance; the state of being prevented": *Untrained workers must expect preclusion from jobs requiring skills*.

recluse, reclusive
(REK-loose, ree-KLOO-siv)

The prefix *re-* means "back." A **recluse** is a person who lives, in a sense, back from the world, shunning the company of others. He or she lives as a hermit—that is, in seclusion: *The rich old man had become a recluse*.

Reclusive describes someone who prefers solitude, retirement from the world: *Having a reclusive nature, she seldom mingled in society*.

occlude, occlusion
(a-KLOOD, a-KLOO-zhun)

Some prefixes change in spelling to blend with roots in pronunciation. The prefix *oc-* is a changed spelling of *ob-*, which means "against." To **occlude** is to shut the way against, to close or fill an opening. **Occlusion** is the closure of an opening. **Occlude** and its forms are frequently used as scientific terms. In dentistry, *occlusion* refers to the fitting together of tooth surfaces when the jaws are closed.

Exercise 1.4

In the blank spaces, write the words that fit the descriptions on the right.

1. an _____ neighborhood — where only the rich can afford to live, one that shuts out those less wealthy

2. _____ evidence — evidence that closes all doubt

3. the _____ of the speech — the close or end

4. a shy _____ person — one who prefers retirement from society

5. to _____ the light — to shut the way; block the passage

6. a _____d place — a private place, one where a person can be apart from others

7. the _____ from political office because of a criminal record. — prevention by a prior action

8. a life of _____ — a life lived alone, shut away from others

The word *patronymic*, from the "onym" list, is related to a group of words based on the root **pater** or **patr**, which means "father."

paternal, paternity
(pa-TUR-nul, pa-TUR-na-tee)

Paternal means "fatherly; pertaining to a male parent; pertaining to the relation of a father to his children." **Paternity** means "fatherhood."

paternalism (pa-TUR-na-liz-um)

A system of government that treats its citizens in a paternal manner—a manner that suggests a father's care and control of his child—is called **paternalism**.

This term also applies to the treatment of employees as children, or to any other system wherein adults are controlled in this manner.

patriarch (PAY-tree-ark)

The root **arch** means "rule." **Patriarch** means "a male ruler of a family; an elder or father figure who is regarded as leader or ruler of a large family, clan, or tribe; a founding father of a church or nation."

patriot (PAY-tree-ut)

A **patriot** is one who loves the fatherland or has loyalty to his or her country.

expatriate (eks-PAY-tree-ate)

To be **expatriated** is to be banished or exiled from one's country. As a noun, **expatriate** (eks-PAY-tree-it) means "one who leaves his native land and lives abroad."

repatriate (ree-PAY-tree-ate)

The literal meaning of *repatriate* is "back to the fatherland." To be **repatriated** is to be sent back to one's native land.

patron, patronize (PAY-trun, PAY-tra-nize)

A **patron** is a person who gives fatherly support and encouragement to someone engaged in an enterprise. In past centuries, talented artists often had **patrons** who helped them succeed by providing financial support. This practice led to the second meaning of **patron**, which is "a regular customer of a business." To **patronize** a business is to frequent it, or to be a regular customer.

The second meaning of **patronize** is "to act in a superior or condescending way toward another." To **patronize** is to "talk down" to someone in a manner of a father toward a child.

patricide (PA-tra-side)

The root **cide** means "kill; murder." **Patricide** is the murder of one's own father.

patrimony (PA-tra-mow-nee)

A patrimony is an inheritance from a father or other male ancestor.

A group of words naturally associated with *pater* and its derivatives are those based on *mater* or *matri*, meaning "mother."

maternal, maternity
(ma-TUR-nul, ma-TUR-na-tee)

Maternal means "motherly; pertaining to a female parent; pertaining to the relation of a mother to her children." **Maternity** means "motherhood; the relation of a mother to her children."

matriarch (MAY-tree-ark)

A **matriarch** is a female ruler of a large family or tribe; a motherly figure who rules a large family or tribe.

matron, matronly (MAY-trun, MAY-trun-lee)

A **matron** is (1) a middle-aged married woman, usually a mother; (2) a female superintendent of an institution; (3) a female guard in a women's prison. **Matronly** describes a mature, dignified, motherly-looking woman.

matrimony (MAT-ra-mow-nee)

Matrimony is marriage, or wedlock, an institution whose original purpose was to provide for having children. Thus, the word *matrimony* was derived from *mater*, a child-bearing woman.

matricide (MAT-ra-side)

Matricide is the killing of one's own mother.

matrix (MAY-triks)

Derived from *mater*, **matrix** is the Latin word for "womb." Actually a **matrix** is that in which anything originates, develops, or is contained, such as rock in which minerals are embedded. Another definition is "a mold in which anything is cast or shaped."

matriculate (ma-TRICK-yoo-late)

An institution for higher learning that one has attended is called *alma mater*, meaning "fostering mother." To enroll in a college or university is to **matriculate**. (From *matricula*, meaning "roll" or "register.")

metropolis (ma-TROP-a-lis)

The root **metr** is a changed spelling of *matr*, meaning "mother." *Polis* means city. A **metropolis**, then, is the "mother city" or chief city of an area.

The Latin word for brother is *frater*. Words derived from *frater* are similar to those derived from *pater* and *mater*.

fraternal (fra-TUR-nul)

Fraternal means (1) pertaining to a brother; brotherly; (2) pertaining to an association of men organized for a common purpose, as a *fraternal* order.

Another meaning of **fraternal** relates to human twins. Identical twins are formed from one fertilized ovum (egg) that has divided. **Fraternal** twins are formed from two separate fertilized ova, and therefore they do not share identical characteristics. **Fraternal** twins may be sisters, brothers, or brother and sister.

fraternity (fra-TUR-na-tee)

A **fraternity** is a brotherhood in the sense of a society of men organized for a common purpose. College **fraternities** are societies of male students. Other **fraternities** consist of people who share the same interests.

fraternize (FRAT-er-nize)

To **fraternize** is to associate with people in a friendly, brotherly way. In wartime, however, **fraternize** can mean to associate in a friendly manner with the enemy or conquered people.

fratricide (FRAT-ra-side)

The murder of one's own brother is called **fratricide**.

The Latin word for sister is *soror*. The most common word based on *soror* is **sorority** (sa-ROR-a-tee), which means "a sisterhood, especially a women's association in a university."

Exercise 1.5

Test your understanding of family roots and their derivatives by completing the sentences below.

1. The word *patrician*, meaning "one of high birth; an aristocrat," is based on the root **patr**, which means _____.

2. The word *matrilineal* means "descending from the maternal family line"; *patrilineal* refers to the _____ line.

3. A matronymic (or metronymic) is a name taken from a _____.

4. Sororicide is the murder of one's own _____.

5. The first recorded case of _____ in history was the murder of Abel by his brother Cain.

6. In Greek mythology, Oedipus (ED-a-pus) was a king who murdered an old man. Later, Oedipus learned that the old man was his own father. This murder was a case of _____.

7. Electra was a Greek princess who plotted with her brother to kill their mother to avenge their father's murder. The crime Electra planned is called _____.

8. *The Man Without a Country* is the story of a man who has been _____d for disloyalty and doomed to live his life aboard a ship.

9. _____ twins are not identical.

10. A rock in which a fossil is embedded is called a _____.

11. _____ was instituted to provide for the care of children; a _____ provides an inheritance.

Exercise 1.6

Practice using the words in context by choosing appropriate ones to complete the following sentences.

1. None of the heirs to her large fortune dared to contradict the old woman. In her position as _____, she held a tight rein on her family.

2. Adorned with pearls and frilly hats, the dignified _____s stared disapprovingly at the guest who had come for tea wearing faded jeans.

3. "Don't bother your pretty little head with business matters," he said. "You wouldn't understand such things." "How dare you _____ me! I'm not a child," she replied angrily.

4. Slaves were subjected to the worst form of _____. Regarded by their masters as innately inferior, they endured not only backbreaking labor but the humiliation of being treated as mindless children.

5. Following the tradition of the homeland, Uncle Theo, as the eldest family member, became our _____ after Grandfather died. We all respected Uncle Theo's word as law.

6. His wife enjoyed associating with the townspeople, but he was too proud to _____ with those whom he considered his social inferiors.

7. I believe that true love of country demands wisdom in dealing with the grave issues facing us, and not the hysterical mouthings of jingoists. These pseudo _____s do nothing to promote the nation's welfare.

8. Large cheering crowds greeted the _____d soldiers on their arrival home. As prisoners of the enemy, some had not seen their country since the beginning of the war.

The preceding group of "family words" contains links to two more sets of words. They are words based on the roots **cide**, meaning "kill," and **arch**, which means "rule."

Numerous words contain the root **cide**. Here are a few familiar ones:

insecticide   a chemical substance for killing insect pests

herbicide   a weed killer

homicide   the crime of killing a human (from *Homo sapiens*, the scientific term for a human being)

Among the most important words to have in your vocabulary are those that relate to government. The root **arch** or **archy** means "govern; rule." A second set of words relating to government are based on the root **crac** or **crat**. Following are words from both sets.

anarchy (AN-ar-kee)

The prefix *an-* means "without." **Anarchy** means (1) without government; absence of government; (2) lawless disorder.

monarch, monarchy (MON-ark, MON-ar-kee)

The Greek word *mono* means "one"; **monarch** means "one ruler; a supreme, or sovereign (SAHV-rin) ruler; a king or queen." A **monarchy** is a government by one; rule by a king or a queen.

oligarchy (OL-a-gar-kee)

The Greek word *oligos* means "few." An **oligarchy** is a government controlled by a few wealthy, powerful people.

aristocracy, aristocrat
(ar-iss-TOK-ra-see, a-RISS-ta-krat)

The Greek word *aristos* means "best"; **aristocracy** literally means "rule by the best." In Europe, the **aristocracy** was a land-owning class of people who held noble titles such as *duke, earl, baron.* **Aristocrats**, the members of this privileged class, lived off the labor of the common people and ruled over them. **Aristocrats** considered themselves greatly superior to commoners. Thus, **aristocracy** means "rule by the best."

hierarchy (HI-er-ar-kee)

The Greek word *hieros* means "sacred"; **hierarchy** is literally defined as "sacred rule." A **hierarch** is a chief priest, or one who holds the highest authority in religious matters. The Pope is the **hierarch** of the Roman Catholic Church, but its **hierarchy** consists of the clergy divided into successive ranks of authority—pope, cardinals, bishop, priests. The word *hierarchy* has broadened in usage to refer to any organization of people or things which is arranged in successive orders. Simply defined, a **hierarchy** is a graded system of people or things.

autocracy, autocrat
(aw-TOK-ra-see, AW-ta-krat)

Auto- means "self," but *autocracy* does not mean "self-rule." Rather, it means "rule by a dictator." An **autocrat** rules by himself and does not share power. *Autocracy* can be used to mean "autonomy," which is self-government or

independence. More often the term refers to government by
a leader who holds absolute power.

democracy, democratic
(da-MOK-ra-see, dem-a-KRAT-ic)

The Greek word *demos* means "people": **democracy** is
rule by the people. A **democratic** form of government is
based on the will of the majority of people.

theocracy (thee-OK-ra-see)

The Greek word for God is *theos*. **Theocracy**, in the strict-
est sense, means "government by God." Actually, **theocracy**
is government by religion. **Theocracies** base their laws on
what their leaders claim to be God's laws.

Exercise 1.7

Test your understanding of "government" words by completing the sentences below.

1. Bureaus are government departments, which often become
   powerful. Government by bureaus is called _____.

2. An autarchy means absolute rule by a dictator. This word
   is a synonym for _____.

3. *Plutocracy* means government by the wealthy, or a class
   that controls a government by means of its wealth. This
   word is similar in meaning to _____.

4. The army is composed of ranks, *general* being the highest
   rank, *colonel* next highest, *major, lieutenant*, and so on
   down to *private*. A word that could apply to this kind of
   power structure is _____.

5. _____ is government by the people;
   _____ is government by no one.

6. A *hierocrat* is a ruling member of a *hierocracy*, which
   is a government headed by priests or religious leaders.
   A _____ might consist of hierocrats.

7. Government by "the best" is called _____.

Exercise 1.8

Carefully read the paragraphs below and supply the missing words.

1. In 1215, King John of England was forced by a group of English barons to sign the Magna Carta, the Great Charter of English liberties, which limited the king's power. Like all European rulers, John had enjoyed absolute power, but he was a cruel and ruthless _____ whose corrupt practices were deeply resented by the nobles.

2. The Magna Carta was designed primarily to give more privileges to the nobility. Commoners did not gain a voice in the affairs of government. Most were peasants who worked on the estates of nobles. Having no property of their own, these laborers comprised a large, powerless class controlled by the _____.

3. After America won its independence from England, some Americans wanted to make George Washington a king, but the founding fathers did not want a _____ in power. They wanted power to reside in the people. The Constitution established what was then a unique form of government. Governing power had always been exercised downward from the head of state through the ranks of his ministers and held over those of the lowest class, the masses. In a _____, power goes upward from the people to their representatives, who make laws reflecting their will, and last, to the head of state, who executes the laws. It was, in a sense, an upside-down _____.

4. Thomas Jefferson warned that the people could not be both free and ignorant. If citizens did not hold informed views and insist that their views be presented, their government would begin to serve only the interests of the wealthy few. Instead of self-government, it would be an _____, government by a selfish minority.

5. The Puritans came to this continent because they wanted freedom to practice their religion, but they did not tolerate religions other than their own. They had set up

a _____, which, like most governments based on religion, tended to restrict expression of differing views.

6. If all people treated one another fairly, if all citizens valued the welfare of others as much as their own, there would be no need for laws. _____ would work if selfishness and greed could be erased.

2
Roots and Branches

English contains more words than any other language. Like a vast garden, our language gives us a tremendous number of words that we can pick to give variety to our speech and writing. Like plants that grow in different ways, some word roots produce only a few "sprouts," or words, but dozens of words may branch out from other roots. Below are some of the smaller "plants"—that is, smaller groups of words that have grown from a single root.

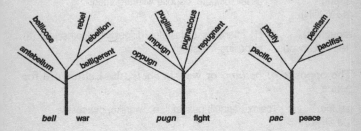

The words shown above relate to war and peace. Below are their definitions.

antebellum
(an-tee-BEL-um)
before the war, especially the American Civil War; from *ante-*, before, and *bellum*, war

bellicose
(BEL-a-kose)
warlike; favoring war to settle dispute

rebel
(ree-BEL)
from *re-*, back, plus *bel*, war, or fight; to fight back against a government or other authority; also, a **rebel** (REB-ul), one who fights back

rebellion
(ree-BEL-yun)
uprising; revolt against a government or other authority

belligerent
(ba-LIJ-er-unt)
waging war; inclined to fight; quarrelsome

pugilist
(PYOO-ja-list)
a boxer; (from *pugnus*, fist)

pugnacious
(pug-NAY-shus)
belligerent; inclined to fight; (from *pugnare*, to fight)

impugn
(im-PYOON)
attack, especially with words; call into question another's motives or trustworthiness

oppugn
(a-PYOON)
assail; dispute; oppose with argument

repugnant
(ree-PUG-nunt)
(1) offensive; distasteful; disgusting; loathsome; (2) opposing; resisting

The opposite of *bellum*, or war, is *pacis*, the Latin word for peace.

pacific
(pa-SIF-ic)
calm; tranquil; peaceful; not warlike; peaceable

pacify
(PAS-a-fie)
(1) bring peace to; end war or strife; (2) to calm; soothe; placate; appease

pacifism
(PAS-a-fiz-um)
a doctrine that opposes war, military force

pacifist
(PAS-a-fist)

one who opposes war or physical force to settle disputes

Exercise 2.1

Supply the missing words in the sentences below.

1. During the _____ period of the South, plantation owners, who used slaves to produce their wealth, lived much like European aristocrats, but after the war, their slaves were freed.

2. Gandhi was a great spiritual leader who, as a _____, rejected violence as a means of freeing India from British control.

3. Because of the _____ tone of his recent speeches, the President's critics are calling him a warmonger.

4. His drunken leer disgusted her. The thought of his touch was _____.

5. I tended to avoid fights, but my _____ brother never hesitated to confront the enemy with his fists.

6. They were a _____ people. Violence was not part of their tribal culture.

7. "I oppose this war, but I am not a traitor," he said angrily. "How dare you _____ my patriotism!"

8. In 1831, Nat Turner, a slave, led a slave revolt known in American history as the Nat Turner _____.

9. Under Hitler's regime, no one dared to _____ the evil doctrines of racial purification.

10. His pugnacious behavior has resulted in suspension from school. He seems to be in a _____ mood lately, always quarreling or picking fights.

In the groups below, as in previous groupings, not all of each word's derivatives are shown. Those that have different

or added meanings, such as *pedagogy* and *congregation*, are
included.

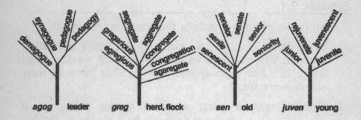

The words below relate to leaders.

demagogue
(DEM-a-gog)

From *demos*, people, and *agogos*, leader, a leader of
people; a rabble-rouser; one who leads by appealing
to prejudices, stirring passions; an unprincipled agita-
tor

pedagogue
(PED-a-gog)

teacher; dull, formal teacher, one who is overly concerned with unimportant scholarly points; from *ped*,
child, and *agogos*, leader, originally a Greek or Roman
slave whose duty was to lead a child to school

pedagogy
(PED-a-goe-jee)

the science of teaching

synagogue
(SIN-a-gog)

a meeting place for Jewish worship, religious instruction; from *syn-*, together, and *agog*, leader, a place
where people are led together in worship

The words below have to do with herding together.

congregate
(KON-gra-gate)

to meet together as a body of people; from *con-*,
together, and *greg*, flock.

congregation
(kon-gra-GAY-shun)

(1) a gathering; (2) a group of persons assembled
for worship; literally, to herd together

aggregate
(AG-ra-gate)

(1) collect into a total or sum; comprise a total; (2) added together; total (adjective and noun form, AG-ra-git)

segregate
(SEG-ra-gate)

From se-, apart, and *greg*, flock, literally apart from the flock; to keep separate; keep a group apart from the rest

gregarious
(gra-GAIR-ee-us)

(1) living in flocks, herds; (2) sociable; enjoying the company of others; preferring company above solitude.

egregious
(a-GREE-jus)

From e-, out, and *greg*, herd, literally standing out from the herd; extraordinarily bad; glaring; flagrant; shocking.

These are ''young'' and ''old'' words.

juvenile
(JOO-va-nile)

(1) a young person; a youth; (2) relating to juveniles; (3) immature (adjective form, JOO-va-nul)

rejuvenate
(ree-JOO-va-nate)

make young again

juvenescent
(joo-va-NES-unt)

becoming young again; making young; rejuvenating

junior
(JOON-yer)

younger; younger of the two, especially as pertains to a son with the same name as his father; lower in rank; a third-year high school or college student

senate
(SEN-it)

upper house of legislature; in ancient Rome, the supreme governing body; literally, council of old men (old, therefore wisest, most fit to govern)

senator
(SEN-a-ter)

member of the Senate; literally, old man

senile
(SEE-nile)

aged; doting; characteristic of old age; deteriorating in physical and mental abilities because of old age

senior
(SEEN-yer)

oldest; highest ranking; a last-year high school or college student

seniority
(sen-YOR-a-tee)

priority due to age or length or service

senescent   growing old; decaying
(sa-NES-unt)

Exercise 2.2

Supply the missing words.

1. In South Africa, apartheid laws were designed to _____ blacks.

2. The English teacher placed a great deal of importance on the metric patterns of poetry. Misinterpreting a poem's meaning was a lesser crime in her eyes than not recognizing a Spenserian stanza. Luckily, the other teachers were not such _____s.

3. The _____ has one hundred members; the lower house has many more representatives.

4. Only two _____s may be elected from each state.

5. The church pastor regarded the _____ as truly his flock.

6. The governor's racist remarks, openly spoken, were not only an insult to minorities, but an _____ political mistake.

7. Your _____ behavior is getting you no place. It's time for you to grow up.

8. She may be in the _____ stage of life, but she has the energy of someone half her age.

9. His enemies had portrayed him as a ruthless _____, but his followers, held sway by his fiery speeches, saw him as their savior.

10. On the Sabbath, Jews worship in the _____.

A second root that means "old" is **archaeo**, which actually means "ancient." This root seems similar to *archi* (or *arch*), which means "first" or "chief." Some word experts associate both roots with the *arch* that means "ruler." This connection seems logical, but other authorities distinguish among the three roots.

The first three words below come from *archaeo*.

archaeology
(ar-kee-OL-a-jee)
the study of the remains of ancient cultures

archaic
(ar-KAY-ik)
belonging to an earlier time; no longer in use, antiquated (like an antique); relating to words or phrases from an earlier period that are not in current usage

archives
(AR-kives)
historical documents; public records; a place where speech records are kept (from Greek *archion*, town hall)

These words relate to *first* or *chief*:

archetype
(AR-ka-tipe)
the original model, pattern from which something is reproduced or copied; prototype; from *archi-*, first, and type, model

archipelago
(ark-a-PEL-a-go)
group of islands; a sea scattered with islands; originally the Aegean Sea; from *archi-*, chief, and *pelago*, sea

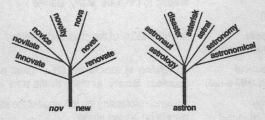

In the following words, *arch* means "chief": archbishop, archangel (ark-), archenemy, archrival.

This root can be attached to a number of nouns, and it is the base root of **architect** and **architecture**. An architect is a "chief worker" who designs buildings. **Architecture** means "the style or design of buildings; the art of building."

These roots have produced a few more word branches.

nova (NO-va)	a new star
novel (NAHV-ul)	(1) new; unusual; (2) book-length fictional story
novice (NAHV-us)	someone new at an occupation; a beginner
novelty (NAHV-ul-tee)	something new and unusual; a small manufactured item for adornment or entertainment
innovate (IN-a-vate)	literally, to bring in something new; introduce a new idea, method, or design
renovate (REN-a-vate)	repair; restore; renew

These words from *astron* are "star words."

astral (AS-trul)	relating to the stars; starry; starlike
astronomy (a-STRAHN-a-mee)	scientific study of the stars and planets
astronomical (as-tra-NAHM-a-kull)	(1) relating to astronomy; (2) of great number; countless; literally, as many as the stars
astrology (a-STRAHL-a-jee)	a science professing the influence of the stars and planets on human affairs
disaster (dis-AS-ter)	a great misfortune; calamity; literally "not in the stars"

asterisk
(AS-ter-isk)

a star-shaped printed symbol (*) placed on a page to indicate footnotes; from Greek *asterikos*, little star

astronaut
(AS-tra-nawt)

one who travels in space; from *astro*, star, and *naut*, sail, one who "sails the stars"

The root *astro* is also used in terms for specialized fields of astronomy, such as *astrophysics* and *astrophotography*.

Exercise 2.3

Write the words that are associated with these phrases.

1. _____ where you might go to do historical research

2. _____ the profession of Indiana Jones, a seeker of ancient, lost relics

3. _____ the science of making astral predictions (some call it a pseudoscience)

4. _____ a new (when first introduced) kind of story with realistic characters

5. _____ a synonym of *neophyte*, or beginner

6. _____ a synonym of *stellar*, meaning "relating to heavenly bodies"

7. _____ too many to count

8. _____ item you would find in a gift shop (Pet Rocks once belonged in this category)

9. _____ antonym of novel

10. _____ to fix up an old house, make it like new

In this chapter, you have seen fifty-five words that have sprung from ten roots. We have compared these minor roots to small plants, because they have produced relatively few words that have remained in English. Later, you will be introduced to some "trees" of the language—individual roots, each of which has produced dozens of words.

3

How Prefixes Work

A prefix is a word part placed before a root in order to direct or change the root's meaning. Like a car's transmission, a prefix makes the word go: in, out, back, forward, and so on. Just as adverbs tell the where, when, and how of verbs, prefixes give the same kinds of signals to roots. In fact, most Latin and Greek prefixes can be translated as English adverbs, as shown in the case of the root **port**—*import*, carry in; *export*, carry out. *Carry* is an action verb; *in* and *out* are adverbs because they tell the "where" of the action.

The word *prefix* itself shows a verb-adverb relationship, *fix* being the verb part, meaning "affix, attach," and *pre-*, the adverb, meaning "before." Because of the *pre-* in *prefix*, the word almost defines itself. It means, of course, a word part attached before a root.

Not all words are as simple to figure out, obviously, but their prefixes provide the first clue. Prefixes have their own definitions; some have more than one meaning. Another characteristic of prefixes is that many have synonyms—that is, other prefixes that mean the same.

This chapter contains a dictionary of the Latin and Greek prefixes that appear most frequently in English, along with exercises using the example words. Learn these words well.

Many are included in college- and graduate-school entrance examinations.

The prefixes are grouped under their English translations.

Four prefixes mean "away" or "apart." They are *ab-* (also *abs-*, *a-*), *dis-*, *se-*, and *de-*.

abnormal (ab-NOR-mull)	apart from what is normal or standard; not normal
aberrant (AB-er-unt)	abnormal; straying from the usual course; mentally deranged
abject (AB-jekt)	sunk to a hopelessly low condition of worthlessness, baseness, or misery; from *ab-*, *away*, and *ject*, throw; literally, thrown away
abrogate (AB-row-gate)	do away with; abolish; repeal, as a law
abrasive (a-BRAY-siv)	scraping away; wearing or rubbing away of a surface
absent (AB-sent)	away, not present; to stay away (ab-SENT)
abscond (ab-SKOND)	go away suddenly and secretly
avert (a-VERT)	turn away from; avoid
dissect (dis-SEKT)	cut apart; cut into sections
disperse (dis-PURSS)	scatter; drive away
dissipate (DIS-a-pate)	scatter; throw away; squander
distinguish (dis-TING-gwish)	to recognize differences between, among; keep apart, distinct
discern (di-SURN)	discriminate; distinguish clearly (by sight or the mind); have keen insight; literally, sift apart

separate
(SEP-a-rate)

keep apart; disjoin

sequester
(si-KWES-ter)

seclude; shut away from

sever
(SE-ver)

cut apart; cut off; break a bond or tie

depart
(dee-PART)

go away; leave

deviate
(DEE-vee-ate)

from *de-*, away, and *via*, path; to turn away from the usual or straight; one whose conduct differs greatly from societal standards

Exercise 3.1

Complete the sentences below with words from the list.

1. *Dispel* means scatter, dissipate, or _____.

2. _____ means cut something apart in order to examine it.

3. To cut off a ribbon or cut off a friendship is to _____ it.

4. Laws requiring racial segregation have been abolished or _____ d.

5. To _____ is to stray from the normal way or go apart from society's standards.

6. _____ describes a scouring powder that cleans by scraping, or a person's sharp-tongued, insensitive manner.

7. _____ describes any condition in which one has, in a sense, hit bottom or become an outcast of society.

8. To stay away from a meeting is to _____ one-self.

9. To _____ is to leave; to leave in haste and se-crecy is to _____.

10. *Disseminate* means to scatter as seed or spread something such as information. A verb that means "waste by scattering" is _____.

The prefixes meaning "in" or "within" are *im-*, *in-*, *em-*, and *en-*.

imbibe (im-BIBE)	drink, drink in; absorb
immerse (im-MERSS)	plunge into, as a fluid
immigrate (im-a-grate)	move from one country into another
incipient (in-SIP-ee-ent)	beginning; just coming into existence
infuse (in-FYOOZ)	inspire; instill; pour in, from *fus*, pour
inject (in-JEKT)	insert; force or shoot into; throw in, from *in-* and *ject*, throw
intrinsic (in-TRIN-sik)	originating from within; belonging to a thing in itself; inherent; having internal value
envelop (en-VEL-up)	enclose; surround with
embrace (em-BRASE)	hold in one's arms; accept willingly as a doctrine, a philosophy

Exercise 3.2

Write the words that fit these phrases:

1. _____ plunge into water; plunge into work
2. _____ move into a country
3. _____ drink liquor; drink in; absorb teachings
4. _____ inspire; instill or "pour in" ideals or feelings for

5. _____   hold, accept a philosophy; hug
                    someone

6. _____   inherent; born into; existing within

7. _____   throw in a joke, a comment; shoot into
                    a blood vein

8. _____   barely beginning

9. _____   enfold in darkness or fog

The prefix *ex-* or *e-* means "out."

exit (EKS-it)	the way out; a departure
exodus (EKS-a-dus)	a departure, especially of a large crowd
exterior (eks-TEER-ee-ur)	external; the outer side
extrinsic (eks-TRIN-zik)	external; originating from outside
exculpate (EKS-kull-pate)	to clear from charges of guilt; vindicate
exonerate (eks-ZAHN-er-ate)	declare free from guilt; vindicate
extricate (EKS-tra-kate)	free from an entanglement or a complicated situation
emerge (ee-MERJ)	come out of, as water, darkness; appear
evanescent (ev-a-NES-ent)	fleeting; vanishing quickly
emigrate (EM-a-grate)	move out of a country
eject (ee-JEKT)	throw out; remove by force

effusive   pouring out; gushing
(ef-FYOO-siv)

effervescent   bubbling; lively
(ef-er-VES-ent)

Note: The prefix *ef-* is a changed spelling of *ex-*.

Exercise 3.3

Supply the missing words.

1. The adjective *ephemeral* is related to the word *ephemerid*, which is a mayfly that lives only one day. *Ephemeral*, meaning very brief, fleeting, is a synonym for
_____.

2. An *onus* is a burden; *onerous* means burdensome. A verb that comes from the same root and means to free from the burden of guilt is _____.

3. Philosophers such as Rousseau believed that goodness was an intrinsic quality. Others believed that humans were born neither good nor bad, but that virtues were acquired from outside influences. Goodness, in their view, was an _____ quality.

4. *External* means outer; the external part of something is its _____.

5. The Latin word *culpa* means blame; a culprit is one who is guilty of or blamed for a wrongdoing. _____ comes from the same root and means remove from blame.

In the words *effusive* and *effervescent*, the prefix *ex-* is assimilated (made similar) with the roots to which it is attached. In other words, the letter *x* has changed to *f* to match the beginning letters of the roots. Prefixes are changed this way to make pronunciation easier. Your study of prefixes will show many such assimilations.

together

The Latin prefix *con-* (also *com-* and *co-*) means "together," as well as the Greek prefixes *syn-* and *sym-*. Both assimilate with roots beginning with the letter *l*, as shown in the words below.

confluence
(KAHN-flu-ens)

a flowing together of streams; a place where streams meet; a large gathering (from *flu*, flow)

confuse
(kun-FYOOZ)

to perplex; bewilder; jumble, mix up together; literally pour together

combine
(kum-BINE)

put things together; blend; unite

commiserate
(ka-MIZ-er-ate)

sympathize with; condole; share another's pain or sorrow

coalesce
(koe-a-LES)

merge; join; unite

cohere
(koe-HEER)

stick together; be logically connected in speech or writing

collaborate
(ka-LAB-a-rate)

labor together; work together, especially on a literary or scientific project

collusion
(ka-LOO-zhun)

a scheme by two or more people to commit fraud; an illegal conspiracy

syndrome
(SIN-drome)

a set of symptoms occurring together (from *syn-*, together, and *drome*, run)

synthesis
(SIN-tha-sis)

a blending of elements or parts to form a whole

syllable
(SIL-a-bull)

a word part uttered in one sound

symmetrical
(sim-MET-tre-kull)

well balanced in shape, arrangement; literally, measured together

Exercise 3.4

Write the words that fit the phrases below.

1. _____ a conspiracy to cheat people of their money

2. _____ word part joined with others to form a word

3. _____ to glue or stick together; to keep thoughts logically connected

4. _____ fever, nausea, and headache running together

5. _____ write a book together

6. _____ a place where rivers merge

7. _____ to muddle; mix up

8. _____ mix ingredients together; blend

9. _____ join forces; form a coalition

10. _____ having harmonious proportions in shape, size, and position; well arranged

against

The prefix *contra-* (also spelled *contro-*) is a form of *counter-*, meaning "against" or "opposing."

contrast
(kun-TRAST)

literally, stand against; be opposite of; compare opposite things

contraband
(KAHN-tra-band)

smuggled goods; forbidden by law; literally, banned against

controvert
(KAHN-tra-vert)

argue against; dispute

counterstrike
(KOWN-ter-strike)

strike back against, especially with military force

| **counter**mand (kown-ter-MAND) | to give a command that is the opposite of a previous order; cancel an order |
| **counter**part (KOWN-ter-part) | the same thing in a different place; (2) the opposite part of something, as *night and day* (both being part of the 24-hour day) |

The prefix *anti-* combines with any number of words to mean "opposing" or "against": antiwar; anticommunist; antislavery. In some words, *anti-* is shortened to *ant-*.

antidote (AN-tee-dote)	something given to counteract the effects of a poison or an evil
antagonize (an-TAG-a-nize)	make an enemy of; incur hostility; oppose; turn against
antarctic (ant-ARK-tik or AR-tik)	pertaining to the region of the South Pole, which is opposite of the Arctic region

A third prefix meaning "against" is *ob-*.

obstacle (AHB-sta-kull)	a hindrance; something standing in the way; literally, stand against
object (ub-JEKT)	argue against; state disapproval; literally, throw against
obstinate (AHB-sta-net)	stubborn; unyielding; literally, standing against
obdurate (AHB-dyoor-it)	stubborn; unyielding; hardened against (*ob-* + *dur*, hard)
obviate (AHB-vee-ate)	make unnecessary; counteract problems so that something else is prevented; preclude; avert

Exercise 3.5

In the sentences below, substitute words from the lesson for those in parentheses.

1. Mass transit could (preclude) _____ the need for more highways.

2. The cardboard shelters, housing ragged children, (were opposite of) _____ sharply with the luxurious apartment buildings looming in the background.

3. The (counterattack) _____ came swiftly.

4. He won't listen to any suggestions. It's impossible to work with someone so (obstinate) _____.

5. They set out to explore the (region opposite the North Pole) _____.

6. They must find the (remedy for poison) _____ quickly.

7. The captain (gave an opposite order) _____ ed the order to fire on ships entering territorial waters.

8. Using the Bible to (dispute) _____ the theory of evolution, the religious group strongly (argued against) _____ ed to its being taught in the schools.

9. The government (incurred hostility of) _____d the tribe by violating their cultural traditions.

10. I had to overcome several (hindrances) _____s to reach my goal.

through and across

Two prefixes that mean ''through'' or ''across'' are *trans-* and *dia-*.

transfer (trans-FER)	carry across; convey; move from one place to another
transact (trans-ACT)	carry through, as a business deal
transfuse (TRANS-fyooz)	pass across, from one to another; literally, pour across

transformed (trans-FORMD)	changed throughout in form, appearance, or condition
transient (TRAN-zhunt)	passing through; not staying; ephemeral; fleeting
transparent (trans-PAIR-unt)	(1) showing through; (2) easy to see through, obvious
diameter (die-AM-a-ter)	the length of a line going through the center of a circle
diaphanous (die-AF-a-nus)	showing through; allowing light through; transparent; translucent

Exercise 3.6

Below are some rather loose definitions of the words you just studied. Write the words that fit them.

1. _____ easy to see through, like clear glass or a thin excuse

2. _____ to ''pour'' blood from one person to another

3. _____ momentary, not permanent; also, a person who doesn't stay long in any one place

4. _____ the measurement across the center of a round cake pan

5. _____ like the ugly duckling who became a swan, completely changed

6. _____ showing through like a sheer fabric; transparent

7. _____ carry through a business deal

8. _____ change to another bus; move an employee to another job

through and throughout

The prefix *per-* means "through," "throughout," and "thoroughly."

perforate
(PER-fa-rate)
punch through, make holes in; penetrate

permeate
(PER-mee-ate)
spread throughout; go through every part; pervade

perpetual
(per-PET-choo-ull)
lasting throughout time; not stopping

perennial
(per-EN-ee-ull)
lasting through the years; lasting a long time

perdition
(per-DISH-un)
damnation throughout eternity

persuade
(per-SWADE)
convince thoroughly

Note: Another meaning of *per-* is "by," as in *percent*, "by the hundred."

Exercise 3.7

Substitute words from the chart for those in parentheses in the sentences below.

1. Toxic fumes (pervaded) _____d the residential area.

2. "Sin is the road to (damnation) _____," the preacher warned.

3. We couldn't (convince) _____ him to stay.

4. We (made holes in) _____d the box so that the trapped animal wouldn't suffocate.

5. Marriage is a state of (lasting forever) _____ bliss only in fairly tales.

6. The singer's popularity was (lasting for years) _____. The public never tired of his music.

between and within

The prefix that means "between" or "among" is *inter-*, which should not be confused with *intra-*, which means "within." (*Intro-* is another form of *intra-*.)

interfere
(in-ter-FEER)
to come between; enter into the concerns of others

interject
(in-ter-JEKT)
introduce abruptly; inject; insert; literally, throw in between

interval
(IN-ter-vull)
a space of time or distance between; a pause; an interim

interrogate
(in-TAIR-a-gate)
question formally; examine; ask; literally, ask between

interstate
(IN-ter-state)
between states

intrastate
(IN-tra-state)
within a state

intravenous
(in-tra-VEE-nus)
within a blood vein

Exercise 3.8

Substitute words from the list for those in parentheses.

1. (question) _____ the suspect

2. (between states) _____ highway

3. (within a state) _____ phone call

4. in the (time between) _____

5. (butt in) _____ in someone else's business

6. give a medicine (within a vein) _____ly

7. (throw in between) _____ a joking remark

under

The prefixes *hypo-* and *sub-* mean "under," "below," or "beneath."

hypodermic (hie-pa-DERM-ik)	under the skin (*hypo*, under + *dermis*, skin)
hypothermia (hie-po-THER-mee-a)	abnormally low body temperature (*hypo*, under + *therm*, heat)
subway (SUB-way)	underground railway or passage
submerge (sub-MERJ)	plunge into water or a liquid; dive under; sink
subtle (SUT-ul)	(1) hardly noticeable; not apparent on the surface: *the subtle use of makeup*; (2) clever; keen: *subtle humor*; (3) insidious; working under the surface: *a subtle scheme*; literally, finely woven (*sub-*, under + *tela*, web)
subpoena (sa-PEE-na)	a writ requiring a person to appear in court to give testimony; literally, under penalty
subterfuge (SUB-ter-fyooj)	a pretense or deception used in order to escape something or gain an end
suffix (SUF-iks)	a word part affixed to the end of a base root (under or last in arrangement)

Exercise 3.9

Complete the sentences below.

1. _____ is an underhanded trick.

2. The survivors were rescued from the icy waters and treated for _____.

3. _____ describes a needle used to inject medicines into the bloodstream.

4. The sunken ship was still intact a century after it had _____d.

5. The antonym of *prefix* is _____.

6. He didn't say outright that I was stupid. His way of insulting me was more _____.

7. The quickest means of getting across the city is the _____.

8. A _____ is a court summons that places a person under threat of legal punishment for failure to appear.

over

Super and its contraction *sur-* mean "over," "above," or "beyond." Two other prefixes meaning "over" are *extra-* and *hyper-*. All four are used in some words to mean "exceeding" or "excessive." *Superstition*, for example, literally means "excessive fear of the gods."

supernatural (sooper-NACH-er-ull)	beyond the natural; existing or occurring through some power beyond natural forces; miraculous or divine
superfluous (soo-PER-floo-us)	overabundant; exceeding what is needed; unnecessary; literally, overflowing (*flu*, flow)
surmount (sur-MOWNT)	to overcome, rise above difficulties or obstacles
surpass (sur-PASS)	exceed; go beyond; excel
extraordinary (eks-STROR-da-nair-ee)	beyond the ordinary; exceptional; exceeding the usual
extraneous (eks-STRAY-nee-us)	unrelated to the matter at hand or what is being discussed; unessential

hyperactive   overactive; excessively active
(hie-per-AK-tiv)

hyperbole   an exaggerated statement not meant to be
(hie-PER-ba-lee)   taken literally

Exercise 3.10

Using the list you have just studied, choose words associated with the ideas expressed in the phrases below. Synonyms are given in parentheses for the words you will write.

1. miracles, ghosts, mind reading, and such (beyond the natural) _____

2. "She cried a river of tears," for example (overstatement) _____

3. too much rain, too many words, too much of anything (overabundant) _____

4. break an old record; set a new one (excel) _____

5. always moving, can never sit still (overactive) _____

6. conquer difficulties and come out a winner (overcome) _____

7. very unusual; not run-of-the-mill (exceptional) _____

8. details thrown in that have little to do with the topic (unessential) _____

around

The prefixes *circum-* and *peri-* mean "around."

circumference   the distance around a circle
(sir-KUM-fer-unss)

circumnavigate   sail around
(sir-kum-NAV-a-gate)

circuitous (sir-KEW-a-tuss)	roundabout; taking an indirect path; devious; sly; erring
perimeter (pa-RIM-a-ter)	the distance around a square, triangle, circle, or any two-dimensional figure; a boundary line around
periphery (pa-RIF-a-ree)	perimeter; circumference; outer boundary; a surrounding region or area

A prefix meaning "around," "on both sides," or "both" is *amphi-* or *ambi-*.

ambiguous (am-BIG-u-us)	(1) having a double meaning; capable of being interpreted two ways. Example: *Jim told Joe he got the job.* (2) unclear; indefinite
ambivalent (am-BIV-a-lent)	having mixed feelings; having different or opposite feelings at the same time, such as feeling both love and hate for someone or something
amphitheater (AM-fa-thee-a-ter)	an oval-shaped theater having tiers of seats around the stage or arena

Exercise 3.11

Complete the sentences below.

1. _____ means to sail around the earth, a continent, or island.

2. "I want to go to Europe, but I don't want to leave my family." The speaker of the preceding sentence has two opposing feelings that can be described as _____.

3. "Mary told Marge she got a raise." The preceding sentence doesn't make clear whether Mary or Marge got the raise. The meaning, which can be taken both ways, is _____.

4. Someone who is sly or devious doesn't take a direct path toward an end, but uses clever, tricky means. Another adjective that describes such strategies is _____.

5. A word that specifically means the distance around a circle
is _____.

6. A measurement around a square or rectangle is
the _____.

7. Both *perimeter* and _____ mean the outer boundary of an area.

8. In ancient Greece, actors performed plays in out-
door _____s.

down

The most common prefix meaning "down" is *de-*. Several
de- words are "put-down" terms, words used to belittle or
disparage persons. Two such words are on the list below.
Others convey the idea of decreasing or becoming less in
some way. *De-* also acts to undo actions in words such as
detach, deprogram, and *dehumidify.*

descend
(di-SEND)

come down

dejected
(di-JEK-ted)

despondent; depressed; cast down in spirit (from
de-, down + *ject, throw*)

deciduous
(di-SID-yoo-us)

shedding leaves or fruit; literally, falling down (from
de-, down, and *cid*, fall)

derogatory
(di-ROG-a-tor-ee)

belittling; disparaging; designed to lesson esteem
or respect for another

deride
(di-RIDE)

scorn; mock; ridicule (from *de-*, down + *ridere*,
laugh)

decline
(di-KLINE)

decrease in number, quality; turn down an offer or
request

deteriorate
(di-TEER-ee-er-ate)

decline in quality or condition; become worse

decadent
(DEK-a-dent)

decaying; falling low in morals or conduct

Another meaning of *de-* is "away from."

deprive   take away from
(di-PRIVE)

derive   draw from a source
(di-RIVE)

Exercise 3.12

Substitute words from the list for the words in parentheses.

1. The other boys (laughed at) _____d him because he dressed differently.

2. As punishment, the girl's parents (took away) _____d her of all the privileges she had enjoyed.

3. The heckler made several (belittling) _____ remarks about the speaker.

4. Most English word roots were (drawn from) _____d from Latin and Greek.

5. *Ascend*, meaning go up, is the antonym of (come down) _____.

6. Her health gradually (worsened) _____d.

7. He (turned down) _____d the invitation to speak at the banquet. The number who attended the dinner (decreased) _____d from last year.

8. The little boy was (downcast) _____ because he lost his dog.

9. Trees that lose their leaves in autumn are called (shedding) _____.

10. Roman society became morally (low) _____.

back and forth

One of the most common and least complicated prefixes in English is *re-*. Seldom does *re-* mean anything other than

"back" or "again." A few exceptions are words such as
redoubtable and *refrigerate*, in which *re-* means "thoroughly."

reject   refuse; not accept; literally, throw back
(ri-JEKT)

retaliate   pay back in kind for an attack; insult; take revenge
(ri-TAL-ee-ate)

reiterate   say again and again; repeat for emphasis (from *re-*,
(ree-IT-er-ate)   again, and *iter*, a second time)

redundant   superfluous; repetitious; unnecessarily wordy
(ree-DUN-dant)

remunerate   pay back; compensate; reward
(ri-MYOON-er-ate)

recalcitrant   disobedient; obstinate; rebellious; literally, kicking
(ri-KAL-sa-trent)   back

forth

The prefix *pro-* means "forth, forward; toward; ahead of
or before."

progress   go forward
(pra-GRESS)

project   throw forward; make a plan
(pra-JEKT)

profuse   pouring forth in abundance; lavish; extravagant
(pra-FYOOS)

prolific   bringing forth offspring, fruit; producing abundantly
(pra-LIF-ik)

propensity   a natural tendency; a leaning toward
(pra-PEN-si-tee)

prologue   a preface, foreword, or introduction to a play or book
(PRŌ-log)

The prefix *ob-* and its forms can mean "toward."

offer
(AW-fer)
present for acceptance; show willingness to do something (from *ob-*, toward, and *fer*, bring)

opportune
(op-er-TOON)
favorable; convenient; occurring at a favorable time; literally, favorable winds blowing toward port

Exercise 3.13

Write words that match the definitions below.

1. _____ pay back for an insult

2. _____ pay back for a favor or service

3. _____ repeat for emphasis

4. _____ repeating unnecessarily

5. _____ stubborn; unmanageable

6. _____ a natural talent for something; a leaning

7. _____ go forward; advance

8. _____ throw back; refuse to accept

9. _____ producing much fruit or works, such as an author's abundant writings

10. _____ lavish; abundant; extravagant

before and after

A common prefix that means "before in time or order" is *pre-*.

preview
(PREE-vyoo)
to view before; a private viewing of art works or a film preceding a public showing

prejudice
(PREJ-oo-dis)
the act of prejudging; an unfair judgment formed without knowledge of facts

previous
(PREE-vee-us)

existing or happening before; literally, going on the path before

premonition
(prem-a-NISH-un)

a forewarning not based on tangible information; a foreboding

presume
(pree-ZOOM)

(1) take for granted; act in a forward manner; (2) assume to be true before having proof

preposterous
(pri-POS-ter-us)

from *pre-*, before, and *post*, after; **preposterous** means absurd, against reason, since, obviously, nothing can be both before and after

Earlier, you learned that the prefix *ante-* means ''before.'' In some words, *ante-* is shortened to *ant-* and *an-*.

antedate
(AN-ta-date)

predate; happen before another event or time period

anticipate
(an-TISS-a-pate)

foresee; expect to happen

ancient
(AYN-shent)

existing long before; very old

Post- means ''after.'' Like *pre-*, *post-* can be attached to a number of words. It is less frequently attached to roots.

postwar
(PŌST-war)

after a war

post meridiem
(pōst-ma-RID-ee-em)

after the sun has passed the meridian

posthumous
(PAHS-cha-mus)

occurring after death; published after the author's death

posterity
(pas-TAIR-a-tee)

future generations; those who will come after the present generation

Exercise 3.14

Supply the missing words.

1. _____ describes an award given after one's death.

2. One o'clock in the afternoon is 1:00 P.M., or 1:00 _____ _____.

3. _____ is a warning especially by intuition that something is going to happen.

4. The _____ owner means the one who owned the property before the present owner.

5. _____ means absurd, because nothing can be before and after at the same time.

6. _____ means existing a long time ago.

7. What kind of world will we leave to _____ if we don't clean up the environment?

8. _____ is the antonym of postdate.

9. _____ comes from the verb prejudge, which means to judge unfairly.

OTHER PREFIXES

to

All the prefixes listed so far have been adverbs. An exception is the Latin prefix *ad-*, which acts as the *to* of infinitive verbs—that is, verbs without tense, such as to see, to go, to do. Examples of infinitive verbs derived from Latin are *adhere* and *admonish*, which translate literally as "to stick" and "to warn." Hundreds of English verbs and their derivatives contain the prefix *ad-* and its disguised forms, or forms created by assimilation with roots. *Accuse, affair, allow,* and *appoint* are examples.

to make

Prefixes that mean "to make, cause, or put within" are *in-* or *im-*, and *en-* or *em-*. Examples are *inflame*, "cause to burn"; *implant*, "to plant into"; *enable*, "to make able"; *embellish*, "to make beautiful [from the French word *belle*, beauty] by adding ornaments." The *im-* form of *in-* is used when the attached base word begins with *b, m,* or *p.* The *em-* form of *en-* attaches to roots or words beginning with *b* or *p,* but *en-* is used with *m* words, as *en*mesh.

THE NEGATIVE PREFIXES

Negative prefixes are those that negate, or cancel out, the quality or condition expressed by the attached base word. The most common negative prefix is the Old English *un-*, which has been added to thousands of Latin- or Greek-derived words. Its Latin counterpart is *in-*, whose two basic meanings are "in," or "within," and "not," or "without." Examples are *invalid*, not valid; *incapable*, not capable.

Exercise 3.15

Test your understanding of prefix assimilations and spelling changes by adding prefixes to complete the words below.

Assimilate *ad-* with these words:

1. _____breviate   to make brief, shorten

2. _____nihilate   to destroy; make *nihil* or nothing

3. _____preciate   to increase in price; be grateful for

4. _____fluent   flowing, especially with wealth (from *flu,* flow)

5. _____gravate   to make worse, more serious (from *gravis,* heavy)

As you know, *in-* changes to *im-* when attached to words and roots beginning with *m, b,* or *p.* Also, *in-* assimilates with *l* or *r* words, as in these examples: *in-* plus *logical*, illogical; *in-* plus *rational*, irrational.

Choose the correct form of *in-* to complete these words:

6. _____carnate — to make into flesh, give a physical body to

7. _____poverish — make poor

8. _____bue — to put in (ideals, emotions)

9. _____discriminate — not discriminating; not making distinctions

10. _____reparable — not able to be repaired

11. _____relevant — not relevant; not relating to the matter at hand

12. _____licit — not lawful

13. _____mutable — not changeable

14. _____superable — not surmountable; not able to be overcome

Following the spelling rules, choose either *en-* or *em-* for these words.

15. _____slave — to put into slavery

16. _____body — to put into a body; unite

17. _____large — to make larger

18. _____power — to give power to

Some prefixes are negative in the sense that they undo or reverse the action indicated in the base word. The prefix *dis-* functions this way in words such as *disappear* and *dissatisfy*. Another negative prefix is *mis-*, which can be translated as the adverbs *wrongly* and *badly* or as the adjective *bad*. Infrequently, *mis-* means "not," as in *mistrust* and *misdoubt*, but normally it means "wrongly" or "bad."

Exercise 3.16

Use *dis-* or *mis-* to complete the words below.

1. _____connect   break connection with

2. _____fortune   bad fortune

3. _____take   err; take one thing for another

4. _____assemble   dismantle

5. _____enchant   disillusion

6. _____suade   persuade not to do something

7. _____apprehend   misunderstand

8. _____treat   treat badly

9. _____deed   bad or evil deed

10. _____entangle   extricate; free from a tangle or complicated situation

The Greek prefix *an-* or *a-*, meaning "without" or "not," combines with words and roots to make some interesting words. Amazon was the name of a mythological race of female warriors. According to a Greek myth, these women cut off their right breasts to give themselves better use of the bow. The name Amazon means literally "without breast"; from *a-*, without, and *mazo*, breast.

Combine the negative *a-* with other roots and words to produce more words.

11. _____typical   not typical, not according to type

12. _____political   not political; not inclined toward politics

13. _____nomaly   an abnormality; irregularity; deviation

14. _____symmetric   having unequal sides; not proportioned

15. _____mnesia   loss of memory, from the root *mne*, to remember

16. _____mnesty   a general pardon given offenders by a government; literally, a forgetting

PREFIXES FOR NUMBERS AND SIZES

Greek and Latin prefixes have furnished English with several words used for indicating numbers. Use the lists below to do the exercise that follows.

Numbers	Greek	Latin
one	mono-	uni-
two	di-	bi-; du-
three	tri-	tri-
four	tetra-	quadr-; quart-
five	penta-	quint-
six	hexa-	sex-
seven	hepta-	sept-
eight	oct-	oct-
nine	ennea-	nov-
ten	deca-	dec-
one-half	hemi-	semi-
one hundred		cent-
one thousand		mille-
one-and-one-half		sesqui-

Exercise 3.17

1. The Latin word *corn* means "horn," as in *cornucopia*, or "horn of plenty." How many horns does a unicorn have? _____

2. How many pairs of wings does a monoplane have? _____ A biplane? _____

3. A three-wheeled cycle is a _____.

4. How many people fight a duel? _____

5. Quadrupled means multiplied by _____.

6. How many years comprise a decade?

7. How many babies are there in a set of quintuplets? _____. How many babies in a set of sextuplets? _____

8. How many singers comprise a barbershop quartet? _____ How many musicians form a sextet? _____

9. The verb *decimate* means "to reduce the numbers of something considerably." Literally, *decimate* means "to kill one out of every _____. (From an ancient Roman custom of choosing a man by lot to be killed as punishment for a group.)

10. December is the twelfth month of the year. In the old Roman calendar, December was the _____ month. According to the Roman calendar, the seventh month of the year was _____; the eighth month was _____; the ninth month was _____.

11. The United States Department of Defense is housed in a famous building called the Pentagon. How many sides does the Pentagon have? _____

12. How many sides does a hexagon have? _____

13. How many legs does an octopus have? _____

14. The root *ped* means "foot." How many feet does a centipede supposedly have? _____ How many feet does a millipede seem to have? _____

15. The Latin root *annu* or *enni* means "year." In 1926, the United States celebrated its sesquicentennial. How old was the United States then? _____ In what year did the United States hold its bicentennial celebration? _____

Exercise 3.18

Other prefixes and roots that indicate amounts are *poly-*, meaning "many," and the prefix *a-*, which means "without" or "none." The Latin root *omni-* means "all; every." The Greek prefix that means "all" is *pan-*, as in pan-African—*all* the African countries. In doing the following exercise, be aware that, except for the word *bigamy*, Greek and Latin elements are not combined in the same word.

This exercise deals with numbers in marriage and religion. Use the numbers chart (p. 63) to answer some of the questions.

1. The Greek root *gam* means marriage. *Polygamy* (pa-LIG-a-mee) is the practice of having _____ spouses at the same time.

2. In most countries, *polygamy* and *bigamy* (BIG-a-mee) are illegal. What is bigamy? _____

3. The practice of being married to only one person at a time is called _____, a Greek word.

4. The Greek root meaning "God" is *the*, as in *theology*, the study of religion. *Theism* is a belief in God or other divinities. A belief that there is no God is called _____.

5. Jews, Christians, and Moslems believe in one God. This belief is called _____, a Greek word.

6. The ancient Greeks were polytheists. *Polytheism* is a belief in _____ gods.

7. The Pantheon was a temple built to honor _____ of the gods.

8. A belief that God's spirit lives in all things is called _____, a Greek word.

9. The doctrine of the Holy Trinity teaches that there are _____ persons in one God.

10. The Unitarian Church rejects the doctrine of the Trinity and stresses complete freedom of religious opinion. In the early Christian era, Unitarians were those who believed in the _____ness of God, rather than the Trinity.

11. *Pandemonium* (pan-da-MONE-ee-um) now means "noisy disorder." The poet John Milton coined this word as the name of Satan's palace in Hell. Literally, *pandemonium* means "the place of _____ demons."

12. Many religions teach that God is a Supreme Being who is omnipotent (ahm-NIP-a-tent). *Potent* means "powerful." *Omnipotent* means _____-_____.

13. The faithful in every part of the world believe that God can hear their prayers because he is *omnipresent*. *Omnipresent* means _____.

14. The word *omniscient* (ahm-NISH-unt) is a combination of the roots *omni-* and *sciens*, which mean "knowing." An omniscient God is _____-_____.

15. Some Christians believe that Christ will come again to rule the earth, and that all nations and people will live in peace during his reign. This peace will last for a *millennium*. How long is a millennium? _____

The prefixes *macro-* and *mega-* (or *megal-*) mean "large." *Micro-* means "small." Chapter 1 presented the words *microphone* and *microscope*. The list below includes two more "micro" words.

microcosm (MY-krow-koz-um)	from *micro*, little, and *cosmos*, world or universe; a little world; miniature universe; the small world surrounding an individual as opposed to the bigger world
microorganism (my-krow-OR-ga-niz-um)	a minute, one-celled organism; a bacterium or disease germ
megaphone (MEG-a-fone)	a funnel-shaped device for increasing the sound volume

megalith
(MEG-a-lith)

a huge stone; an ancient stone monument

megalomaniac
(meg-a-le-MANE-ee-ak)

a person who has delusions of grandeur or lust for power

macrocosm
(MAK-ra-koz-um)

the whole universe

Exercise 3.19

Supply the missing words.

1. *Lithos* means "stone"; a monolith is a single large stone block used in architecture or sculpture. Huge stone monuments such as the monoliths of Stonehenge, England, erected by prehistoric people, are called _____s.

2. *Phon* means "sound." A _____ makes voices sound louder.

3. A microbe is a unicellular organism visible only through a microscope. The synonym for *microbe* is _____ .

4. The smaller world in which one carries out the daily functions of life is a _____, compared to the _____, which is the whole universe.

5. A _____ has a giant ego. He may even think he's God.

GOOD AND BAD PREFIXES

Most prefixes are similar in function to prepositions or adverbs. They give information about the "where, when, or how" of a root. Some examples are *re-*, back; *pre-*, before; *con-*, together. Other prefixes such as *in-* or *non-* serve to give roots negative meanings. A few prefixes, however, act as descriptive adjectives. In this lesson, you will learn the descriptive prefix *mal-* or *male-*, meaning "bad" or "badly," and the root **bene**, meaning "good." The prefix *mal-* functions as the adverb "badly" in these words: maltreat—treat badly; malfunction—function badly; malnourish—nourish badly. In other words in which *mal-* or *male-* appear, its meaning is "bad" or "evil."

Exercise 3.20

You may be able to answer the following questions just from what you've already learned about how words work. Use a dictionary to guide you if you need a hand.

1. *Malaise* (ma-LAYZ) comes from the prefix *mal-* and the root **aise**, meaning "ease." In what way are *malaise* and *malady* (MAL-a-dee) related in meaning? In what way do they differ?

2. What *mal-* word means "ill will; spite; desire to injure another"?

3. What do the adjectives *benign* (ba-NINE) and *malicious* (ma-LISH-us) mean?

4. As medical terms, what are the definitions of *benign* and *malignant* (ma-LIG-nunt)?

5. If someone *maligns* (ma-LINE) your character, does that person say nice things in your behalf or spread false, ugly rumors about you?

6. Antonyms are words that have opposite meanings. The words *benevolent* (be-NEV-a-lent) and *malevolent* (ma-LEV-a-lent) are antonyms based on the root **vol**, which means "will," as in *volition* and *voluntary*. Which antonym means "bearing ill will"? _____ Which means "bearing good will"? _____

7. *Malediction* (MAL-a-dik-shun) and *benediction* (BEN-a-dik-shun) are antonyms based on the root **dict**, meaning "say; speak." Which antonym means "a spoken blessing"? _____ Which means "a curse"? _____

8. The antonyms *benefactor* (BEN-a-fak-ter) and *malefactor* (MAL-a-fak-ter) are built on the root **fac**, meaning "do; make." Which of the pair means "an evildoer"? _____ Which means "a person who does good things for another"? _____

9. The root **fact** means "do; make." Which antonym means "a person who does good things for another"? _____ Which means "an evildoer"? _____

10. Another form of the root **fac** is **fic**, on which the antonyms *beneficent* (be-NEF-a-cent) and *maleficent* (ma-LEF-a-cent) are based. Of this pair, which means "kindly, generous"? _____ Which means "doing evil or harm"? _____

4

Combining Prefixes and Roots

Nearly all of the roots you are learning require the attachment of prefixes, suffixes, or other roots in order to make fully formed words. Such roots are called "bound roots." Unlike free roots, such as *run, song,* or *war,* bound roots cannot stand alone. The root **vert** or **vers,** meaning "turn," is an example of a root that must be bound to other elements to form a complete word. The word *vertical,* meaning "turned upright," is formed by adding a suffix. The word *anniversary* comes from two roots, **anni,** meaning "year," and **vers,** meaning "turn," plus the suffix -**ary.** An *anniversary,* literally "the turning of a year," recurs annually on the same date each year and commemorates a past event.

The root **vert** combines with several prefixes to form words. The first exercise in this lesson deals with ten prefixes that combine with **vert** or **vers.**

Exercise 4.1

Form words with each prefix listed below. Then match each word you have formed with its definition at the right, writing its letter in the blank space at the left.

Example:

con + verse =   talk together; have a
converse = turn   conversation; literally,
together   to turn together in
                             thought to certain topics

Before beginning, notice that some basic meanings are the same for different words. You will need to use a dictionary to determine the subtle differences in meanings of these words.

	Basic Meaning	Definition
1. _____ a + vert = _____ = turn away		a. to corrupt; turn something good into something bad or evil; literally, to turn throughout
2. _____ ad + verse = _____ = to turn		
3. _____ contro + versy = _____ = a turning against		b. change completely; turn one thing into another; change from one belief or religion to another
4. _____ con + vert = _____ = turn completely		c. turn away; avoid; prevent; ward off something
5. _____ di + vert = _____ = turn away		d. to turn back to a former state, condition, habits, etc; turn property back to a former owner
6. _____ extro + vert = _____ = turn outside		e. to turn away from a set or regular course; to turn the mind away from care by entertainment; to distract attention
		f. argument; debate; dispute

7. _____ intro +
   vert = _____ = turn
                  inward

8. _____ per +
   vert = _____ = turn
                  throughout

9. _____ re +
   verse =
   _____ = turn
          back

10. _____ re +
    vert = _____ = turn
                   back

g. a person whose
thoughts and interests
are turned inward; an
introspective person,
one who prefers being
alone

h. turn in an opposite
direction; go
backward; overturn a
previous decision or
order

i. turning to
misfortune;
unfavorable; causing
hardship

j. a person who is
outgoing; one whose
interest is focused
outside the shelf; one
who prefers being with
others

Exercise 4.2

Complete the following sentences, choosing words you
wrote in Exercise 4.1.

1. We are going to _____ the garage into a den.

2. Some people feel that Christmas has been _____ed.
   Once considered sacred, Christmas has become just a
   source of big profits for manufacturers.

3. We thought he had reformed and would stay out of trouble,
   but now that he is mixing with that crowd, he
   has _____ed to his old ways.

4. I'm too busy to _____ with you now, but we can talk later.

5. The car, still in _____ gear, backed into a truck.

6. He spends a great deal of time alone reading or writing in his journal. Sometimes he takes long walks by himself just to think. He's an _____.

7. His sister is just the opposite. She's very outgoing and always has plenty of friends. She's a real _____.

8. The nuclear power plant is causing much _____. Some people think that it should continue to operate, but others say the plant is unsafe and should be shut down.

9. In spite of _____ weather conditions, the rescue team managed to save the stranded mountain climbers.

The prefix of *avert* is *a-*, a shortened form of *abs-*, which means "away." The prefix *dis-*, shortened to *di-* in the word *divert*, also means "away." Thus, *avert* and *divert* both mean "turn away." Although their basic meaning is the same, these verbs are used differently. Study the broader definitions of both, and write the one that best fits in each of the sentences below.

10. Traffic is being _____ed until the main road is repaired.

11. Playing tennis _____s my mind from problems.

12. The government must find a way to _____ war.

13. You _____ her attention while I put the candles on her cake.

14. The shy young girl _____ed her eyes to avoid his gaze.

Exercise 4.3

The words in this exercise are based on the root **pon, pos**, or **posit**, which means "place" or "put," as in the words *pose* and *position*. The directions for this exercise are the same as those for Exercise 4.1. First combine the root with its various prefixes. Then find the definition of each newly formed word, placing its letter in the space provided. Use a dictionary if necessary.

1. _____ com +
   pose
   = _____ = put
           together

2. _____ de +
   pose
   = _____ = put
           down

3. _____ de +
   posit
   = _____ = put
           down, away

4. _____ dis +
   pose
   = _____ = put away

5. _____ ex +
   pose
   = _____ = place
           outward

6. _____ im +
   pose
   = _____ = place on

7. _____ op +
   pose
   = _____ = place
           against

a. reveal what has been hidden, uncover; open to light; to put outside in an unsheltered place; to leave unprotected

b. to assume to be true; to place under assumption without actually knowing; to guess

c. to place on as a burden; to intrude; to force upon as by law

d. to place after; to delay a scheduled event or action

e. to put forth an idea or plan; to make a suggestion

f. to put something down; to put money or valuables away, as in a bank, for safekeeping; a partial payment made to secure something; something that has been put down

g. to deprive of rank and power; to force a ruler to step down

8. _____ post +
   pone
   = _____ = place
            after

from office, oust; (as
a legal term) to put
testimony down in
writing

9. _____ pro +
   pose
   = _____ = put forth

h. to put together the
elements of something;
create, arrange; to
"put" oneself together
in the sense of
becoming calm

10. _____ sup +
    pose
    = _____ = place
             under

i. to take a contrary
position; to fight or
compete against

j. to get rid of; sell,
give, or throw away;
to settle a matter; to be
inclined toward

Exercise 4.4

To complete the sentences below, choose words from those
you wrote in Exercise 4.3. You will be writing some of the
words more than once.

1. This closet is full of junk. I really should _____
   of these worthless old things.

2. It's very important that I _____ of these business
   matters right away.

3. The owner is not _____d toward selling the
   property.

4. The investigation _____d a scheme to steal the
   old man's fortune.

5. Don't _____ yourself to danger by walking
   alone at night.

6. You should not _____ your skin to sunlight for
   long periods of time.

7. If it rains, we will have to _____ the game.

8. I hate to _____ on my cousin, but I have no other place to stay.

9. The judge _____d a fine of fifty dollars.

10. The people were suffering hardships because the king _____d heavy taxes on them.

Exercise 4.5

The words in this exercise are based on the root **mit** or **miss**, which means "send; let go; allow." A *mission* is the act of sending or the duty on which one is sent. Other words based on **miss** and **mit** contain the prefixes listed below.

ad-	to
com-	together
dis-	away
e-	out
o-	toward
per-	through
re-	back
sub-	under
trans-	across

Combine prefixes from the list above with the root **mit** or **miss** to form words that match the literal definitions given.

Example:

admit   to send or allow in

1. _____ miss   send away

2. _____ mit   send together

3. _____ mit   send across

4. _____ mit   send back

5. _____ mit   send out

6. _____ mit   send through, allow

7. _____ mit   send under

8. _____ mit   send toward

Some of the words you have just formed have usages that relate closely to their basic definitions. The verb *transmit*, for instance, is used to mean "send something across." Other words in the list, however, are not as clearly connected in usage with their literal meanings. For example, the word *admit* also means "confess." The verbs *submit* and *commit* are now only loosely connected to their original meanings. Before beginning the next exercise, find the various definitions of *submit* and *commit* in the dictionary.

Another word you will need to find is *omit*. Formed from *obs-* and *mit*, *omit* originally meant "send something toward someone," but this definition is no longer used.

Exercise 4.6

Complete the sentences below, using the words you formed in Exercise 4.5.

1. If they find him guilty, they will _____ him to prison.

2. She spent months planning how to _____ the crime.

3. I'm much too busy to _____ myself to more responsibility.

4. I need to _____ a message to the company's president in London.

5. This disease is not infectious. One person cannot _____ it to another.

6. He is going to _____ his manuscript to a publisher.

7. Your ideas are good. You should _____ them to the supervisor.

8. I refuse to _____ to such unreasonable demands.

9. You should _____ this paragraph from your letter.

10. You must _____ your payment within ten days.

5

Suffixes

A suffix is a word part that is attached to the end of a root. Most suffixes carry little meaning by themselves. Instead, they help identify words as verbs, nouns, adjectives, or adverbs. For instance, many words ending in the suffix *-ate* are verbs. *Motivate* and *terminate* are examples. The suffix chart on page 80 is built on the verb *create*.

NOUN SUFFIXES

Noun suffixes help identify words that mean persons, places, and things. The suffix *-er* (also spelled *-or* and *-ar*) means "one who" in these words: bak*er*, one who bakes; sail*or*, one who sails; begg*ar*, one who begs.

Another suffix meaning "one who" is *-ant* and its variant spelling *-ent*. A *participant* is one who participates; a *president* is one who presides. The suffix *-ant* or *-ent* also means "that which" in words such as *repellant*, that which repels, and *precedent*, that which precedes.

The suffix *-ary* means "that which" in words such as *dictionary*, literally, "that which contains diction." Attached to other roots, the suffix *-ary* can mean "one who." A *secretary* is one who deals with the papers and correspondence of

Suffix	Meaning	Example	Meaning	Part of Speech
-or	one who	creat**or**	one who creates	noun (a person)
-ion	the act of; that which	creat**ion**	the act of creating; that which is created	noun (a thing)
-ure	that which	creat**ure**	that which is created	noun (a thing)
-ive	having the quality of; ability to	creat**ive**	having the ability to create	adjective
-ly	in a certain way or manner	creative**ly**	in a creative way	adverb

a business, or literally "one who keeps secrets." A suffix that indicates a place is *-ory*. A *dormitory* is a large room or place where many people sleep. The root **pos**, as you learned, means "put." A *repository* is a place where things are put back for safekeeping, or stored. A *depository* is a place where anything is deposited. *Note*: Like some other noun suffixes, the suffix *-ory* may also be used as an adjective, as in *satisfactory*.

The words below are made by combining suffixes with roots that you learned in an earlier lesson on prefixes. Remember that **vers** and **vert** mean "turn"; **pos** and **pon** mean "put"; **mit** and **miss** mean "send."

adver**sary**   one who has turned against another; an enemy; an opponent

compon**ent**   a part of the whole; an element; ingredient

compos**er**   one who composes—especially one who writes music

emis**sary**   one who is sent out on a secret mission; a secret agent, spy; a representative of a country

impost**or**   one who poses as another person; that is, one who
             deceives by pretending to be someone else

oppon**ent**   adversary; one who opposes another; antagonist; one
             who opposes a plan or idea

propon**ent** one who puts forth a plan; one who is in favor of a plan or
             cause; an advocate

mission**ary** one who is sent to a foreign country for the purpose of
             religious work

Many noun suffixes mean "act," "result," "state," "condition," or "quality of." A few are listed below.

-al	renew**al**	the act of renewing
-ence	confid**ence**	the state of being confident
-ance	resist**ance**	the act of resisting
-ion	confu**sion**	the state of being confused
-ment	amaze**ment**	the state of being amazed
-ness	polite**ness**	the quality of being polite
-ty	penal**ty**	the result of being penalized
(also **-ety,**	sobri**ety**	the condition of being sober
-ity)	sincer**ity**	the quality of being sincere
-ure	pleas**ure**	the state of being pleased;
		also, that which pleases

Of the suffixes that denote an act, state, or condition, the suffix *-ion* seems to appear most frequently. Variant spellings of *-ion* are *-sion*, *-tion*, *-ation*, and *-ition*. There are few, if any, rules to rely on in deciding which spelling to use. However, certain patterns occur when *-ion* is added to some syllables. In changing verbs ending in *-de* to nouns, notice that *-de* is dropped and *-sion* is added.

divi**de**	divi**sion**
persua**de**	persua**sion**
intru**de**	intru**sion**

Roots follow patterns when combined with *-ion*. The root **port**, for example, combines with *-ation*.

deport	deport**ation**
export	export**ation**
transport	transport**ation**

Exercise 5.1

Practice adding *-ion* to the roots **vert, pose,** and **mit**. This will result in changing verbs into nouns. Add *-ion* to **vert** by dropping *t* and adding *-sion*.

Example:

| verb | noun |
| avert | aversion |

	verb	noun
1.	convert	_____
2.	divert	_____
3.	pervert	_____
4.	subvert	_____

When adding *-ion* to the stem **pose**, drop *e* and add *-ition*.

5.	compose	_____
6.	depose	_____
7.	dispose	_____
8.	expose	_____
9.	impose	_____
10.	oppose	_____
11.	propose	_____
12.	suppose	_____

Before adding *-ion* to the root **mit**, change **mit** to its other form, **miss**.

Example:

verb	*noun*
admit	admission

13. commit   _____

14. emit   _____

15. intermit   _____

16. omit   _____

17. permit   _____

18. remit   _____

19. submit   _____

20. transmit   _____

Exercise 5.2

Choose the definition that best fits each word. Write its letter in the space provided. Use a dictionary to guide your choices.

1. _____ conversion

2. _____ subversion

3. _____ diversion

4. _____ deposition

5. _____ imposition

a. a guess; an assumption

b. a witness's sworn statement put down in writing

c. a failure to do something; the act of leaving out something

d. an interval of time between activities; the time between acts of a play; a pause

e. the act of overthrowing a government

6. _____ opposition

7. _____ supposition

8. _____ emission

9. _____ intermission

10. _____ omission

f. (1) amusement; the act of turning the mind away from care; (2) the act of drawing attention away from something

g. the act of turning a thing into something else; a transformation; a change of belief or religion

h. the sending out of something

i. the state of being opposite; a contrary position; resistance

j. intrusion; a burden placed on someone; the forcing of one's will on another

Roots in this exercise can be combined with suffixes other than -*ion* to become nouns. Postpone*ment*, dismis*sal*, rever*sal*, and adver*sity* are examples. *Postponement* is the act of "placing after" or delaying something. *Dismissal* means "the act of sending away; the act of discharging someone from a job." *Reversal* means "the reversing of an earlier decision or policy." *Adversity* is misfortune, hardship.

Other roots have another noun ending in addition to -*ion*. The addition of a different suffix can give the same base word other meanings. As examples, both *proposal* and *proposition* mean "a plan or suggestion offered for consideration," but *proposition* also means "a theory; a stated idea which one believes to be true; an assertion."

Exercise 5.3

Using a dictionary to guide you, choose from the word pairs below the word that best fits each definition. Write the word in the blank space at the right.

Example:

admission, admittance

a. permission to enter _____ admittance _____

b. permission to enter; a confession _____ admission _____

1. *commission, commitment*

    a. a group of people appointed to perform a task; the act of committing a deed, such as a crime _____

    b. a pledge to do something _____

2. *composition, composure*

    a. calmness, serenity _____

    b. the act of putting together parts to form a whole; something that has been put together; a musical or literary work _____

3. *disposition, disposal*

    a. the act of getting rid of something; also, the means of disposing _____

    b. the getting rid of something; inclination; temperament; one's usual frame of mind _____

4. *exposition, exposure*

    a. the act of exposing; disclosure of what has been hidden; the act of revealing _____

    b. an exhibition; a large public display of products, arts; an explanation of a theory _____

5. *remission, remittance*

   a. a temporary lessening of the   _____
progress of a disease; a lessening;
relaxation of effort; pardon of a
debt, sin, or crime

   b. the sending of a payment   _____

Exercise 5.4

Complete these sentences with nouns from this chapter.

1. A word that means "opponent" or "enemy"
is _____.

2. _____ is misfortune and hardship.

3. That man is not the real Dr. Sommers. He is
an _____.

4. To stay calm in stressful situations is to keep
one's _____.

5. Every sentence has a verb. A verb is a necessary _____ of a sentence.

6. A court reporter takes _____s from witnesses.

7. A confession is an _____ of guilt.

8. A sign that reads "No _____tance" means that
no one is allowed in.

9. A kitchen _____ gets rid of garbage.

10. A person who is usually in a light-hearted mood has a
cheerful _____.

11. Too much _____ to sunlight can damage the
skin.

12. Products from all over the world were exhibited at
the _____.

13. Some diseases spread from one person to another very quickly. The _____ of a disease to large numbers of people is called an epidemic.

14. A disease in _____ is one in which the symptoms have temporarily lessened or disappeared.

15. The _____ of toxic fumes from the chemical spill forced residents to evacuate. The spill sent out fumes over a wide area.

16. A secret agent is an _____.

17. My sister brought her three unruly children to my party. I really resented the _____.

18. By mistake, we left out the name of the groom's father on the wedding invitation. He is deeply offended by this _____.

19. A change from one religion to another is called _____.

20. An opponent is against a proposal; a _____ is in favor of the proposal.

21. Many voters were against the tax increase and voiced their _____ at the town hall meeting.

22. The pickpockets work in pairs. One creates a _____ so that the victim isn't aware that the other thief is stealing his wallet.

23. Marriage is a _____ to live together the rest of your lives. You should be very sure before making such a pledge.

24. In that country, penalties for the _____ of even lesser crimes are extremely harsh.

25. The reason for her _____ was that she was always late for work.

VERB SUFFIXES

Verbs are action words. The verb suffixes *-ate*, *-fy* (or *-ify*), *-ish*, and *-ize* (or *-ise*) mean "to do, make, cause, become, have."

-ate	complic**ate**	to make something complex
-ify	terr**ify**	to cause terror
-ish	fin**ish**	to cause to end
-ize	sympath**ize**	to have sympathy

Two verbs based on the root **vert** are formed by adding suffixes. They are *diversify* and *advertise*. The adjective *diverse* originally meant "turned in different directions," but now means "several; different; various; marked by differences": *America's diverse cultures*. The verb *diversify* means "to vary; have variety."

The literal definition of *advertise* is "to cause to turn." *Advertise* means "to turn public attention toward something, especially a product for sale, by means of the press or broadcasting; to give public notice of something, especially products or services."

ADJECTIVE SUFFIXES

Adjectives are words that describe nouns.

Example:

adjective	*noun*
beautiful	flower
joyous	day

The suffixes *-ful* and *-ous* mean "full of." Thus, a beaut*iful* flower is full of beauty; a joy*ous* or joy*ful* day is full of joy.

The suffixes below are combined with the roots **mit**, **vers**, and **pos**. These combinations form adjectives.

Suffix	Adjective	Meaning
-ent	intermitt**ent**	occurring at intervals; ceasing from time to time, not steady; literally, sent between
-ible (variant spelling of **-able**)	permiss**ible**	allowable
	revers**ible**	capable of being turned in the opposite direction; capable of being worn inside out (a garment)
	irrevers**ible**	incapable of being turned, changed, or undone
-ile	versat**ile**	having many abilities or uses; literally, able to turn
-ing	unremitt**ing**	not stopping; not lessening; constant
-ite	oppos**ite**	contrary; placed on the other side; placed in a contrary position
-ive	permiss**ive**	not strict in discipline; lenient; allowing
	submiss**ive**	obedient; yielding to the will of others
	subvers**ive**	tending to overthrow or destroy, especially a government

Exercise 5.5

Choose from the above chart the adjective that best fits each phrase below. Write the adjective in the blank space.

Example:

permissive	parents who allow their children a great deal of freedom

1. _____ a person who usually gives in to the demands of others, or who tends to readily obey another's commands

2. _____ a musician who can play all types of music

3. _____ a coat that can be worn inside out

4. _____ damage that cannot be undone

5. _____ pain that comes and goes

6. _____ pain that doesn't stop

7. _____ an activity that is allowable

8. _____ the wall that faces another wall on the other side of a room

9. _____ an organization that plans to overthrow a government

THE ADVERB SUFFIX -*ly*

Adverbs modify verbs. They describe the manner in which an action is performed.

Example:

verb	*adverb*
walk	fast

Adverbs also modify adjectives and other adverbs.

Examples:

adverb	*adjective*
very	beautiful

verb	adverb	adverb
walk	very	fast

Only one suffix, *-ly*, is used to form adverbs from other words. The suffix *-ly* is joined to adjectives to make adverbs.

Example:

adjective	adverb
beautiful	beautiful*ly*

The suffix *-ly* means "in a certain way or manner": permissive*ly*, in a permissive manner.

Note: Not all words ending in *-ly* are adverbs. The suffix *-ly* is also part of some adjectives, such as *friendly* or *lovely*.

When the suffix *-ly* is added to an adjective, the adjective's spelling usually does not change:

Example:

adjective	adverb
polite	politely
real	really

A few adjectives, when converted to adverbs, do not follow this rule: *true-truly; due-duly*. Other exceptions are adjectives ending in *y* and *le*.

Examples:

adjective	adverb
easy	easily
possible	possibly

Exercise 5.6

In the blank space on the right, substitute the appropriate adverb for each phrase below.

Example:

In a polite way   ___politely___

1. in a permissive manner   _____

2. in an unremitting way   _____

3. in an intermittent way   _____

4. in a submissive manner   _____

5. in an irreversible way   _____

Exercise 5.7

In the sentences below, substitute words from this chapter for the definitions given in parentheses. Be sure to use the part of speech indicated below the parenthesized words. Write the substituted word in the blank space at the end of each sentence.

Example:

The child's parents are too ___(lenient)___.   ___permissive___
                              adjective

1. The steamy jungle heat was ___(constant)___.   _____
                                adjective

2. To sell products, you must ___(turn attention to)___ them.
                                (verb)

3. The rain has been ___(not steady)___.   _____
                       adjective

4. The men worked ___(without stopping)___ in a desperate
                      adverb
   effort to rescue the child from the well.   _____

5. The decision is ___(able to be changed)___.
                      adjective

   _____

6. The child is very ___(obedient)___.   _____
                        adjective

7. This coat is _____(can be turned inside out)_____.
                              adjective

   _____

8. The rumors and lies harmed her good name
   _____(in a way that cannot be undone)_____. _____
                        adverb

9. With new facilities, we can _____(give variety to)_____ our
                                    verb

   sports program. _____

10. The brothers fought on _____(contrary)_____ sides in the Civil
                             adjective

    War. _____

6

Language Trees

So far, you have studied roots producing small families of words, which we called word plants. Compared to these minor roots, major roots, which produce large numbers of words, can be called the trees of the language. In this chapter, you will learn one such tree—the root **ten**, which is also spelled **tain** and **tin**, depending on the derived word's part of speech. *Ten* means to have, hold, keep, occupy, or possess. Of course, you already know some of the words from this root: *contain*, hold together; *content*, that which is held together, or happy with what one has; *continent*, a body of land held together in one mass. In all, there are over one hundred words that came from this single root.

Following are some of them. Practice pronouncing the words as you read them.

tenacious (ten-Ā-shus), tenacity (ta-NAS-a-tee)
Tenacious means "holding on to something tightly or stubbornly." The ability to hold on to something in spite of difficulty is called **tenacity**.

tenant (TEN-unt)
A **tenant** is a person who holds land or occupies a property, especially property rented from someone else. Other defini-

tions of **tenant** are "occupant, dweller, or one who rents a dwelling."

tenement (TEN-a-munt)

A **tenement** is an apartment building in bad condition usually located in a slum area of a large city.

tenet (TEN-it)

A teaching or principle that is held to be true by a religion or an organization is called a **tenet**.

tenure (TEN-yur)

A **tenure** is a holding of something such as land, but a common usage of **tenure** is related to employment, especially in a profession. In this sense, **tenure** means "permanent status given to a professional after a trial period."

lieutenant (loo-TEN-unt)

The phrase "in lieu of" means "in place of." Literally, **lieutenant** means "holding the place of or acting in the place of another." A **lieutenant** is one who has the power to act in the place of a superior. In the armed forces, a **lieutenant** is an officer who ranks below a superior officer. A **lieutenant** governor acts as governor of a state during a governor's absence from office.

abstain (ab-STAYN), abstinence (AB-sta-nens), abstemious (ab-STEEM-ee-us)

The prefix *abs-* means "away"; the root *ten* means "hold" or "keep." **Abstain** means "to keep or hold oneself away from something; to refrain from something, such as alcohol. **Abstain** also means "to keep oneself from doing something, such as voting." **Abstinence** means "the act or practice of abstaining; the act of denying oneself something such as food or pleasure." An **abstemious** person is one who eats and drinks sparingly.

tenable (TEN-a-bull), untenable (un-TEN-a-bull)

Tenable means "capable of being held or supported";

untenable means "insupportable." A theory or belief that is found to be inaccurate or flawed and therefore insupportable can be described as **untenable**.

continue (kun-TIN-yoo), continuity (con-ta-NOO-a-tee)

To **continue** is to keep on doing something, to go on in some action, or to go on after an interruption. **Continuity** is an unbroken sequence of thoughts or actions, or the quality of being continuous.

detain (de-TANE), detention (de-TEN-chun)

The prefix *de-* means "down" or "away." **Detain** means (1) keep one away; keep from going on; stop; delay; (2) hold away from others; confine. **Detention** is the state of being held in confinement.

maintain (mane-TANE), maintenance (MANE-ta-nuns)

The verb **maintain** is formed from the roots **manu**, meaning "hand," and **tain**, meaning "keep." Literally, **maintain** means "to keep by hand." Its broader meanings are (1) to keep in good condition; to keep in existence, preserve; (2) to claim to be true; (3) to give financial support; pay the expenses of. **Maintenance** means (1) the act of maintaining; the work of keeping buildings, roads, or machines in good condition; the act of keeping anything in good condition: *the maintenance of health*; (2) the means of support; livelihood.

obtain (ob-TANE)

Obtain means "to gain possession of; get."

pertain (per-TANE), pertinent (PUR-ta-nunt), impertinent (im-PER-ta-nunt)

The prefix *per-* means "through." The literal meaning of **pertain** is "to hold throughout." Its broader meaning is "to relate; to belong to or have to do with the subject or matter at hand." **Pertinent** means "pertaining to; relevant." **Imper-**

tinent means "not pertinent; irrelevant." A second meaning of **impertinent** is "disrespectful; impudent; unmannerly." This definition is not related to the root **ten** because **impertinent**, used in this sense, comes from another root.

pertinacious (per-ta-NAY-shus)

Like *tenacious*, **pertinacious** means "holding on stubbornly," but unlike *tenacious*, it is not used to indicate physically gripping something. **Pertinacious** means "to hold on to a goal or aim throughout all difficulties or opposition." In the sense of conveying dogged persistence, the two words are synonyms.

retain (re-TANE), retention (re-TEN-chun)

The prefix *re-* means "back." **Retain** means (1) to hold back something; to keep back something for oneself; (2) to keep in mind, remember; (3) to obtain the services of a lawyer or other professional by paying a fee in advance. **Retention** is (1) the act or condition of being held back; (2) the ability to remember.

sustain (sus-TANE), sustenance (SUS-ta-nens)

The prefix *sus-*, a variant spelling of *sub-*, means "under." **Sustain** means "hold up, support, keep from falling": *The bridge will sustain the weight of heavy trucks*. **Sustain** also means "to support life with water, nourishment, etc.; to keep up courage, give comfort": *Food is necessary to sustain life. That Bible verse sustains me during difficult times.* Other definitions of **sustain** are "endure, suffer, or undergo something; continue, prolong, keep something going": *The victim sustained injuries to his head and neck.* To succeed, you must **sustain** your efforts. As a legal term, **sustain** means "to uphold something as being valid": *The judge sustained the defense attorney's objections.*

Sustenance means "the act of sustaining; that which supports life, especially food; that which gives comfort and encouragement to the spirit."

Exercise 6.1

In each pair of sentences below, substitute a verb that matches both parenthesized definitions in the sentences. Write the verb in the blank space at the left.

1. _____
   a. The old man is giving his sons the land, but will (keep back for himself) the business.
   b. I can't (keep in mind) all this information. I'll have to write it down.

2. _____
   a. What you're saying doesn't (relate, belong to) this case.
   b. The terms *marinate* and *broil* (relate) to cooking.

3. _____
   a. Food, water, and oxygen are required to (support) life.
   b. Your comforting words helped (support) me during a trying time.

4. _____
   a. I am determined to (get) an education.
   b. He wants to (gain possession of) that property.

5. _____
   a. The storm will (delay) us if we don't leave soon.
   b. The police tried to (stop) the suspect, but he got away.

6. _____
   a. (Keep on) working.
   b. If the rain stops soon, we will (go on with) the game.

7. _____
   a. Vegetarians (keep away) from meat.
   b. To lose weight you must (keep away) from fattening foods.

8. _____   a. In order to (financially support) his
                       large family, he has to do two
                       jobs.
                    b. Do you still (claim) that you are
                       innocent of the crime?

Exercise 6.2

Choose words from the list below to complete the sentences
that follow.

abstinence	detention	impertinent	tenacity
abstemious	lieutenant	retain	tenement
continuity	maintenance	retention	tenet
untenable	pertinent	sustain	tenure
			pertinacious

1. That property needs _____. The paint is peeling
   and the yard is overgrown with weeds.

2. This bridge will not _____ the weight of heavy
   trucks.

3. Christians hold the belief that Christ died and arose from
   the dead. This teaching is a basic _____ of
   Christianity.

4. Being _____ by habit, she never eats much.

5. That information isn't _____ to this discussion.
   We were talking about a completely different matter.

6. Fasting is _____ from food.

7. Without a _____ing wall to hold back the soil,
   the rain will cause a mudslide.

8. The tenants complained about the terrible conditions in
   the _____.

9. It takes courage and _____ to win when everything seems to be against you.

10. That theory is _____, because it contains major
    errors.

7
Making and Breaking

As we have already seen, the basic meaning of any word is given to it by its middle building block (the meaning base or word root). The prefix gives the word direction; the suffix simply helps identify it as a noun, adjective, and so forth. In this chapter we will look at two basic concepts that everyone is familiar with: making and breaking. There are two word groups for each concept, an easy one to help you familiarize yourself with the concept, and a harder group to help you learn to recognize and identify more difficult words. This chapter shows how the words go together, then explains their derivation. After reading the explanations, take the tests to make sure you understand the way these words work. Now, let's start with "making."

MAKING

The word *factory* comes from the Latin verb *facere*, which means "do" or "make." The roots from *facere*—**fac, fact, fect**, and **fic**—are contained in such words as manu*fac*ture, which literally means "make by hand," per*fect*, whose literal definition is "thoroughly done," and *fic*tion, meaning "a made-up story."

The Word Building Chart
for *fact, fac, fect,* and *fic*

Word	Beginning block	Middle block	End block	Quick definition
artifact	the root **arti** (art)	**fact** (to make)	none	object made by human art or skill
faction	none	**fact** (act)	**-ion** (noun)	a subgroup acting in opposition to a larger group
facile	none	**fac** (do)	**-ile** (adj. meaning "able")	easily done; able to do with ease
facilitate	none	**facil** (do easily)	**-itate** (form of verb suffix *-ate*, meaning "make")	make easy to do
facility	none	**facil** (do easily)	**-ity** (noun)	a ready ability; means by which something can be done, room, equipment, etc.
affect	**af-** (meaning to)	**fect** (act)	none	to act on, influence; touch emotionally
effect	**ef-** (form of *ex-*, meaning "out")	**fect** (produce)	none	outcome of an action
effective	**ef-** (out)	**fect** (produce)	**-ive** (adjective)	producing desired outcome, result

defect	de- (not, away)	fect (make, do)	none	(1) a lack; an imperfection (2) desert, do away with allegiance
infect	in- (within)	fect (produce)	none	produce something within, especially a disease
infectious	in- (within)	fect (producing within)	-ious (adjective)	tending to produce within; contagious
efficient	ef- (ex-, out)	fic (produce)	-lent (adjective)	producing results with minimum effort

---

Group One

artifact (n.) (AR-ta-fakt)

This word is formed by two roots, **art** and **fact**. Its literal meaning is "to make art," but, in usage, **artifact** can mean "any object made by human work or art."

Archaeologists learn about ancient cultures by studying artifacts.

faction (n.) (FAK-shun)

A **faction** is a group of people, usually dissenters, operating within a larger group to gain its own ends. **Faction** refers especially to subgroups within political parties.

Following the Civil War, the Radical Republicans, a faction of the Republican Party, began promoting citizenship for Blacks.

facile (adj.) (FAS-ill)

The root **fac** means "do"; the suffix *ile* means "able." **Facile** is defined literally as "able to do" and comes from the Latin word *facilis*, meaning "easy to do." Something that is **facile** is easily done. Other definitions of **facile** are (1) requiring little effort; achieved or performed easily; (2) skillful; dexterous; (3) smooth of speech, glib.

> Countless hours of practice lie behind his facile performances at the keyboard.

facilitate (v.) (fa-SIL-a-tate)
Facilitate means "to make easier to do; to free from hindrances or obstacles; to expedite (speed up) an action."

> For people in wheelchairs, ramps and automatic doors facilitate access to buildings.

facility (n.) (fa-SIL-a-tee)
Facility means "ease in doing something; ready skill or ability."

> Having a facility for languages, he spoke German, Japanese, and Russian fluently.

Another definition of **facility** (especially when pluralized) is "a room, building, area, or equipment that makes an activity possible or easier."

> Our school has facilities for all kinds of sports.

affect (v.) (a-FEKT)
Affect comes from the prefix *af-*, a changed spelling of *ad-*, meaning "to," and *fect*, meaning "do." **Affect** means "to do" in the sense of acting upon, influencing, changing, or having an effect.

> Gloomy weather affects my mood.

Affect can also mean "to touch or move the emotions."

> He was deeply affected by the plight of the homeless.

Another definition of **affect** is "pretend; imitate; act in an unnatural, artificial way."

> She affects a British accent just to impress people.

effect (v. & n.) (a-FEKT)

Effect is formed from the prefix *ef-*, a changed spelling of *ex-*, meaning "out," and *fect*, meaning "do." An **effect** is an outcome of something that has been done, a result of some action or event.

> Exercise has a good effect on the mind as well as the body.

As a verb, **effect** means "bring about a result or outcome."

> By concentrating on her studies, she was able to effect an improvement in her grades.

Note: People often confuse **affect** and **effect**. Remember that the noun **effect** means "result" or "outcome." If you keep in mind that the prefix *ef-* means "out," you will automatically associate "out" with "outcome," which means "result." The verb **effect** means "produce a result or outcome." **Affect** means "act upon, change, influence, or have an effect," but it does not mean "an outcome" or "a result." These three sentences illustrate the differences.

> The noisy party next door affected (acted upon) my concentration.
> The effect (result) was that I couldn't study.
> Finally, a warning from the apartment manager effected (produced as a result) peace and quiet.

effective (adj.) (a-FEK-tiv)

Effective means "producing the desired result; efficient; producing a strong impression."

> Combining exercise with a reducing diet is an effective way to lose weight.

defect (n.) (DEE-fect)

The prefix *de-* is sometimes used as a negative. In the word **defect**, *de-* means "not." Literally, **defect** means "not made complete." A **defect** is an imperfection, a failing, blemish, or flaw.

His frequent lying indicates a serious defect in his character.

As a verb, **defect** (de-FEKT) means "do away" in the sense of doing away with allegiance to one's country or political alliance. To **defect** is to abandon one's country, political party, etc.

Once a loyal supporter of the revolution, he became dissatisfied with the leadership and defected.

infect (v.) (in-FEKT), **infectious** (adj.) (in-FEK-shus)
Infect is formed from the prefix *in-*, meaning "into" or "within," and **fect**, meaning "made" or "produced." **Infect** means "produced within" in the sense of producing a disease within the body.

In the tropics, he was infected with malaria.

Infectious, the adjective form of **infect**, means "producing disease; contagious."

Influenza is a highly infectious disease.

Infect and **infectious** do not always apply to the producing or spreading of disease, but may pertain to spreading a mood, spirit, or attitude.

Her laughter was infectious; soon we were all laughing.

efficient (adj.) (i-FISH-ent)
Efficient and *effective* have the same basic meaning— "producing an intended effect or result"—but **efficient** also implies producing results with little wasted effort. Other definitions of **efficient** are "capable; competent."

In order to finish the work on time, we must find more efficient methods.

Group Two

Some words in this advanced group and those in later chapters will be variant forms of words you have already learned. Other words may be fairly common but have been placed in the advanced groups because of their length or spelling difficulty. Other words in these groups will be less common. Their common root connections, however, provide a clue to their meanings. Along with recognition of roots, knowledge of how word blocks fit together solves some of the difficulty in recognizing and spelling new words. Like the words you have just studied, the words here are built on the root forms related to doing, producing, or making.

affectation (n.) (af-fek-TAY-shun)
an artificial manner or appearance; a pretense

Actually, she grew up in Kansas. Her British accent is an affectation.

artifice (n.) (ART-a-fiss)
deception; trickery

He used charm and artifice to win her confidence and easily persuade her to withdraw her life's savings.

de facto (adv. & adj.) (de-FAK-tow)
Latin phrase often used as an adjective to mean "actual" or "true"; "actually existing with or without legal sanction"; literally, "in fact."

Although not legally recognized, the de facto government maintains its power by force.

efficacious (adj.) (ef-a-KAY-shus)
producing a desired result or intended effect

Walking is efficacious for reducing tension and building health.

facsimile (n.) (fak-SIM-a-lee)
an exact copy or reproduction; literally, "to make alike"

This dress is a facsimile of the one worn by the Queen at her coronation.

factious (adj.) (FAK-shus)
inclined to form factions; promoting dissension; *in a sense* "making trouble"

His factious statements already have caused some members to band into opposing groups.

factitious (adj.) (fak-TISH-us)
artificial; affected, not spontaneous

Her factitious smiles failed to impress the beauty-contest judges.

factotum (n.) (fac-TOTE-um)
handyman; one employed to do all kinds of work (from *fac*, do + *totum*, all)

Hired as a gardener, he soon became a general factotum on the large estate.

fictitious (adj.) (fik-TISH-us)
imaginary; invented

The suspect gave a fictitious alibi.

In the two words below, the root **fic** is a changed form of the suffix *-fy*, which means "to make."

deification (adj.) (dee-a-fa-KAY-shun)
the act of deifying, making a god of; the regarding of a person as a deity (*deus*, a god + *fic*, make)

Mad with power, the emperor decreed his own deification and ordered his subjects to worship him.

reification (adj.) (ray-if-a-KAY-shun)
the act of materializing, as an idea or plan; the act of making real or concrete

The Nazi death camps were a horrible reification of Hitler's insane ideas.

Exercise 7.1

Complete the sentences below by substituting **verbs** from Group One for the words in parentheses.

1. Word processors (make easier) _____ writing books.

2. Losing sleep (acts on, influences) _____ your grades.

3. Doing your homework will (bring about, result in) _____ better grades.

4. He is going to (abandon) _____ from the party.

5. At the rich old man's funeral, his greedy nephew (pretended) _____ed a sorrowful look.

6. Dirty bandages will (produce disease in) _____ a wound.

Exercise 7.2

Complete the sentences below by substituting **nouns** from Groups One and Two for the words in parentheses.

1. The school has no (building, place) _____ for basketball.

2. That (subgroup) _____ plans to walk out of the meeting if their demands aren't met.

3. That painting has a (flaw) _____.

4. He does a little of everything around the office. Because his duties are so varied, his only job title is that of (handyman) _____.

5. By using clever (deception) _____, the couple gained the old man's confidence and then took all his money.

6. Early Egyptians regarded their kings as divine beings whose authority they dared not question or disobey.

Through (making a god of) _____, Egypt's monarchs enjoyed immense power.

7. She's no more a countess than I am. That accent of hers is an (pretense) _____.

8. Close to the Indian burial ground, we found arrows, pottery, and other (human-made objects) _____.

9. The counterfeit painting was an almost perfect (duplicate) _____ of the original.

10. Exercise has a beneficial (result) _____ on your health.

Exercise 7.3

In the phrases below, substitute **adjectives** from Groups One and Two for the words in parentheses.

1. (producing results) _____ teacher

2. (producing intended results) _____ treatment for disease

3. a very (capable) _____ secretary

4. (contagious) _____ disease

5. (invented) _____ excuse

6. (easily done) _____ dance performance

7. (in fact) _____ government

8. (affected; artificial) _____ enthusiasm

9. (promoting dissension) _____ statements

Exercise 7.4—Synonyms

From Groups One and Two, choose words that are most nearly the same as the words listed below.

1. _____ in fact

2. _____ efficacious

3. _____ reproduction

4. _____ handyman

5. _____ materialization

6. _____ pretense

7. _____ contagious

8. _____ flaw

9. _____ subgroup

Exercise 7.5—Antonyms

Choose words that mean the opposite of those listed below.

1. _____ difficulty

2. _____ harmonious

3. _____ true

4. _____ incompetent

5. _____ ineffectual (two possible answers)

6. _____ hinder

BREAKING

The Latin verb *frangere* means "to break." Its root, **frag,
frac, frang,** or **fring,** forms the base of these words in the
following group, all of which relate to breaking.

The Word Building Chart
for *frag* and *frac*

Word	Beginning block	Middle block	End block	Quick definition
fragile	none	**frag** (break)	**-ile** (adjective suffix meaning "able")	breakable; easily broken
fragment	none	**frag** (break)	**-ment** (noun)	a piece broken off
fragmented	none	**frag** (break)	**-ment** **-ed** (noun converted to adjective)	broken; disconnected
fracture	none	**frac** (break)	**-ture** (noun or verb suffix)	a break; to break
fraction	none	**frac** (break)	**-tion** (noun)	a piece broken off from the whole; small part
infraction	**in-** (into)	**frac** (break)	**-tion** (noun)	break into another's rights, territory; break a law, contract, etc.

fragile (adj.) (FRAJ-ill)

Fragile comes from the root *frag*, meaning "break," and the suffix *-ile*, meaning "able." **Fragile** literally means "breakable," but its usual meaning is "easily broken or damaged; frail; delicate."

This antique vase is very fragile, so pack it carefully.

fragment (n.) (FRAG-ment)

A **fragment** is (1) a piece broken off; a small detached part; (2) a small isolated bit.

I heard only fragments of their conversation, but they seemed to be quarreling about something.

fragmented (adj.) (FRAG-ment-ed)

Fragmented means "broken into fragments; disconnected."

The vase is so fragmented that it would be impossible to glue it together again.

fracture (v. & n.) (FRAK-chur)

To **fracture** is to break something.

She fell and fractured her wrist.

As a noun, **fracture** means "a break, rupture, or crack."

The x-ray revealed three bone fractures in her left leg.

fraction (n.). (FRAK-shun)

In arithmetic, a **fraction** means "a division of a unit." The broader definition of **fraction** is "fragment; a disconnected part; a small portion."

Only a fraction of the art collection was saved from the fire.

infraction (v.) (in-FRAK-shun)

The noun **infraction** is based on the infrequently used verb **infract**, which comes from the prefix *in-*, meaning "in," and *frac*, meaning "break." An **infraction** is the act of violating or breaking a pledge, rule, or law. Another definition of **infraction** is "infringement."

> The two were suspended for fighting, an infraction of the rules at this school.

Another group of words that mean "break" or "burst" is based on the Latin root **rupt**.

The Word Building Chart
for *rupt*

Word	Beginning block	Middle block	End block	Quick definition
rupture	none	**rupt**	**-ure** (verb or noun suffix)	to break; a break
abrupt	**ab-** (away)	**rupt** (break)	none	break away; ending suddenly
corrupt	**cor-** (form of *com-* meaning "thoroughly")	**rupt** (break)	none	to thoroughly break down or deteriorate (especially in a moral sense)
corruption	**cor-** (thoroughly)	**rupt** (break)	**-ion** (noun)	deterioration; breakdown of integrity, moral values
disrupt	**dis-** (apart)	**rupt** (break)	none	break apart, break up an activity; impede progress by causing disorder
disruption	**dis-** (apart)	**rupt** (break)	**-ion** (noun)	disturbance; a halt
erupt	**e-** (from *ex-*, meaning "out")	**rupt** (break)	none	break out
eruption	**e-** (out)	**rupt** (break)	**-ion** (noun)	a breaking out

| interrupt | inter-
(between) | rupt
(break) | none | to break in
between |
| interruption | inter-
(between) | rupt
(break) | -ion
(noun) | a breaking in
between |

---

rupture (v. & n.) (RUP-chur)

The verb **rupture** means "to break or burst."

Her appendix may rupture if it isn't removed immediately.

A **rupture** is a breaking or a bursting.

A rupture in the tanker caused a large oil spill.

abrupt (adj.) (a-BRUPT)

Abrupt comes from the prefix *ab-*, meaning "away," and *rupt*, meaning "break." The literal meaning of **abrupt** is "break away." More usual definitions are (1) broken off; steep; (2) ending or changing suddenly; sudden, as in departure; 3) brusque, rude, or curt in manner or speech.

A shrill whistle brought an abrupt end to the clamor.

corrupt (v. & adj.) (ka-RUPT),
corruption (n.) (ka-RUP-shun)

Corrupt is formed from a variant spelling of the prefix *com-*, meaning "thoroughly," and *rupt*, meaning "break." **Corrupt** means "to 'break down thoroughly' in a moral sense; become dishonest, wicked; to morally decay."

There is a saying that absolute power corrupts absolutely.

As an adjective, **corrupt** means "dishonest; evil; morally decadent."

Dictators become corrupt because no one is allowed to question or protest what they do.

Corruption is dishonesty; moral deterioration; moral decay; vice.

Wars, greed, and corruption caused the fall of the Roman Empire.

Note: **Corrupt** may also mean "contaminate, taint; physically decay, rot."

disrupt (v.) (dis-RUPT), disruption (n.) (dis-RUP-shun)

The prefix *dis-* means "apart." **Disrupt** means "break apart" in the sense of breaking up an activity by throwing it into disorder. **Disruption** means "the act of disrupting; a disturbance."

The accident disrupted traffic.

erupt (v.) (i-RUPT), eruption (n.) (i-RUP-shun)

Erupt comes from the prefix *e-*, meaning "out," and *rupt*, meaning "break" or "burst." **Erupt** means "to break out" or "burst forth suddenly and violently." An **eruption** is a violent outbreak or a bursting forth.

A fight erupted in the hall when one of the students accused another of stealing.

interrupt (v.) (in-ter-RUPT), interruption (n.) (in-ter-RUP-shun)

Interrupt comes from the prefix *inter-*, meaning "between," and *rupt*, meaning "break." **Interrupt** means "break in between, hinder, or temporarily stop an activity."

A fire drill interrupted class this morning.

An **interruption** is the act of interrupting or something that interrupts.

A power failure caused an interruption of the broadcast.

Exercise 7.6

Complete the sentences below with words from the last two groups.

1. A break, crack, or rupture is a _____.

2. A piece broken off or a small fraction of something is a _____.

3. The breaking of a law or rule is an _____.

4. An object that is easily broken is _____.

5. A sudden, unexpected departure can be described as _____.

6. A division of a unit, a fragment, or a small portion of something is a _____.

7. A break, fracture, or bursting is a _____.

8. To burst out violently is to _____.

9. To break apart or break up (an activity) is to _____.

10. A noun that means moral breakdown or moral deterioration is _____.

HIGHER-LEVEL WORDS

fractious (adj.) (FRAK-shus)
unruly; rebellious; quarrelsome, peevish

Confined too long without diversion, the prisoners became fractious.

fragmentary (adj.) (FRAG-mun-tair-ee)
composed of fragments; broken; incomplete

Archaeologists have found a fragmentary skeleton of a man who may have lived thousands of years ago.

frangible (adj.) (FRANJ-a-bull)
fragile; brittle; easily broken

Removing these frangible artifacts from the site will require expert care.

infringement (n.) (in-FRINJ-ment)
the breaking of an agreement, oath, regulation, or law; violation of another's rights

Opening my mail without permission is an infringement of my privacy.

refraction (n.) (ri-FRAK-shun)
the change of direction of a ray, as of light or heat, in passage from one medium to another; literally, the "breaking" of direction

Rainbows are caused by light refraction, which occurs when sunlight passes through a raindrop, breaking the light's rays into colors.

refractory (adj.) (ri-FRAK-ta-ree)
obstinate; unmanageable; resistant to control; heat resistant; resistant to treatment, as a disease

Mules have great strength and endurance, but are better known for their refractory dispositions.

8

Coming and Going

Language began with the need to talk about the ordinary things required for human survival. Alphabets came from pictures of everyday things. The first letter of the Greek alphabet, *alpha*, meant "ox." *Beta*, the second letter, meant "house." Both letters symbolized things necessary for survival.

People needed to tell about such basic actions as eating, running, and hunting. In the beginning, words for these activities meant only those actions and nothing more. The Latin-derived word *current*, for example, originally meant "running"—not "latest" or "up-to-date," as in current events or current fashions—but simply the physical action of running. As civilizations developed and life became more complex, words had to become more versatile to fit new situations. Definitions went through a stretching process to accommodate wider human experience, so that a word like *profuse*, for *pour*, would mean more than pouring forth a liquid. *Profuse* might describe an abundant harvest or feast or someone's wordy speech. The essential idea of pouring is still there, however, to convey the idea of abundance.

In the chapters that follow, it will become apparent that most long words are based on everyday experiences and actions that everyone can understand. From there, it is not such a big step to understand broader definitions. In this chapter, you will first study words based on the simple idea of coming. The Latin root **ven** or **veni** is part of Julius Caesar's famous victory message sent to Rome upon his conquest of a part of Asia: *Veni, vidi, vici*—"I came, I saw, I conquered."

The **ven** root includes the stems **vene** and **vent**.

The Word Building Chart
for ven, veni, vene, vent

Word	Beginning block	Middle block	End block	Quick definition
advent	**ad-** (to)	**vent** (come)	none	a coming; an arrival
adventure	**ad-** (to)	**vent** (come)	**-ure** (that which)	that which comes or happens, especially as an exciting experience
convene	**con-** (together)	**vene** (come)	none	come together; meet
convention	**con-** (together)	**vent** (come)	**-ion** (the act of)	the act of coming together; a meeting
convenience	**con-** (together)	**veni** (come)	**-ence** (the quality of)	the quality of coming together handily; efficiency
convenient	**con-** (together)	**veni** (come)	**-ent** (having the quality of)	having the quality of ease and efficiency
event	**e-** (out)	**vent** (come)	none	a coming about; a happening
eventful	**e-** (out)	**vent** (come)	**-ful** (full of)	full of important happenings
intervene	**inter-** (between)	**vene** (come)	none	come between; interfere
intervention	**inter-** (between)	**vent** (come)	**-ion** (the act of)	the act of intervening; interference

invent	in- (on; upon)	vent (come)	none	to come upon an idea; create
invention	in- (on)	vent (come)	-ion (the act of)	the act of inventing, devising something
inventive	in- (on)	vent (come)	-ive (tending to)	tending to invent; clever
prevent	pre- (before)	vent (come)	none	to come before in order to stop something; forestall
prevention	pre- (before)	vent (come)	-ion (the act of)	the act of preventing; prior measures taken to avoid something
preventive	pre- (before)	vent (come)	-ive (tending to)	tending to ward off something
revenue	re- (back)	ven (come)	-ue (that which, French suffix)	money that comes back; income

---

Group One

advent (n.) (AD-vent)

The approach or arrival of something new can be called an **advent**, meaning "coming" or "that which is about to arrive."

> The advent of the automobile brought sweeping changes in American culture.

In Christian religions, Advent is a holy season before Christmas that marks the time approaching Christ's coming to earth.

adventure (n.) (ad-VEN-chur)

Something exciting that comes about in the way of a risky undertaking can be called an **adventure**.

For a real adventure, try sky-diving.

convene (v.) (kun-VEEN),
convention (n.) (kun-VEN-chun)

The prefix *con-* means "together"; *ven* means "come." **Convene** means (1) to come together; to assemble; (2) to call together, as for a meeting.

The superintendent convened the teachers in an emergency meeting yesterday.

Convention, the noun form of **convene**, means "an assembly; a formal meeting of members of social, political, or professional purposes."

A riot erupted in Chicago during the Democratic Party's 1968 convention.

convenience (n.) (kun-VEEN-yenss),
convenient (adj.) (kun-VEEN-yent)

Literally, **convenience**, like *convention*, means "the act of coming or meeting together," but in modern usage it means "that which fits or comes together easily." In other words, **convenience** refers to something that is efficient, trouble-saving, or handy. **Convenient**, the adjective form of *convenience*, means "handy; affording ease; saving trouble."

More buildings are designed now for the convenience of people in wheelchairs.

event (n.) (e-VENT), eventful (adj.) (e-VENT-full)

Event contains the prefix *e-*, meaning "out," and the root **vent**, which means "come." The literal meaning of **event** is "outcome." In modern usage, however, **event** translates more as "something that comes about; an occurrence; a happening."

> The most important event of this century was the development of the atomic bomb.

The suffix *-ful* means "full." **Eventful** means "full of exciting or important events; momentous."

> What began as an ordinary working day became the most eventful day of my life.

intervene (v.) (in-ter-VEEN), intervention (n.) (in-ter-VEN-chun)

Intervene is a combination of the prefix *inter-*, meaning "between," and the root **ven**, meaning "come." To **intervene** means "to come between or interfere, usually in order to settle disputes." **Intervention** is the act of *intervening*.

> The teacher intervened when the two boys began to fight.

invent (v.) (in-VENT), invention (n.) (in-VEN-chun)

In some words, the prefix *in-* means "on," as in **invent**, which means literally "to come upon something, such as a new idea; to devise something new; create."

> There seems no limit to what the human mind can invent, except ways to live in peace.

Invent can also mean (1) create fiction; (2) deceive; lie.

> Hans Christian Andersen invented children's stories that are still popular.

An **invention** is (1) the act of inventing; (2) an original device or contrivance; (3) deceit; (4) fiction.

> The invention of the steam engine helped bring about the Industrial Revolution.

inventive (adj.) (in-VENT-iv)

Inventive means "clever, resourceful; creative."

> He has an inventive mind.

prevent (v.) (pri-VENT),
prevention (n.) (pri-VEN-chun)

Prevent is formed from the prefix *pre-*, meaning "before," and **vent**, meaning "come." **Prevent** means "come before." Its full meaning is "to come before to keep something from happening; forestall." **Prevention** is the noun form of **prevent**.

> Unless the weather prevents traveling, she will come tomorrow.

preventive (adj.) (pri-VENT-iv)

Preventive, as an adjective, means "tending to ward off disease or harm; precautionary."

> Smoke alarms are preventive devices that can save lives and property.

revenue (n.) (REV-a-nyoo)

Money that comes back from a sale, investment, or rent is **revenue**, which means also "the income of a government collected by taxation."

> The Internal Revenue Service is the agency that collects taxes for the federal government.

Group Two

adventitious (adj.) (ad-ven-TISH-us)
coming about by chance; accidental

> The sisters, separated since childhood, were reunited in an adventitious meeting through a mutual friend.

venturesome (adj.) (VEN-chur-sum)
inclined to take risks; bold; daring

> The venturesome boys attempted to scale the steep cliff.

circumvent (v.) (sir-kum-VENT)
literally, to come around; to get around something; to outwit; avoid something by use of trickery

You can circumvent rush-hour traffic by taking the side streets.

conventional (adj.) (kun-VEN-chun-ull)
adhering to society's conventions; conforming to accepted customs and practices

Conventional methods are being challenged by new ideas.

eventuate (v.) (i-VEN-chu-ate)
to come about or bring about as a final consequence of something else

Pollution could eventuate in the destruction of the earth's resources.

eventual (adj.) (i-VEN-chu-ull)
finally coming about as the result of something else; ultimate

Talent and hard work led to her eventual success.

covenant (n.) (KUV-a-nent)
a solemn agreement or contract entered into by two or more persons; literally, a coming together of minds (from *co-*, together, and **ven**, come)

The Constitution is, in a sense, a covenant between the nation's government and its citizens.

supervene (v.) (soo-per-VEEN)
to follow closely upon; happen in addition or unexpectedly; literally, come upon

Famine and disease supervened the coming of the terrible floods.

venue (n.) (VEN-yoo)
in law, the district where a crime is committed and the case is tried; also, a gathering place for any large event

Venue is the place where a case must come to trial.

Exercise 8.1

For each word listed below, find a synonym from Word Group One and write it in the space provided.

1. _____ interfere

2. _____ assemble

3. _____ handy

4. _____ momentous

5. _____ forestall

6. _____ creative

7. _____ precautionary

8. _____ contrivance

9. _____ arrival

10. _____ (a) happening

11. _____ income

Exercise 8.2

From Group Two, supply the missing words.

1. Hard work _____d in the success of the project.

2. When there is doubt that a defendant can receive a fair trial in the place where the crime was committed, a defense lawyer may request a change of _____.

3. The discovery of gold at Sutter's Mill was purely _____.

4. With word of the discovery, the Gold Rush _____d.

5. The Mayflower Compact, a _____ signed by the Pilgrims, established self-government in the Plymouth Colony.

6. Accustomed to rigid standards of propriety, the staid club members shunned anyone whose conduct was not _____.

7. He tried to _____ paying income tax by falsifying his tax report.

8. The _____ young man set out alone to explore the deep cave.

9. Heavy gambling losses led to his _____ ruin, both financial and professional.

WORDS THAT RELATE TO GOING

A large number of words that relate to *going* are derived from the root **ceed**, or **ced**. Other spellings are **cede**, **ces**, and **cess**. This root, with all its spelling variations, is from the Latin word *cedere*, meaning "go" or "yield."

The Word Building Chart
for *ceed, ced, cess*

Word	Beginning block	Middle block	End block	Quick definition
access	ac- (to)	cess (go)	none	to go; a way to go in
ancestor	an- (before)	cest (form of cess, go)	-or (one who)	one who has gone before; forefather
cede	none	cede (yield)	none	yield; give
exceed	ex- (beyond)	ceed (go)	none	go beyond limits
excess	ex- (beyond)	cess (go)	none	go beyond amount needed; surplus
excessive	ex- (beyond)	cess (go)	-ive (tending to)	tending to exceed; too much
intercede	inter- (between)	cede (go)	none	go between; act as a go-between
precede	pre- (before)	cede (go)	none	go before, ahead of
proceed	pro- (forward)	ceed (go)	none	go forward
procession	pro- (forward)	cess (go)	-ion (the act of)	the act of proceeding; a line going forward
procedure	pro- (forward)	ced (go)	-ure (means)	a means of going forward; method
process	pro- (forward)	cess (go)	none	an ongoing operation

recede	re- (back)	cede (go)	none	go back; withdraw
recession	re- (back)	cess (go)	-ion (the act of)	a going back; decline
recess	re- (back)	cess (go)	none	time of withdrawal; an indentation
secede	se- (apart)	cede (go)	none	to go apart; disunite
secession	se- (apart)	cess (go)	-ion (the act of)	separation
succeed	suc- (from sub-, after)	ceed (go)	none	go after; achieve
success	suc- (after)	cess (go)		achievement
successful	suc- (after)	cess (go)	-ful (full of)	full of success; achieving

---

Group One

access (n.) (AK-ses)

An **access** is a way of getting to something, an approach, or a passage.

She had access to the records of that office.

ancestor (n.) (AN-ses-ter)

The first syllable of the word **ancestor**, *an-*, is a shortened spelling of the prefix *ante-*, meaning "before." Literally, an **ancestor** is one who goes before. The precise meaning of **ancestor** is "forefather; one from whom a person is descended." The word **ancestor** does not usually apply to a grandparent, but to one who lived further back in time.

My ancestors came to America from Ireland in the midnineteenth century.

cede (v.) (SEED)

Yield, relinquish, and surrender (something) are synonyms of **cede**. To **cede** is to give up something, especially territory.

> The tribes were forced to cede their lands to the settlers.

exceed (v.) (ek-SEED), excess (n.) (ek-SES)

Exceed is formed from the prefix *ex-*, which means "out; beyond," and *ceed*, meaning "go." **Exceed** means (1) go beyond the limits; (2) to be greater; surpass.

> If you exceed the speed limit, you risk having an accident or getting a ticket.

Excess is (1) the act of going beyond what is needed or proper; (2) an overabundance of something; an amount that is more than what is needed; (3) a surplus; an amount that is more than expected.

> Some of the people had an excess of wealth, while others in that same city had nothing to eat.

Excess is sometimes used as an adjective meaning "extra; being over and above what is needed; left over."

> The excess grain could be used to relieve famine in Africa.

excessive (adj.) (ek-SES-iv)

Excessive is an adjective meaning "too much; more than necessary or proper; immoderate."

> Excessive drinking ruined his life.

intercede (v.) (in-ter-SEED)

Intercede is based on the prefix *inter-*, meaning "between," and **cede**, meaning "go." To **intercede** is to go between, or to act as a "go-between," especially in the sense of pleading someone's case to another.

> The principal was ready to expel the girls from school, but their teacher interceded for them.

A second meaning of **intercede** is "intervene in a dispute; mediate; make peace."

The major purpose of the United Nations is to intercede in disputes between nations in order to avoid wars.

precede (v.) (pree-SEED)

The verb **precede** is derived from the prefix *pre-*, meaning "before," and cede, meaning "go." **Precede** means "to go before."

Carter preceded Reagan as president.

proceed (v.) (pro-SEED),
procession (n.) (pra-SESH-un)

The prefix *pro-* means "forward"; ceed means "go." **Proceed** means "go forward, go on, continue."

Finish the lesson and proceed to the next page.

A **procession** is (1) a line of people or cars moving forward in a formal way, as in a parade or a funeral procession; (2) a continuous course.

The groom waited nervously as the wedding procession moved slowly up the aisle.

procedure (n.) (pra-SEED-jer)

A **procedure** is a way of proceeding or going forward, a step-by-step method of accomplishing something.

What is the procedure for enrolling in this school?

process (n. & v.) (PRAH-ses)

A **process** is an ongoing operation in the production of something, or a series of actions that bring about a result. **Process** is also used as a verb.

The students went to a textile mill to see the process of cloth-making.
It will take three days to process this application.

recede (v.) (re-SEED), **recession** (n.) (ri-SESH-un)
Recede means the opposite of *proceed*. The prefix *re-* means "back." **Recede** means "to go back; withdraw."

That road is closed until the floodwaters recede.

Recession means "withdrawal, the act of receding," but it is frequently used to mean "economic setback" or "a slight economic depression."

Many people have lost their jobs because of the recession.

recess (n.) (REE-ses)
A **recess** is (1) a period of withdrawal from usual activities; (2) an indentation or cavity.

Congress is in recess and will reconvene in January.
In the wall, we found a recess apparently carved out by a prisoner.

Recess (ree-SES) is also a verb.

The court recessed for lunch.
The safe where she kept her jewelry was recessed in the wall.

secede (v.) (si-SEED), **secession** (n.) (si-SESH-un)
The prefix *se-* means "away; apart." The literal definition of **secede** is "go apart from." **Secede** means "to withdraw from a union or an alliance." **Secession** is the noun form of **secede**.

The southern states seceded from the United States after the election of President Lincoln.
The secession of the South led to the Civil War.

succeed (v.) (suk-SEED), **success** (n.) (suk-SES),
    successful (adj.) (suk-SES-full)
The words *succeed*, *succession*, *successive*, *successor*, *success*, and *successful* are all based on the Latin word

succedere, which means "go after; follow." The first syllable, *suc*, is actually a changed spelling of the prefix *sub-*,
meaning "under" or "after."

Succeed has two definitions, the first being "go after" or
"follow."

> *B* succeeds *A* in the alphabet.

The second meaning of **succeed** is "achieve what is at-
tempted," or, more literally, "to achieve what one goes
after."

> I want to succeed in being a good teacher.

The noun form of **succeed** in the sense of "achieve" is
success.

> Your success in this work will depend on how much
> effort you make.

The adjective **successful** means "obtaining what is intended." Literally, **successful** means "full of success."

> Edison failed at thousands of experiments in his attempt
> to invent the first successful electric light bulb.

successor (n.) (suk-SES-er)

Successor has the opposite meaning of *predecessor*. A
successor is one who follows in the place of another.

> Prince Charles will be the successor of his mother,
> Queen Elizabeth, to the throne of England.

Group Two

accede (v.) (ak-SEED)

to go along with; give in to; agree to

> We have no choice but to accede to their demands.

accession (n.) (ak-SESH-un)

a "going to," or attainment of a right or office

The accession of James I to the English throne ended the Tudor reign.

accessory (n.) (ak-SES-a-ree)
(1) an additional object, not the main thing; (2) an accomplice but not the **principal** in the commission of a crime

That silk scarf would be a perfect accessory for the dress. Driving the getaway car made her an accessory to the bank robbery.

antecedent (n.) (ANT-a-seed-ent)
a person or thing that goes before in the order of time

The horse-drawn carriage was the antecedent of the automobile.

concede (v.) (kun-SEED)
admit to be true; grant as a right or privilege; yield to

I concede that you are right on that point.

concession (n.) (kun-SESH-un)
the act of conceding or yielding; a privilege granted

The warden refuses to make any concessions to the prisoners' demands.

intercession (n.) (in-ter-SESH-un)
the act of interceding; a plea or prayer on behalf of others; the mediation of a dispute

They had hoped that the statesman's intercession would bring about the hostages' release.

precedent (n.) (PRESS-a-dent)
something that has gone, or happened, before and serves as an example for similar cases

The establishment of democracy in America set a precedent for democratic reforms in other nations.

precedence (n.) (PRESS-a-denss)
priority; that which ranks first in importance

My family takes precedence over my career.

predecessor (n.) (PRED-a-ses-er)
someone who has gone before another in point of time; a previous office-holder who is replaced by another (from *pre- + decedere*, "to go away")

The predecessor of President Bush was Ronald Reagan.

succession (n.) (suk-SESH-un)
the act of following in order; a series; a sequence

A succession of uprisings brought about the downfall of the hated government.

successive (adj.) (suk-SES-iv)
consecutive; following one after another

Franklin Roosevelt was elected president for four successive terms.

Exercise 8.3

Selecting words from Group One, write antonyms for the words below. Remember that antonyms have opposite meanings.

1. proceed (v.) _____

2. precede (v.) _____

3. predecessor (n.) _____

4. failure (n.) _____

5. join (v.) _____

6. scarcity (n.) _____

7. descendant (n.) _____

8. withhold (v.) _____

9. exit (n.) _____

Exercise 8.4

Substitute words from Group Two for the parenthesized words in the phrases below.

1. to (admit) _____ defeat

2. to (give in) _____ to their demands

3. to set a (example for following) _____

4. (attainment) _____ to the throne

5. a (series) _____ of disastrous events

6. the (antecedent) _____ of the present governor

7. (contributor) _____ to a crime

8. (mediation) _____ by the United Nations

9. a (grant) _____ provided in the treaty

10. (following one after another) _____ rulers

Exercise 8.5

Mark the statements below either true or false.

_____ 1. Henry III *preceded* Henry II to the English throne.

_____ 2. E *succeeds* D in the alphabet.

_____ 3. The antonym of *predecessor* and *antecedent* is *successor*.

_____ 4. To *precede* is to go forward.

_____ 5. A parade is a *procession*.

_____ 6. A person who achieves what she or he goes after is *successful*.

_____ 7. Both *precede* and *antecede* mean "go before."

_____ 8. *Intercede* means "go between"; *exceed* means "to go beyond."

_____ 9. In 1862, the South *succeeded* from the United States.

_____ 10. A *recessional* hymn is played when people are entering a church; the *processional* hymn is played as they are leaving.

9
More Words
That Mean "Go"

The preceding chapter dealt with a major group of words that mean "go." The words in this chapter relate to going by steps, stages, or grades. They are based on the roots **grad** and **gress**, which are forms of the Latin verb *gradi* or *gradus*, meaning "walk, go, and step." The word *degree* is a form of **gress** and means "a grade or step in a series of advances."

The Word Building Chart
for *grad* and *gress*

Word	Beginning block	Middle block	End block	Quick definition
gradual	none	**gradu** (stem of **grad**, go, step)	**-al** (tending)	tending to go step by step; happening by degrees
graduate	none	**gradu** (step)	**-ate** (make)	advance by steps; finish a course
graduation	none	**gradu** (step)	**-ation** (the act of)	the act of graduating; completion of a course
degrade	**de-** (down)	**grade** (stem of grad, step)	none	to lower in rank; debase
degrading	**de-** (down)	**grade** (step)	**-ing** (tending)	tending to lower, debase
ingredient	**in-** (in)	**gredi** (form of grad, go)	**-ent** (that which)	that which goes into a mixture
aggress	**ag-** (ad, toward)	**gress** (go)	none	go toward to attack; attack first
aggression	**ag-** (toward)	**gress** (go)	**-ion** (the act of)	the act of moving toward; an attack
aggressor	**ag-** (toward)	**gress** (go)	**-or** (one who)	one who makes the first move; attacker

aggressive	ag- (toward)	gress (go)	-ive (tending)	tending to go toward; attack first
congress	con- (together)	gress (go)	none	a meeting; body of lawmakers
digress	di- (away)	gress (go)	none	go away from the main path or the matter at hand; ramble
digression	di- (away)	gress (go)	-ion (the act of)	the act of wandering away
progress	pro- (forward)	gress (go)	none	go forward; advance
progression	pro- (forward)	gress (go)	-ion (the act of)	the act of going forward; advancement
progressive	pro- (forward)	gress (go)	-ive (tending)	tending to progress
regress	re- (back)	gress (go)	none	go back; return to an earlier state
regression	re- (back)	gress (go)	-ion (the act of)	the act of regression
transgress	trans- (across)	gress (go)	none	step across a boundary; break a law
transgression	trans- (across)	gress (go)	-ion (the act of)	the act of transgressing; violation of a law
transgressor	trans- (across)	gress (go)	-or (one who)	one who transgresses; a lawbreaker

Group One

gradual (adj.) (GRAJ-oo-ul)

Gradual means "step by step" and describes a process or change that happens slowly or by degrees.

Education is a gradual process.

graduate (v.) (GRAJ-oo-ate), graduation (n.) (graj-oo-Ā-shun)

The base word of **graduate** is **grade**. Students go through school by steps or grades until they graduate. Although its basic meaning is "move by steps or degrees to higher levels," **graduate** most commonly means "to receive a diploma upon finishing a course of study." A **graduate** (n.) (GRAJ-oo-it) is a person who has been granted a diploma or a university degree. **Graduation** is the act of graduating.

Many employers will not hire people who have not graduated from high school.

Remember that **graduate** has a broader meaning than simply "completion of school." For instance, scales and thermometers are marked with **graduated** units of measure, and a **graduated** income tax is a tax rate that increases according to the level of income.

degrade (v.) (di-GRADE), degrading (adj.) (di-GRADE-ing)

Degrade comes from the prefix *de-*, meaning "down," and the root **grad**, meaning "step." To **degrade** oneself is to "step down" in the sense of lowering self-respect, dignity, character, or morals. To **degrade** another person is to demean or humiliate him by insults. The precise definition of **degrade** is "demean; reduce in status."

I refuse to degrade myself by begging him for money.

Degrading means "humiliating; debasing; lowering in esteem, honor, morals, etc."

It's degrading for me to work here for so little pay and suffer your insults day after day.

ingredient (n.) (in-GREED-ee-ent)

The Latin word *ingredientis*, which means "entered into," was derived from the prefix *in-*, meaning "into," and *gradi*, meaning "go." **Ingredient** means "anything that goes into a mixture; a component of something."

The right choice of words is an ingredient of good writing.

aggress (v.) (a-GRES),
aggression (n.) (a-GRESH-un),
aggressor (n.) (a-GRES-er)

The prefix *ag-*, a changed spelling of *ad-*, means "to, toward, or near." **Aggress** means "to step" or "walk toward," but in usage, **aggress** has come to mean "attack; begin a quarrel." **Aggression** means "the act of aggressing; the act of attacking first; an unprovoked attack." An **aggressor** is one who attacks first, or who takes a hostile action.

The government agreed by treaty not to aggress against neighboring countries.

After Japan's aggression at Pearl Harbor, the United States was forced to enter the war.

aggressive (adv.) (a-GRES-iv)

Aggressive means "characterized by aggression or the tendency to attack."

Aggressive behavior can be caused by emotional problems.

A second definition of **aggressive** is "inclined toward vigorous activity; inclined to be assertive." **Aggressive**, in this sense, is closer to the literal meaning of **aggress**, which is "to go toward." **Aggressive** can describe people who are "go-getters"—those who don't hesitate to take the first step toward what they want.

Salespeople must be aggressive.

congress (n.) (KAHN-gres)

The noun **congress** has lost some connection with its origin. The prefix *con-* means "together." Originally, a **congress** was "a walk together." Now **congress** means a "going together" or meeting of people, especially elected representatives or delegates selected for the purpose of solving problems or enacting laws.

> The Congress of the United States was formed for the purpose of making laws.

digress (v.) (die-GRES), digression (n.) (die-GRESH-un)

The prefix *di-* is a shortened spelling of *dis-*, meaning "away." **Digress** means to "go away," especially in the sense of rambling or wandering away from the main subject of a discussion or speech. *Digression* is the noun form of **digress**.

> The students were growing impatient with the instructor's frequent digressions.

progress (v.) (pra-GRES), progression (n.) (pra-GRESH-un)

The prefix *pro-* means "forward." To **progress** is to go forward, to advance by steps or stages. Various definitions of the verb *progress* are:

1. advance toward a goal or the completion of something
2. improve
3. spread through all parts, as a disease
4. move forward in space

> After learning English, he progressed easily through school.
> Although she didn't progress in math this term, she has improved in all her other subjects.
> The disease progresses through the body, destroying muscle tissue.
> Traffic is progressing slowly because of the fog.

As a noun, **progress** (PRAH-gres) means "the act of moving forward; advancement; development; improvement."

> Our progress through the rough terrain was painfully slow.

Progression has the same basic meaning as **progress**—advancement; development; a moving forward—but **progression** is often used to mean an advancing sequence, especially a series of numbers that increase by the same amount.

> The following is a mathematical progression: 4, 8, 12, 16.

progressive (adj.) (pra-GRES-iv)

The adjective **progressive** describes something that goes forward or advances.

> In technological advancement, Japan is among the most progressive countries in the world.

Progressive is also used to describe something that spreads from one part to another.

> Some progressive diseases can be arrested by treatment.

Progressive also describes social, educational, or political ideas that stress change through reforms.

> Progressive schools of the 1930s were harshly criticized for discarding traditional teaching methods.

regress (v.) (ree-GRES),
regression (n.) (ree-GRESH-un)

Regress has the opposite meaning of *progress*. *Pro-* means "forward"; *re-* means "back." **Regress** means "to go back, return." In another sense, **regress** means "go back to an earlier or worse condition." **Regression** is the noun form of **regress**.

> During the Dark Ages, European civilization regressed to a primitive condition.

transgress (v.) (trans-GRES), **transgression** (n.)
(trans-GRESH-un), **transgressor** (n.) (trans-GRES-er)

Trans- means "across." To **transgress** is to step across a limit, especially a limit set by law or a moral code. Simply put, to **transgress** is to break a law or to sin. **Transgressions** are violations of the law or are sins. A **transgressor** is a lawbreaker or a sinner.

> In some countries, transgressions of the law are dealt with severely.

Group Two

Earlier, we spoke of stretched definitions. Some of the "step" words seemed to have been stretched a long way from their basic definitions. For instance, *congress* once meant simply "go together," but now it means "a body of legislators." In nearly every word-root group, a few words will appear more loosely connected than others. But even these more vaguely linked words are easy to remember when they are learned by association with their family roots.

In Group Two are two nouns, *ingress* and *egress*, which, although a little less common in usage than the other words in this group, are very closely connected to their original meanings.

degradation (n.) (deg-ra-DAY-shun)

a lowering of character, moral standards, respect, etc.; debasement

> Greed and dishonesty led him to utter degradation.

gradient (n.) (GRAY-dee-unt)

an incline, ramp, or slope; rising by degrees

> The distant gradient appeared in relief to the vast flat terrain.

gradation (n.) (gray-DAY-shun)

a change by imperceptible degrees; the degree or intensity of color

Gradations are varying shades of the same color.

egress (n.) (EE-gres)
a way out; an exit

A faint shaft of light signaled an egress from the tunnel.

ingress (n.) (IN-gres)
a way in; entrance; the right to enter

They discovered a secret ingress to the palace by way of an underground passage.

retogress (v.) (ret-row-GRES)
regress; revert to an earlier worse condition; go backward (*retro*, backward)

During the Dark Ages, European civilization retrogressed to a primitive stage.

retrogression (n.) (ret-row-GRES-shun)
decline; deterioration; regression

Retrogression of societies is characterized by ignorance, violence, and greed.

Exercise 9.1

Substitute nouns and adjectives from Group One for the parenthesized words in the sentences below.

1. The main (element) _____ of success is hard work.

2. The United States declared war because of Japan's (attack) _____.

3. We must confine our discussion to the topic. There's no time for (rambling) _____.

4. I believe he is guilty of this (crime) _____.

5. The Puritans punished (sinners) _____s harshly.

6. Without cause, the (attackers) _____ invaded the small neighboring country.

7. The United Nations condemned the (attacking) _____ actions of the invaders.

8. Her grades have shown (improvement) _____ since she transferred to this school.

9. We were accustomed to hard work, but he regarded manual labor as (demeaning) _____.

10. This is an example of a mathematical (advancement) _____: 3, 9, 27, 81.

Exercise 9.2

Write synonyms from Group Two for the words listed below.

1. _____ return

2. _____ slope

3. _____ shade

4. _____ entrance

5. _____ exit

6. _____ regression

7. _____ debasement

Exercise 9.3

This chapter included ten Latin prefixes that served as beginning building blocks for words you have just studied. Below are their definitions. In the spaces beside them, write the seven verbs and three nouns in which these beginning blocks appear.

1. in   _____

2. out   _____

3. away   _____

4. down   _____

5. across   _____

6. back   _____

7. backward   _____

8. forward   _____

9. toward   _____

10. together   _____

10

Leading and Following

WORDS RELATING TO LEADING

The words in this chapter are based on the Latin root **duc** and **duct**, which means "lead, bring, or convey."

Word Building Chart
for *duc, duct*

Word	Beginning block	Middle block	End block	Quick definition
educate	e- (out)	duc (lead)	-ate (cause)	lead (the mind) outward; teach
conduct	con- (together)	duct (lead)	move	direct; lead together
conductor	con- (together)	duct (lead)	-or (one who; that which)	one who conducts; something that conveys
conducive	con- (together)	duc (lead)	-ive (tending)	tending to lead; leading toward
deduct	de- (away)	duct (lead)	none	lead, or take away; subtract
introduce	intro- (within)	duce (lead)	none	lead within; bring in; make known
introduction	intro- (within)	duct (lead)	-ion (the act of)	act of introducing
produce	pro- (forth)	duce (bring)	none	bring forth; yield
production	pro- (forth)	duct (bring)	-ion (act of)	the act of producing
productive	pro- (forth)	duct (bring)	-ive (tending)	tending to produce
productivity	pro- (forth)	ductive (bringing)	-ity (state of)	the state of bringing forth, producing
reduce	re- (back)	duce (bring)	noun	bring back in number, amount; lessen

reduction	re- (back)	duct (bring)	-ion (act of)	act of reducing, lessening
abduct	ab- (away)	duct (lead)	none	lead away; kidnap
abduction	ab- (away)	duct (lead)	-ion (act of)	the act of abducting; kidnapping
aqueduct	aque (water)	duct (convey)		a water duct, conveyance
viaduct	via (way)	duct (convey)		a roadway carried by a structure over a valley or river

---

Group One

educate (v.) (ED-jou-kate)

The literal definition of **educate** is "to lead out." To educate is to teach, develop the mind by instruction, to give knowledge, and, in a literal sense, lead out of ignorance.

Democracy cannot exist if people do not educate themselves about governmental affairs.

conduct (v.) (kun-DUKT),
conductor (n.) (kun-DUKT-er)

The prefix *con-* means "together." **Conduct** means "to lead together; direct; guide."

The vice president conducted the meeting.

Conduct also applies to leading or guiding oneself. In this sense, **conduct** means "behave."

He conducted himself badly at the party.

As a noun, **conduct** (KAHN-dukt) means "behavior."

That child's conduct is intolerable.

A **conductor** is a leader, guide, or director, especially of a choir or an orchestra. On passenger trains, a **conductor** is one who has charge of the passengers.

Another meaning of **conductor** is "a material or substance that conducts heat, electricity, etc."

Metal is a conductor of electricity.

conducive (adj.) (kun-DOOS-ive)
Conducive is an adjective meaning "leading to; helping with; promoting."

Physical exercise is conducive to good health.

deduct (v.) (di-DUKT)
From *de-*, away, and **duct**, bad, **deduct** means "lead away from," literally, or "remove; take away from; subtract."

We will have to deduct the cost of the broken plates from your pay.

introduce (v.) (in-tra-DOOS),
introduction (n.) (in-tra-DUK-shun)
Intro- means "within" or "into." **Introduce** means "bring in; lead into" in the sense of acquainting persons with someone or something, or to bring into use something new.

Americans introduced the Japanese to baseball, now Japan's most popular sport.

An **introduction** is (1) the act of formally acquainting persons with one another; (2) a first knowledge of something; initiation; (3) something that leads into what follows, such as a preface of a book.

I started to make the introduction, but I forgot her name.
The course was an introduction to classical music.
After reading the introduction, I decided the book wouldn't interest me.

induce (v.) (in-DOOS),
inducement (n.) (in-DOOS-ment)

A verb that literally means "lead in" is **induce**. In usage, however, **induce** often implies leading someone to do something by persuasion or enticement.

> She induced the child to eat the vegetables by promising him his favorite dessert.

Another definition of **induce** is "cause something to happen; produce a condition." In this sense **induce** means "lead into."

> The doctor gave him a sedative to induce sleep.

The noun **inducement** means (1) that which persuades, such as a reward or enticement; (2) that which causes something to happen, or produces a condition.

> They offered the actor a huge sum of money as an inducement to star in the film.

produce (v.) (pra-DOOS)

Pro- means "forward" or "forth." **Produce** means "lead forth" or "bring forth" in the sense of yielding, creating, or manufacturing.

> The drama students produced their own play.

Produce also means "bring about" or "cause to happen."

> The chemical leak produced a cloud of toxic gas.

product (n.) (PRAH-dukt)

A **product** is something that is produced.

> Crime is one of the products of illiteracy.

production (n.) (pra-DUK-shun)

Production is (1) the act of process of producing; (2) a product; something that is produced, especially a play for television, stage, or motion pictures.

> The invention of the steam engine, along with the production of cast iron, brought about the Industrial Age.

productive (adj.) (pra-DUK-tive), productivity (pra-duk-TIV-it-ee)

Productive is an adjective meaning "creative, fertile; having the tendency to produce."

> The workers would be more productive if they had decent working conditions.

Productivity is the power to produce.

> The decline of agricultural productivity was a major cause of the Roman Empire's collapse.

reduce (v.) (ri-DOOS), reduction (n.) (ri-DUK-shun)

The prefix *re-* means "back"; **reduce** literally means "bring back." To **reduce** is to bring back down in size, number, amount, or, in other words, become less.

> The company has reduced its personnel.

Reduce also means "to become less in rank or position."

> His superiors reduced the corporal to the rank of private.

Reduction is the noun form of **reduce**.

> The President has ordered a reduction of troops in that area.

abduct (v.) (ab-DUKT), abduction (n.) (ab-DUK-shun)

The prefix *ab-* means "away." **Abduct** means "to lead away," and specifically "to lead someone away by force." In other words, to abduct is to kidnap.

> The banker's wife was abducted and held for ransom.

Abduction is the noun form of **abduct**.

> The two men were charged with abduction and extortion.

aqueduct (n.) (AK-wa-dukt)

A duct is a pipe, tube, or channel through which a fluid or air is conducted. *Aque* means "water." An **aqueduct** is a bridge or channel for conveying water above or below ground.

The ancient Romans were masterful engineers who built roads, bridges, and aqueducts, some of which are still in use.

viaduct (n.) (VIE-a-dukt)

Structures that carry roads across valleys and stretches of water are called **viaducts**.

Some viaducts built by the Romans are still used today.

Group Two

adduce (v.) (a-DOOS)
to bring forward as proof

The police adduced evidence that the suspect was at the scene of the crime.

deduce (v.) (di-DOOS)
to lead to a conclusion; trace down by reasoning

By careful examination of all the evidence, the shrewd detective deduced that the butler committed the murder.

educe (v.) (i-DOOS)
to bring out; elicit; infer

There is not enough evidence to educe a solution to the crime.

traduce (v.) (tra-DOOS)
to misrepresent someone's character; slander; bring into disgrace; give misleading, damaging information about someone

His enemies tried to traduce his reputation with malicious lies.

seduce (v.) (si-DOOS)
lead astray; tempt; induce to commit wrongful deeds

No amount of gold could seduce him to betray his leader.

seductive (adj.) (si-DUK-tiv)
tempting; enticing; alluring

> Her seductive beauty entranced him.

counterproductive (adj.) (kown-ter-pra-DUK-tiv)
opposite of productive, undermining productivity

> Your harsh criticism of your co-workers is counterproductive to the cooperative spirit we are trying to achieve.

deductive (adj.) (di-DUK-tiv)
relating to a method of reasoning in which a particular truth is derived from a general truth; drawing a conclusion from stated premises

> The following is an example of deductive reasoning:
>> Even numbers are divisible by 2.
>> 12 is an even number.
>> Therefore, 12 is divisible by 2.

inductive (adj.) (in-DUK-tiv)
related to a method of reasoning in which a general truth is derived from a number of particular truths

> The following is an example of the inductive method: Scientists conducted studies in which a number of elderly men participated in an exercise program. Each man gained a great deal of muscular strength. The scientists concluded that exercise benefits elderly men in general.

Exercise 10.1

Write synonyms from Group One for the **verbs** below.

1. _____ kidnap

2. _____ lessen

3. _____ guide

4. _____ entice

5. _____   manufacture

6. _____   instruct

7. _____   subtract

8. _____   acquaint

Exercise 10.2

Match words from Group Two to the definitions below.

1. _____   infer from data; elicit

2. _____   lead astray

3. _____   bring forth proof

4. _____   lead down to a conclusion

5. _____   mislead; slander

6. _____   tempting

7. _____   inferring a general truth from particular truths

8. _____   drawing a particular truth from a general truth

9. _____   working against productivity

Exercise 10.3

Replace the parenthesized words in the sentences below with **verbs** from both groups.

1. Sherlock Holmes (brought forth) _____d evidence of an intruder by way of a footprint found outside the window.

2. From the footprint, Holmes (led down to the conclusion) _____d that the intruder had been a woman of slight build.

3. In shrubs beside the window was found a scrap of paper containing a coded message whose meaning Holmes was finally able to (elicit) _____ through his knowledge of cryptology.

4. The famous detective had been called on to (direct) _____ the investigation into the disappearance of the missing count.

5. The note revealed a plot to (kidnap) _____ the count.

6. The countess's extravagant spending had been a source of displeasure to the count. He had threatened to divorce the countess if she did not (lessen) _____ her expenditures.

7. The servants disliked the countess for her haughty, inconsiderate treatment of them. She had even gone so far as to (subtract) _____ the cost of the food they consumed from their salaries.

8. Scheming to get more riches from the count, she had tried to (lead astray) _____ his greedy nephew with the promise of a large sum of money for helping in her evil plan.

9. At first, the nephew resisted the idea, but promise of half the count's fortune (enticed) _____d him to arrange his uncle's disappearance.

10. "This is a conspiracy by the count's envious relatives to (slander) _____ my good name," the countess replied tearfully upon hearing the charges.

Exercise 10.4

From both word groups, select **adjectives** to complete the sentences below.

1. The following model, formulated by the great philosopher Aristotle, is a well-known example of _____ reasoning, in which a particular truth is derived from a general truth:

All men are mortal.
Socrates is a man.
Therefore, Socrates is mortal.

2. In Holmes's opinion, the constable's unscientific methods were not _____ to solving a mystery as complex as this one.

3. The investigation had not been _____. In fact, his efforts had not yielded the slightest clue.

4. The constable's carelessness was _____ to a thorough investigation of the case.

5. The countess was beautiful and alluring, but her _____ wiles failed to stir Holmes, who had learned her evil designs.

6. Scientists use the _____ reasoning method to infer general truths from facts gathered through experimentation.

WORDS RELATING TO FOLLOWING

The words in this section are based on the root **sec, secut,** or **sequ.** The Latin word *sequor* means "follow." All of the words in this group relate in some way to the act of following.

Word Building Chart
for *sec, secut, sequ*

Word	Beginning block	Middle block	End block	Quick definition
secondary	none	second (from Latin *secundus*)	-ary (relating to)	following the first
consecutive	con- (together)	secret (follow)	-ive (in the manner of)	following together, one after another
persecute	per- (throughout)	secute (follow)	none	pursue in order to harm; harass
persecution	per- (throughout)	secut (follow)	-ion (act of)	the act of pursuing; harassment
prosecute	pro- (forward)	secute (follow)	none	follow forward with legal proceedings
prosecution	pro- (forward)	secut (follow)	-ion (the act of)	the act of conducting legal proceedings
execute	ex- (out)	(s)ecute (follow)	none	follow out; carry out orders, plans, etc.
execution	ex- (out)	(s)ecut (follow)	-ion (the act of)	the act of executing, carrying out, administering
executive	ex- (out)	(s)ecut (follow)	-ive (that which; one who)	administrative; one appointed to administer

sequel	none	**sequ** (follow)	**-el** (that which)	that which follows; a continuing part
sequence	none	**sequ** (follow)	**-ence** (that which)	a number of things that follow one another; a series
sequential	none	**sequent** (follow)	**-ial** (that which)	pertaining to a sequence, arranged as a series

---

Group One

secondary (adj.) (SEK-un-dair-ee)

The word *second* came from the Latin word *secundus*, which means "following." **Secondary** is another form of the adjective *second*, and means "following the first" or "next in order to the first."

After students complete the elementary grades, they attend secondary schools.

Secondary also means "second in rank" or "following in rank."

The office of the vice president is secondary to that of president.

Another meaning of **secondary** is "less important; not primary."

The primary rule that should govern societies is the Golden Rule; all other moral laws are secondary.

consecutive (adj.) (kun-SEK-yoo-tiv)

Consecutive means "successive; following in uninterrupted order." The prefix *con-*, meaning "together," indicates that **consecutive** refers to a group of things arranged together in successive order.

So far, the team has had five consecutive losses.

persecute (n.) (PER-sa-kute),
persecution (n.) (per-sa-KUE-shun)

Both *pursue*, meaning "chase," and **persecute** come from the Latin verb *persequi*, which means "chase; follow with the intention of capturing someone or obtaining something." The basic meaning of **persecute** is "to pursue with cruel intentions." Its definitions include (1) to harass with cruel treatment; (2) to treat badly or oppress because of race, religion, or unpopular beliefs; (3) to harass or annoy persistently.

They persecuted the boy because he dared to be different from the others.
The Ku Klux Klan persecutes Catholics, Jews, and Blacks.
Quakers often have been persecuted because they oppose war.

Persecution is the noun form of **persecute**.

They followed him everywhere, shouting threats and insults, but he did not fear their persecution.

prosecute (v.) (PRAH-sa-kute),
prosecution (n.) (prah-sa-KUE-shun)

Prosecute comes from the prefix *pro-*, meaning "forward," and **secut**, meaning "follow." **Prosecute** is used as a legal term meaning "to pursue justice," or, more specifically, "to bring to trial for the punishment of a crime; to conduct legal proceedings against a suspect of crime or wrongdoing."

There was not enough evidence to prosecute the suspect.

Prosecution means "the act of initiating and carrying out legal proceedings against persons accused of crime or wrongdoing."

Both men are facing prosecution for bribery.

execute (n.) (EKS-a-kute),
execution (n.) (eks-a-KUE-shun)

When a root begins with *s*, as in **secut**, and follows the prefix **ex-**, the *s* is omitted. The word **execute** is actually a combination of *ex-*, meaning "out," and **secute**, meaning "follow." **Execute** means "follow out" in the sense of following through with something or carrying out fully. The most common definitions of **execute** are (1) carry out orders or tasks; (2) administer laws; (3) put someone to death according to a court sentence; (4) carry out the terms of a will; (5) perform (especially something requiring great skill); (6) produce something by following a plan or design.

> The lieutenant executed the captain's orders.
> According to the Constitution, the president must execute the laws passed by Congress.
> The prisoner was executed by a firing squad.
> The court appointed the woman's lawyer to execute her will.
> The pianist executed perfectly each note of the difficult composition.
> Michelangelo executed the magnificent paintings on the ceiling of the Sistine Chapel.

Execution, the noun form of **execute**, means (1) the administration or enforcement of laws; (2) the carrying out of orders, required procedures, or tasks; (3) the carrying out of a death penalty; (4) a performance or production requiring great skill.

> The president is responsible for the execution of laws passed by Congress.
> She was careless in the execution of her assigned tasks.
> The prisoner's execution is scheduled for tomorrow.
> He was awarded an Olympic gold medal for his flawless gymnastic executions.

executive (n.) (ek-ZEK-yoo-tiv)

Executive is used both as an adjective and a noun. As an adjective, **executive** means (1) administrative; carrying out the affairs of government; (2) managing business affairs; carrying out the plans and projects of a business.

The president is the head of the executive branch of government.

As a noun, **executive** means "one who is appointed to administer the affairs of a corporation, company, or government; a high official."

As an executive of the corporation, he earns a large salary.

sequel (n.) (SEE-kwul)
Sequel means "that which follows; a succeeding or continuing part." **Sequel** most commonly refers to a narrative, such as a novel or film, which is a continuation of one that was previously published.

The Empire Strikes Back was the sequel to *Star Wars*.

A second definition of **sequel** is "outcome; final result; upshot."

The sequel to the matter was that he was asked to resign.

sequence (n.) (SEE-kwenss),
sequential (adj.) (si-KWEN-shul)
A **sequence** is a connected series, a succession, a number of things that follow one another.

In poker, a straight flush is a sequence of five numbers of the same suit.

Sequential is an adjective meaning "arranged in a sequence."

I recorded the television series and marked the tapes in sequential order.

consequence (n.) (KON-sa-kwenss)
The prefix *con-* means "with." The literal definition of **consequence** is "with that which follows." A **consequence** is a natural effect of a preceding action, or, in other words, a logical result of something that has happened earlier.

Her illness was a consequence of poor eating habits.

Consequence is used also to mean "importance" or "significance."

> What he does with his life is of no consequence to me.

Group Two

consequent (adj.) (KAHN-sa-kwent)
naturally resulting; following as a natural result

> With good nutrition and the consequent improvement of her health, she was able to return to work.

consequently (adv.) (KAHN-sa-kwent-lee)
as a result; therefore

> He spent all of his money; consequently, he can't afford the trip.

inconsequential (adj.) (in-kon-si-KWEN-chul)
unimportant; trivial; not following as a consequence; irrelevant

> I dislike spending my time on inconsequential tasks.

subsequent (adj.) (SUB-sa-kwent)
succeeding; following; next in the order of arrangement or time; later

> A tip to the police led to the man's arrest and subsequent trial.

subsequently (adv.) (SUB-sa-kwent-lee)
next in the order of time; later; as a result

> He made high grades and was subsequently awarded a scholarship.

Note: Both **consequently** and **subsequently** can mean "as a result." However, **consequently** is used only when speaking of a natural, inevitable result, a result that is bound to happen. In the example sentence above, **subsequently**, rather than

consequently, is used because it does not always follow as a natural consequence that a student who makes high grades is awarded a scholarship.

obsequious (adj.) (ub-SEE-kwee-us)

fawning; following about in the manner of a sycophant; servile

> That obsequious waiter hopes to get a large tip from those wealthy customers.

obsequy (n.) (OB-si-kwee)

a solemn ceremony following a death; a funeral, burial rite

> A eulogy is a part of an obsequy.

non sequitur (n.) (non-SEK-wa-ter)

Latin phrase, meaning "It does not follow," which is used in reference to a statement that does not logically follow a preceding statement, or a conclusion that does not follow from stated facts

> Though he began his speech with a string of facts, his conclusion was a non sequitur.

Exercise 10.5

Substitute words from both groups for the parenthesized words in the sentences below.

1. The (carrying out) _____ of laws passed by Congress is the chief responsibility of the president.

2. He followed the director about in an (fawning) _____ fashion, hoping to gain a promotion.

3. My primary concern is for the children. All other matters are (following the first) _____.

4. The witness's statement led to the arrest and (later) _____ (legal proceeding) _____ of the suspect.

5. He was (later) ＿＿＿＿＿ found guilty and sentenced to serve three (one after another) ＿＿＿＿＿ prison terms for the three crimes he had committed.

6. If you break the rules, you should be aware of the (naturally resulting) ＿＿＿＿＿ penalties.

7. The victory was a (natural result) ＿＿＿＿＿ of determined effort.

8. The Roman emperor Nero ordered the (cruel treatment) ＿＿＿＿＿ of Christians.

9. Their criticisms are (unimportant) ＿＿＿＿＿ to me.

10. Throngs of loyal subjects witnessed the magnificent (funeral) ＿＿＿＿＿ for the fallen king.

11

Pushing and Pulling

PUSHING

The root that means "push" or "drive" is **pel** or **puls**.

The Word Building Chart
for *pel, puls*

Word	Beginning block	Middle block	End block	Quick definition
compel	com- (together)	pel (drive)	none	drive by force; originally, drive together, herd
compelling	com- (drive)	pell (drive)	-ing (tending)	tending to compel; forceful
dispel	dis- (away)	pel (drive)	none	drive away; disperse
expel	ex- (out)	pel (push)	none	push out
impel	im- (on)	pel (drive)	none	drive on; urge on
impulse	im- (on)	pulse (drive)	none	sudden inner urge
propel	pro- (forward)	pel (push)	none	push forward
propeller	pro- (forward)	pel (push)	-er (that which)	that which propels; device that pushes an object forward
propellant	pro- (forward)	pel (push)	-ant (that which)	something that propels; a rocket fuel
repel	re- (back)	pel (push)	none	push back
repellent	re- (back)	pel (drive)	-ent (that which)	that which pushes something back; causing aversion

Group One

In the **pel** words, the *l* is doubled when suffixes are added. The rule for doubling consonants is as follows: When a suffix beginning with a vowel is added to a two-syllable word in which the stress is on the second syllable, the final consonant is doubled. Thus, *propel* becomes prope**ll**ed; expel, expe**ll**ed; repel, repe**ll**ent, and so on.

compel (v.) (kum-PEL)

Com- means "together." The literal meaning of **compel** is "drive together." Originally **compel** meant "drive together" in the sense of herding. Now it means "to drive someone to do something by force, law, or necessity."

> Because of his large debts, he was compelled to hold two jobs.

compelling (adj.) (kum-PEL-ing)

Compelling means "forceful; overpowering."

> The prosecution presented to the jury a compelling argument for its side of the case.

dispel (v.) (dis-PEL)

The prefix *dis-* means "away." **Dispel** means "to push away; to drive away; scatter; cause to disappear."

> Finally, the sun appeared and dispelled the gloom that had hung over us for days.

expel (v.) (ex-PEL)

Ex- means "out"; **expel** means "to push out; drive out by force; force out; eject." **Expulsion** (eks-PUL-shun), the noun form of **expel**, means "the act of driving out."

> She was expelled from school after she was caught stealing.

impel (v.) (im-PEL)

To **impel** is to drive onward, urge on, incite.

> The icy wind impelled us to seek shelter.

impulse (n.) (IM-pulss)

An **impulse** is a sudden urge or inclination to do something with little forethought given to the action.

> She bought the dress on impulse.

propel (v.) (pra-PEL)

The prefix *pro-* means "forward"; **pel** means "push" or "drive." **Propel** means "push forward" or "cause to drive or push forward."

> Bicycles are propelled by muscle power.

propeller (n.) (pra-PEL-er)

A **propeller**, literally meaning "something which propels," is any device that pushes a craft through the air or water, but especially a power-driven, revolving shaft with blades."

> Each summer many people are seriously injured by swimming too close to boat propellers.

propellant (n.) (pra-PEL-unt)

Propellant is another noun meaning "that which propels," but **propellant** more often means "a fuel which serves to propel a rocket or a guided missile."

> Thrusting a rocket beyond the earth's gravity requires a tremendous amount of propellant.

repel (v.) (ri-PEL)

Repel is a combination of the prefix *re-*, meaning "back," and **pel**, meaning "push" or "drive." To **repel** is to push back or drive back. **Repel** can mean (1) drive back by force; (2) cause to feel distaste or aversion. In this sense, a person is "driven back" by a strong dislike of something.

> A heavy bombardment repelled the enemy.
> The gory violence of the movie repelled her.

repellent (n. & adj.) (ri-PEL-unt)

A **repellent** is something that drives something else back or keeps it away.

> When you go camping, be sure to take an insect repellent.

As an adjective, **repellent** describes something that pushes or keeps back.

> A raincoat is water-repellent.

Repellent also means "disgusting; extremely distasteful; horrifying; having qualities that drive one back."

> His constant bragging about his wealth is repellent to me.

Group Two

All the words in this group are derivatives of those in Group One.

compulsory (adj.) (kum-PUL-sa-ree)
required; forced by law; mandatory

> In most states, the wearing of seat belts while driving is compulsory.

compulsive (adj.) (kum-PUL-siv)
driven by an inner urge; having an overpowering urge to behave in a certain way; unable to control or resist certain behaviors

> She is a compulsive spender; she can't resist buying things she doesn't need.

compulsion (n.) (kum-PUL-shun)
the act of compelling; force; an uncontrollable behavior

> In the United States, children attend school under compulsion until they reach a certain age.
> His gambling compulsion led him to poverty.

expulsion (n.) (eks-PUL-shun)
the act of pushing out; ejection; removal by force

President Andrew Jackson ordered the expulsion of the Five Civilized Tribes from their homelands in the South.

impulsive (adj.) (im-PUL-siv)
inclined to act suddenly with little forethought; acting on impulse

By making a shopping list and sticking to it, you can avoid the expense of impulsive buying.

propulsion (n.) (pra-PUL-shun)
the act of propelling; the act of being propelled

Modern airliners are powered by jet propulsion.

propulsive (adj.) (pra-PUL-siv)
tending to propel; inclined to thrust forward

A car's size and speed determines the propulsive force on passengers and objects inside.

repulse (v.) (ri-PULSS)
(1) repel; push back by force; (2) to cause a feeling of aversion, disgust

Our forces were not strong enough to repulse the enemy attack.
His table manners repulsed me.

repulsive (adj.) (ri-PUL-siv)
repugnant; repellent; grossly offensive; causing a feeling of aversion

His table manners are repulsive.

repulsion (n.) (ri-PUL-shun)
(1) the act of repelling by force; (2) aversion; a feeling of disgust or horror; repugnance

The guerrillas' fierce attacks resulted in the repulsion of the invaders.

Although most snakes are harmless, many people feel repulsion toward them.

Exercise 11.1

Add prefixes to the root to make words that match the definitions from Group One.

1. _____pel   drive out

2. _____pel   drive away

3. _____pel   drive (together), to force, (literally, drive together)

4. _____pel   drive onward

5. _____pel   drive back

6. _____pel   drive forward

Exercise 11.2

Choose words from Group Two to place in the sentences below.

1. His gambling is _____. He can't control it.

2. She likes to do things on the spur of the moment. She has an _____ nature.

3. Kleptomania is a _____ to shoplift, but like many other uncontrollable behaviors, this problem can be treated by psychiatry.

4. Cheating on tests will result in _____ from this university.

5. The _____ effect of the impact threw the passenger through the windshield.

6. The thought of eating that stale, grease-soaked food is _____.

7. Extra troops were sent to the border in an effort to _____ the invaders.

8. The filth of the room filled me with _____.

9. Before the steam engine, ships required wind power for _____.

10. Some states have laws making school attendance _____ through age sixteen.

PULLING

The root that means "pull" or "draw" is **tract**. **Tract** is the base of the word *tractor*, meaning "a vehicle that pulls a trailer or farm machinery." *Traction*, meaning "a pulling force," is also based on the root **tract**. Following are more words containing **tract** as their base.

The Word Building Chart
for *tract*

Word	Beginning block	Middle block	End block	Quick definition
attract	at- (to)	tract (draw)	none	to draw attention; pull toward
attractive	at- (to)	tract (draw)	-ive (tending)	tending to draw attention; pleasing
attraction	at- (to)	tract (draw)	-ion (the act of)	the act of drawing something toward
contract	con- (together)	tract (pull)	none	pull together; shorten
contraction	con- (together)	tract (pull)	-ion (the act of)	the act of pulling together; shrinkage
detract	de- (down)	tract (pull)	none	pull down; lessen
distract	dis- (away)	tract (draw)	none	draw attention away from something
distraction	dis- (away)	tract (draw)	-ion (the act of)	the act of distracting; diversion of attention
extract	ex- (out)	tract (pull)	none	to pull out
extraction	ex- (out)	tract (pull)	-ion (the act of)	the act of extracting; descent, lineage
protract	pro- (forward)	tract (pull)	none	pull forward; lengthen

protracted	pro- (forward)	tract (pull)	-ed (forms an adjective)	prolonged
tract	re- (back)	tract (pull)	none	to pull back, with draw
subtract	sub- (under)	tract (draw)	none	take away; literally, draw from underneath

---

Group One
attract (v.) (a-TRAKT)

The first syllable of **attract**, *at-*, is another spelling of the prefix *ad-*, which means "to" and "toward." *At-* combined with **tract** means "to pull toward."

> We left food scraps outside our tent to attract the raccoons.

Attract also means "pull toward" in the sense of gaining notice or admiration.

> In order to attract new customers, we'll have to advertise more.

attractive (adj.) (a-TRAK-tiv)

Attractive means "pleasing; having qualities that draw interest or admiration."

> That window display is very attractive.

attraction (n.) (a-TRAK-shun)

Attraction is (1) the act or power of attracting; (2) something that attracts.

> Although he wasn't handsome, she felt a strong attraction toward him.
> Disneyland is a popular attraction.

contract (v.) (kun-TRAKT),
contraction (n.) (kun-TRAK-shun)

The prefix *con-* means "together." **Contract** means "to draw together," and is used in the following ways: (1) to shorten; shrink; become smaller in size, more compact; (2) to draw together two people in a legal agreement; (3) to acquire, as a disease or debt. In a literal sense, diseases or debts are "drawn" from sources or influences; therefore, they are said to be contracted.

> Darkness causes the pupils of the eyes to enlarge; bright light contracts the pupils.
> His company contracted to build the gym.
> Malaria is a tropical disease contracted by the bite of a mosquito.

As a noun, **contract** (KON-trakt) means "a legal agreement drawn together by two persons."

> A contract must be signed by both parties.

A **contraction** is (1) a pulling or drawing together; a shrinkage; (2) a shortening of a word; two words pulled together into one.

> A muscle cramp is a tight contraction of a muscle.
> The word *though* is a contraction of "although"; *don't* is a contraction of "do" and "not."

detract (v.) (di-TRAKT)

To **detract** from something means to "lessen, reduce, or diminish in quality."

> That hairstyle detracts from her beauty.

distract (v.) (dis-TRAKT),
distraction (n.) (dis-TRAK-shun)

To **distract** is to draw one's attention away from something.

> The loud party next door distracted me from my reading.

A **distraction** is anything that distracts. Another definition is "extreme mental stress caused by worry, emotional conflict, or grief; mental preoccupation with cares, conflict, or anxiety."

All that noise is causing distraction.

A now-rare definition of **distraction** is "insanity or madness." Although people still use **distraction** in this sense, they do not use it in a serious way, but as an exaggeration.

That child's behavior is driving me to distraction!

distracted (adj.) (dis-TRAK-ted)

The adjective **distracted** means "preoccupied with worry or grief; mentally agitated; frantic."

She was in a distracted state of mind over the loss of her life savings.

extract (v.) (eks-TRAKT),
extraction (n.) (eks-TRAK-shun)

The prefix *ex-* means "out." **Extract** means "pull out; draw out; pull out by force, demands, threats, schemes, etc."

She extracted a promise from me not to tell anyone her secret.

As a noun, **extract** (EKS-trakt) means (1) something extracted or drawn out; (2) a passage or excerpt from a book, poem, the Bible, etc., which is selected for some particular purpose.

The bride read an extract from her favorite poem during the exchange of vows.

Extraction, the noun form of the verb **extract**, means: (1) the act of extracting; (2) ancestry; national origin.

A major industry of South Africa is the extraction of gold from extremely deep mines.

protract (v.) (prō-TRAKT),
protracted (adj.) (prō-TRAK-ted)

The prefix *pro-* means "forward." **Protract** means "draw forward" in the sense of time. To **protract** is to prolong, extend, or stretch out for a longer time period than planned.

> Let's not protract this meeting by discussing trivial things.

Protracted is an adjective meaning "prolonged, drawn out for a longer period of time than expected or necessary."

> Mother's nerves were frazzled after Aunt Jane's protracted visit.

retract (v.) (ri-TRAKT),
retraction (n.) (ri-TRAK-shun)

Retract is a combination of the prefix *re-*, meaning "back," and **tract**, meaning "pull." To **retract** is to pull back or withdraw something.

> A tortoise can retract its head and feet into its shell.

Another definition of **retract** is "take back something that has been said; apologize."

> He refused to retract one word of the accusations he made.

Retraction is (1) the act of pulling back something; (2) the act of taking back what one has said or written.

> There were problems with the retraction of the landing gear.
> The editors published a retraction when they learned that their report about the mayor was not true.

subtract (v.) (sub-TRAKT)

Normally, the prefix *sub-* means "under." In a few words such as **subtract**, *sub-* means "away." **Subtract** means "to draw away" in the sense of deducting or taking away part of an amount.

My bank account was overdrawn because I didn't subtract correctly the amount of my checks.

Group Two

abstract (n.) (ab-STRAKT)
(1) literally, to draw away; draw out the essence of something; summarize; as a noun, a summary; (2) existing in the mind only as ideas, emotions, concepts, theories

An abstract is a summary of the main facts of a document.

Happiness is an abstract thing.

contractual (adj.) (kun-TRAK-choo-ul)
connected with a contract; relating to a signed agreement

A contractual agreement is legally binding.

detraction (n.) (di-TRAK-shun)
slander; disparagement; aspersion

Despite her opponent's detractions of her ability, she easily won the election.

detractor (n.) (di-TRAKT-er)
one who disparages, criticizes

In spite of her detractors' scorn, she spoke out fearlessly against corruption.

distraught (adj.) (dis-TRAWT)
a form of the adjective *distracted*, meaning preoccupied with worry; mentally agitated; frantic; crazed with worry or grief

The owner was distraught over the theft of her valuable paintings.

protractive (adj.) (prō-TRAK-tiv)
tending to prolong, draw out; stall, cause delay

The children tried a number of protractive strategies to avoid going to bed.

tractable (adj.) (TRAK-ta-bull)
literally, able to be pulled; easily led, controlled, or managed

The child has a sweet, tractable nature.

intractable (adj.) (in-TRAK-ta-bull)
not able to be pulled; not easily controlled or managed; stubborn; unyielding

Mules are noted for being intractable.

Exercise 11.3

Add appropriate prefixes and suffixes to the root **tract** to complete the meaning of each of the sentences below.

1. Certain exercises _____tract the muscles, causing them to become firm.

2. Cats can extend and _____tract their claws.

3. You forgot to _____tract the amount we spent on decorations from the proceeds.

4. The porch light _____tracted a swarm of flying insects.

5. *House* is a concrete noun; *love* is an _____tract noun.

6. Her constant chatter _____tracts me from my work.

7. The dentist is going to _____tract my wisdom teeth.

8. Her rude manner _____tracts from her beauty.

9. Try not to _____tract this discussion by digressing from the topic.

10. The child is _____tract_____. He refuses to go to bed.

12
Moving and Settling

MOVING

Words that relate to moving are based on the roots **mov, mot** (or **mote**), and **mob**. These roots form the base of the words *move, motor, automobile*, and all of the words in Group One. Although many are familiar, their uses are varied. Don't neglect to explore all their meanings.

The Word Building Chart
for *mov, mot, mob*

Word	Beginning block	Middle block	End block	Quick definition
movement	none	**move** (stem of *mov*, produce motion)	**-ment** (act of)	act of moving
moving	none	**mov** (produce motion)	**-ing** (adj. form)	producing motion or emotion
unmoved	**un-** (not)	**mov** (produce motion)	**-ed** (adj. form)	not moved; untouched
motion	none	**mot** (move)	**-ion** (act of)	the act of moving
commotion	**com-** (thoroughly)	**mot** (move)	**-ion** (state)	violent motion; state of agitation
motive	none	**mot** (move)	**-ive** (causing)	a cause of action; reason
motivate	none	**motiv** (cause)	**-ate** (give)	give a cause to act
locomotive	**loco-** (place)	**mot** (move)	**-ive** (causing)	causing to move from place to place; a railway engine
demote	**de-** (down)	**mote** (move)	none	move down in rank
demotion	**de-** (down)	**mot** (move)	**-ion** (act of)	act of moving down; reducing in rank

emotion	e- (out)	mot (move)	-ion (state)	literally, a moving outward of feelings; a state of strong feeling
emotional	e- (out)	motion (movement)	-al (causing)	causing emotion
promote	pro- (forward)	mote (move)	none	move forward; advance
promotion	pro- (forward)	mot (move)	-ion (act of)	act of moving forward; advancement
mob	none	mob (from *mobilus*)	none	a moving, disorderly crowd
mobile	none	mob (move)	-ile (able)	movable
mobility	none	mobil (movable)	-ity	movability

Group One

movement (n.) (MOOV-ment)

Movement means (1) motion; the act of moving; (2) the manner of moving; (3) activity organized to achieve a result, especially a political result.

> Leonardo Da Vinci tried to devise a flying machine based on his study of birds' movements in flight.
> Women's Suffrage was a political movement organized to obtain the right of women to vote.

moving (adj.) (MOOV-ing)

As an adjective, **moving** means (1) going or capable of going from place to place; (2) impelling or influencing action; (3) arousing the emotions; producing an emotional effect.

An escalator is a moving stairway.
The leadership of Martin Luther King was a moving force in the civil rights struggle.
The Killing Fields was a moving story of friendship and war.

unmoved (adj.) (un-MOOVD)

Un- is an Old English prefix meaning "not." The adjective **unmoved** means "not moved" in the sense of being untouched or remaining in the same place.

The broken glass and overturned furniture were left unmoved until the police made their investigation.

Unmoved is often used to mean "untouched or unaffected in feelings or emotions."

Only the most heartless person could remain unmoved by the sight of starving children.

motion (n.) (MOE-shun)

Motion means (1) movement; (2) a formal suggestion made at an assembly or meeting.

Da Vinci was fascinated by the motion of birds in flight. A new member made the motion that the group help build a shelter for the homeless.

As a verb, **motion** means "to direct or signal by a bodily gesture."

The guide motioned us to follow her.

commotion (n.) (ka-MOE-shun)

A violent disturbance or agitation can be called a **commotion**. Other definitions are "uproar, tumult."

The neighbors heard a commotion and called the police.

motive (n.) (MOTE-iv)

A **motive** is the purpose or incentive that moves a person to an action or a behavior.

What was her motive for stealing the diary?

motivate (v.) (MOTE-i-vayt),
motivation (n.) (mote-i-VAY-shun)

Motivate means "to provide with a motive or an incentive; to induce."

> Using threats and punishment is not the best way to motivate students to learn.

Motivation means "incentive" or "the act of motivating."

> The children were given rewards as a motivation for good behavior.

locomotive (n.) (low-ka-MOE-tiv)

The Latin word *locus* means "place." Literally, a **locomotive** is something that moves from place to place. Its common definition is "an engine used to pull trains on a railway."

> In 1830, near Baltimore, a famous race took place between a horse and a small steam locomotive named the *Tom Thumb*.

demote (v.) (di-MOTE),
demotion (n.) (di-MOE-shun)

Demote comes from the prefix *de-*, meaning "down," and **mote**, meaning "move." **Demote** means "move down in rank or position." The noun form of **demotion** means "a move downward; a reduction in rank."

> The corporal was demoted to the rank of private.

emotion (n.) (e-MOE-shun),
emotional (adj.) (e-MOE-shun-ul)

In the word **emotion**, the prefix *e-* is a shortened spelling of *ex-*, "outward." Specifically, **emotion** means "a stirring of feeling; a strong surge of feeling that is outwardly expressed; any intense feeling, such as love, hate, anger, pity, etc."

Hatred is a very destructive emotion.

Emotional is the adjective form of **emotion** and means "full of feeling; expressing emotion; arousing the emotions."

promote (v.) (pra-MOTE),
promotion (n.) (pra-MOE-shun)

Promote comes from the prefix *pro-*, meaning "forward" or "ahead," and **mote**, meaning "move." **Promote** means (1) advance; move forward in rank or position; (2) to cause something to advance or spread; (3) to put forth an idea or product for public acceptance.

> The lieutenant was promoted to the rank of captain.
> According to psychologists, movies that portray fighting and killing promote violence.
> Manufacturers use television advertising to promote their products.

Promotion means (1) advancement in rank or position; (2) an effort toward advancing something; (3) the effort of making someone or something popular.

mob (n.) (MAHB)

The Latin origin of the word **mob** is the phrase **mobile vulgus**, literally "a movable crowd." The Romans used this phrase to mean "the fickle masses," those whose feelings and opinions could be easily swayed or moved. In modern usage, **mob** means "a large, disorderly, or lawless crowd prone to act mindlessly; a rabble."

> In Boston, a mob, angered by desegregation, overturned a school bus carrying black children.

Mob is also a verb meaning (1) to attack; (2) to crowd around and jostle.

> A throng of adoring fans mobbed the rock star's limousine.

mobile (adj.) (MOE-bull),
mobility (n.) (moe-BILL-a-tee)

The adjective **mobile** comes from the prefix *mob-*, meaning "move," and the suffix *-ile*, meaning "able." **Mobile** means "able to move; able to move freely; movable; easily moved."

> Physical therapy helped the patient to become mobile again.

Mobility is the state of being mobile or the ability to move.

> As his illness progressed, he lost mobility in his legs.

Group Two

emote (v.) (i-MOTE)

a humorous term meaning to display emotions in an exaggerated way, as in acting

> The star of the play doesn't seem to know the difference between acting and emoting.

emotive (adj.) (i-MOTE-iv)

tending or designed to excite emotion

> Martin Luther King spoke with emotive eloquence.

mobilize (v.) (MOE-ba-lize)

to assemble for action; make ready for war; put into activity; organize

> To meet this crisis, we must mobilize all our resources.

demobilize (v.) (de-MOE-ba-lize)

to disband an army or troops

> After the victory, the troops were quickly demobilized.

mobocracy (n.) (mahb-AHK-ra-see)

rule by a mob; a ruling mob

> The frontier town seemed to be in the power of a mindless mobocracy.

remote (adj.) (ri-MOTE)

1) far-removed; distant in place or time; 2) distant in manner; aloof; 3) absentminded; distracted; 4) slight; slightly related

> At times, I long to be on some remote island, far away from all the problems here.
>
> In some remote future time, humans may communicate with beings from outer space.
>
> Because of his remote manner, he has few friends.
>
> His eyes had a remote expression, as if he were remembering something from long ago.
>
> The chances of finding that treasure are remote.

Exercise 12.1

Match words from both groups to their definitions below.

1. assemble an army _____

2. disband an army _____

3. mob rule _____

4. far-removed _____

5. designed to arouse emotion _____

6. exaggerate emotions _____

Exercise 12.2

Substitute **verbs** from both groups for the parenthesized words in the sentences below.

1. (Signal) _____ them to join us at our table.

2. The mercenary soldiers were (given incentive) _____d by greed.

3. She was (advanced) _____d to office manager.

4. He was (moved down) _____d from regional to district manager.

5. Actors in silent movies tended to (exaggerate emotions) _____ in a melodramatic style.

6. We must (organize) _____ our energies in order to save the environment.

7. A huge victory celebration awaited the (disbanded) _____d troops.

Exercise 12.3

Substitute **adjectives** from both groups for the parenthesized words in the sentences below.

1. Her tearful pleas left him (untouched) _____.

2. My father was a very (full of feeling) _____ man, who was not ashamed to weep or show affection.

3. (Movable) _____ libraries serve readers who live in small rural towns.

4. Gandhi's leadership was the (impelling) _____ force of Indian resistance to British control.

5. Her (distant) _____ manner made it clear that she did not desire my friendship.

6. In the days of the silent screen, theaters employed pianists whose job was to play (designed to arouse emotions) _____ music in order to heighten audience's sense of drama.

SETTLING

Most of the words in this part of the chapter have meanings that are quite the reverse of moving or motion. This group of words is based on the root sid (or side), sed, or sess, which means "settle," "sit," or "occupy."

The Word Building Chart
for *sid, sed, sess*

Word	Beginning block	Middle block	End block	Quick definition
preside	**pre-** (before)	**side** (stem of *sid*, to sit)	none	sit before others as leader; to lead
president	**pre-** (before)	**sid** (sit)	**-ent** (one who)	one who presides, leads
reside	**re-** (back)	**side** (settle)	none	literally, settle back; occupy
resident	**re-** (back)	**sid** (settle)	**-ent**	one who settles in a place; dweller; occupant
residence	**re-** (back)	**sid** (settle)	**-ence** (place where)	place where one settles; a dwelling
residue	**re-** (back)	**sid** (settle)	**-ue** (French suffix, that which)	that which is left back; a remaining part
subside	**sub-** (under)	**side** (settle)	none	to settle under; become calm
sedate	none	**sed** (settle)	**-ate** (cause)	cause to settle; make calm
sedative	none	**sed** (settle)	**-ative** (that which)	that which has a settling effect; a medicine for soothing pain, nerves

sedation	none	**sed** (settle)	**-ation** (state of)	state of calm, relief from pain produced by medication
sediment	none	**sedi** (stem of *sed*, settle)	**-ment** (that which)	substance in liquid which settles
assess	**as-** (from *ad-*, to)	**sess** (sit)	none	to sit in judgment; judge a matter
assessment	**as-** (to)	**sess** (sit)	**-ment** (the act)	act of assessing; a judgment
obsess	**ob-** (before)	**sess** (occupy)	none	occupy the mind excessively; literally, sit before the mind
obsession	**ob-** (before)	**sess** (occupy)	**-ion** (state)	a state of being obsessed; that which obsesses
possess	**pos-** (from *potis*, master)	**sess** (sit)	none	to own; literally, sit as master
possession	**pos-** (owner)	**sess** (sit, occupy)	**-ion** state of	state of ownership; that which is owned
dispossess	**dis-** (away)	**possess** (own)	none	to take away possessions
session	none	**sess** (sit)	**-ion** (the act of)	a meeting; "a sitting"

Group One

preside (v.) (pre-ZIDE),
president (n.) (PREZ-a-dent)

The verb **preside** is derived from the prefix *pre-*, meaning "before," and the root **side**, meaning "sit." To **preside** is to sit before others in a position of authority or leadership.

The new chairperson will preside over the meeting.

A **president** is one who presides over or leads an organization or a nation.

The first president to be assassinated was Lincoln.

reside (v.) (re-ZIDE), residence (n.) (REZ-a-denss), resident (n.) (REZ-a-dent)

Reside comes from the prefix *re-*, meaning "back," and the root **sid**, meaning "settle." **Reside** means "settle back" in the sense of living in or occupying a place.

The Smiths reside at 315 Elm Street.

Reside also means "to exist within as a quality."

The strength to overcome difficulties resides in all of us.

Another definition of **reside** is "to be vested in, as a right."

The power to declare war resides in the Congress.

A **residence** is a home or the place where one resides.

That old mansion was once the residence of the town's richest family.

The phrase **in residence** means "officially present" or "residing in an official capacity."

Our school district has a new artist in residence.

Resident means "one who lives in a place; an occupant; dweller."

residue (n.) (REZ-a-doo)

Residue means "matter which settles or remains after a part has been taken away; remainder."

That cleaner left a gritty residue on the floor after it dried.

subside (v.) (sub-SIDE)

The prefix *sub-* means "under"; **side** means "settle." The literal meaning of **subside** is "to settle under," and although it is sometimes used to mean "settle to the bottom, as sediment," **subside** more often means "become less agitated; settle down; become calm."

My anger subsided after she apologized.

sedate (adj.) (sa-DATE), **sedative** (n.) (SED-a-tiv), **sedation** (sa-DAY-shun)

The verb **sedate** means to "administer medicine to ease pain or settle the nerves."

The doctor had to sedate the patient.

As an adjective, **sedate** describes a person who is staid, habitually calm, composed, or "settled" in manner.

A sedate person tends to be unemotional.

The adjective **sedative** means "having a settling effect; calming; soothing."

Soft music can have a sedative effect on frazzled nerves.

As a noun, **sedative** means "a medicine that soothes pain or distress; any means of calming distress."

A warm bath can be a sedative after a hectic day.

Sedation is the state resulting from the administration of sedative medication.

The patient is still under sedation.

sediment (n.) (SED-a-ment)

Sediment is matter that settles to the bottom of a liquid.

On close inspection, the wine remaining in the victim's glass revealed a suspicious sediment.

assess (v.) (a-SES), **assessment** (n.) (a-SES-ment)

The prefix *as-* is a changed spelling of the prefix *ad-*, meaning "to." **Assess** means "to sit by in the manner of a judge," or simply "to judge." The broader meaning of **assess** is (1) to charge a fine, a tax, or other payment after settling upon a fair amount; (2) to determine the amount of something; estimate.

> Damage from the tornado was assessed at several million dollars.

Assessment means "judgment; an estimate."

> The new superintendent has made an assessment of the students' educational needs.

obsess (v.) (ub-SES), obsession (n.) (ub-SESH-un)

One meaning of the prefix *ob-* is "before." **Obsess**—literally, "sitting before"—means "occupying the mind to an excessive degree."

> He suspected that his wife was unfaithful, and the idea of revenge began to obsess him.

An **obsession** is the state of being obsessed.

> Her obsession with clothes is costing a fortune.

possess (v.) (pa-ZES), possession (n.) (pa-ZESH-un)

Possess is formed from the roots **pos**, a contraction of the Latin word *potis*, meaning "master," and **sess**, meaning "sit." Literally, **possess** means "to sit as a master." In early times, *master* was the term for an owner of property. **Possess** means "to own or have as property; to have as a quality."

> She possesses charm, intelligence, and wit.

Possession is (1) ownership; the fact of having, owning, possessing; (2) that which is owned. **Possessions** are belongings.

> They will take possession of the house on the first of the month.
> This trophy is his most prized possession.

dispossess (v.) (dis-pa-ZES)

The prefix *dis-* means "away." **Dispossess** means "to take away possessions, especially houses and land; to oust; drive out."

The Trail of Tears began when the government dispossessed the Cherokees of their homelands in the South.

session (n.) (SESH-un)

Session means (1) the sitting together of a body of lawmakers, a council, or a court for the transaction of business; (2) a single meeting or series of meetings held for a special purpose or activity; (3) a school term.

Little was accomplished toward reducing the federal debt during the last congressional session.
The company conducts training sessions for new employees.
During the summer session, classes are smaller.

Group Two

dissident (n.) (DIS-a-dent)

one who disagrees, dissents; literally, one who sits apart in opinion

In some countries, political dissidents are imprisoned.

insidious (adj.) (in-SID-ee-us)

treacherous; cunning; working unseen to do harm; literally, sitting (or lying) in wait

The investigators exposed an insidious plot to overthrow the government.

assiduous

hardworking; diligent; unremitting in effort; constant in attention (from Latin *assidire*, to sit by)

Completing the project on time will require assiduous work.

residual (adj.) (ri-ZID-yoo-ul)

remaining, left over as residue

Geologists have developed methods to recover residual stores of oil from old wells that have been shut down.

sedentary (adj.) (SED-un-tair-ee)
requiring a sitting posture; sluggish, inactive

Secretarial work is a sedentary occupation.

subsidiary (adj.) (sub-SID-ee-air-ee)
an organization or company under control of a larger organization or company; literally, sitting under

That company is a subsidiary of a major corporation.

subsidize (v.) (SUB-sa-dize)
to grant money through the government to an enterprise; to finance something by assistance from the government; literally, sit under (in the sense of financial dependence)

Congress voted to subsidize the corporation in order to save thousands of workers' jobs.

subsidy (n.) (SUB-sa-dee)
a sum of money granted by a government

Many taxpayers were angered by the subsidy given to the huge corporation.

supersede (v.) (soop-er-SEED)
to set aside, or replace with something that is more important, or superior; literally, "sit above" in authority, importance

The captain's orders superseded those of the lieutenant.

Note: **Supersede** is often misspelled as "supercede." Remembering that the root of supersede is **sed**, meaning "sit," will help you avoid this error.

Exercise 12.4

Substitute words from both groups for the parenthesized words in the phrases below.

1. attending the (meeting) _____

2. (own) _____ great wealth

3. to (judge the amount of) _____ the damage

4. when the trouble (settled down) _____d

5. a (sitting under control of) _____ company

6. to (give government money) _____ the health project

7. to ("sit above") _____ my orders

8. to (soothe, settle) _____ the patient

9. sticky (remaining matter) _____ on the furniture

10. (inactive) _____ lifestyle

13

Seeing, Hearing, Touching

SEEING

The Latin word *visus* means "sight; look; appearance." *Videre* means "to see." *Video* is a Latin word that actually means "I see." Several English words related to seeing are based on the roots **vis** and **vid,** including *visit* and *television.* This section of the chapter provides many other examples.

Word Building Chart
for *vis, vid*

Word	Beginning block	Middle block	End block	Quick definition
visibility	none	**visibil** (see)	**-ity** (ability)	the ability to be seen
vision	none	**vis** (see)	**-ion** (the act of)	the act of seeing; sight
visual	none	**vis** (sight)	**-ual** (relating to)	relating to sight
visualize	none	**visual** (sight)	**-ize** (relating)	to create sights, images in the mind
advise	**ad-** (to)	**vise** (stem of *vis*, see)	none	to give counsel; literally, to see
evident	**e-** (out)	**vid** (see)	**-ent** (having the quality of)	easily seen; seen outright
evidence	**e-** (out)	**vid** (see)	**-ence** (that which)	that which serves as proof
provide	**pro-** (ahead)	**vide** (stem of *vid*, see)	none	to furnish needs; literally, see ahead
provision	**pro-** (ahead)	**vis** (see)	**-ion** (the act of)	the act of providing for; that which is provided
revise	**re-** (again)	**vise** (see)	none	to review and change; literally, look at again

revision	re- (again)	vis (see)	-ion (the act of)	the act of revising
supervise	super- (over)	vise (see)	none	to oversee; direct
supervisor	super- (over)	vis (see)	-or (one who)	one who supervises; an overseer
supervision	super- (over)	vis (see)	-ion (the act of)	the act of supervising

---

Group One

visibility (n.) (viz-a-BIL-i-tee)

Visibility is the ability to be seen, or the degree to which objects can be seen. **Visibility** is often used to mean "the degree of clearness in the atmosphere."

Visibility was very low because of the dense fog.

vision (n.) (VIZH-un)

Vision is the faculty of seeing or eyesight. A second definition of **vision** is "sight" in the sense of something that is seen. An especially beautiful sight may be called a **vision**. **Visions** are also seen in the mind as imagination or dreams.

The doctor tested my vision and prescribed reading glasses.
The bride was a vision of loveliness in her flowing white dress.

visual (adj.) (VIZH-yoo-ul)

Visual is an adjective that relates to sight. The **visual** portion of a television program, for instance, is the part that is seen rather than heard. Painting and sculpture are **visual** arts because they are meant to be seen. **Visual** teaching aids are pictures, films, and graphs that help students learn by seeing examples of what is being studied.

The movie's visual effects are dazzling.

Another definition of **visual** is "used for seeing; optic."

A microscope is an instrument used for visual examination of tiny organisms.

visualize (v.) (VIZH-yoo-ul-ize)

To **visualize** is to form mental images, to picture in the mind, imagine, envision.

She liked to visualize herself as a famous movie star.

advise (v.) (ad-VIZE)

In the literal sense, **advise** means to have insight into a problem, but its definition has been expanded to mean "recommend, suggest, give counsel." A synonym for *counsel* is *advice*, the noun form of **advise**.

The doctor advised her to rest.

A second meaning of **advise** is "inform."

The staff advised the president of the disaster that had just occurred.

provide (v.) (pra-VIDE)

The prefix *pro-* means "ahead" or "forward." Literally "look ahead," **provide** means "foresee" but its broader meaning is "to make ready beforehand." To **provide** is not only to foresee but to prepare. A second meaning is "to supply" or "to furnish," or "to support by furnishing food, clothing, and shelter."

Seat belts provide protection from serious injury in case of an accident.
The students will provide the food for the party.

provision (n.) (pra-VIZH-un)

The noun form of **provide** is **provision**, which means (1) preparation; (2) supplies; (3) stipulation—that is, a certain condition set forth as part of an agreement.

Squirrels make provision for winter by gathering and storing food.

The storm left us stranded and without provisions.

My parents allowed me to work with the provision that I do my homework each day.

evident (adj.) (EV-a-dent),
evidence (n.) (EV-a-denss)

Formed from the prefix *e-*, meaning "out," and the root **vid**, meaning "see," evident means "out in the open, plain to see; apparent."

It's evident that you didn't do your assigned reading.

revise (v.) (ri-VISE), **revision** (n.) (ri-VIZH-un)

To **revise** is to review for the purpose of making changes and corrections. A second definition is "to change, alter."

With the new evidence, the scientists had to revise their opinions about the cause of the disease.

A **revision** is a change or the process of changing.

The manuscript had undergone several revisions.

supervise (v.) (SOO-per-vize),
supervisor (n.) (SOO-per-vize-er),
supervision (n.) (soo-per-VIZH-un)

The prefix *super-* means "over" or "above." To **supervise** is literally "to oversee." A **supervisor** is an overseer, who has authority to direct and control operations. **Supervision** is the act of overseeing, directing, or controlling.

His job was to supervise the construction of the bridge.

Group Two

visage (n.) (VIS-ij)

a facial expression, look; countenance; face

My father's stern visage conveyed his disapproval.

visitation (n.) (viz-a-TAY-shun)
a formal visit; a dispensation of divine favor or disfavor

The prophet predicted a visitation of plague as God's punishment for the people's wickedness.

visionary (n. & adj.) (VIZH-a-nair-ee)
highly imaginative; idealistic; fanciful; an impractical dreamer; idealist; one with unusual insight

Martin Luther King's famous "I have a dream" speech revealed him as a great visionary.

evidential (adj.) (ev-a-DEN-chul)
pertaining to evidence; serving as proof

The judge will examine the evidential documents.

providence (n.) (PRA-va-denss)
foresight; (with capital P) divine protection; God's watchful care of the universe

The missionaries placed their trust in Divine Providence.

provident (adj.) (PRA-va-dent)
having foresight; making ready for future needs; thrifty

The young man was provident, not wasting a penny of his small earnings.

providential (adj.) (pra-va-DEN-chul)
fortunate; lucky; resulting from God's providence

Our rescue from the river was providential.

proviso (n.) (pra-VIZE-ō)
stipulation; provision

According to the proviso, you must finish college in order to receive any money from the estate.

provisional (adj.) (pra-VIZH-un-ul)
tentative; providing a temporary need

Promising free elections soon, the general has installed himself as the provisional head of government.

vista (n.) (VISS-ta)
a view from a distance; prospect; outlook

Education has opened new vistas to these disadvantaged children.

Exercise 13.1

From both groups, find an appropriate word to replace each of the italicized words and phrases below. Write the words in the blank space to the right.

1. a *change* of the rules _____

2. *rewrite* the manuscript _____

3. *God's protection* _____

4. *recommend* changing the plan _____

5. *oversee* the work _____

6. furnish *proof* of guilt _____

7. *a provision* of the treaty _____

8. make a *formal visit* _____

9. exhibits *serving as proof* _____

10. *impractical, fanciful* schemes _____

HEARING

Just as *video* literally means "I see," *audio* means "I hear," although the word in modern usage normally describes electronically reproduced sound. The root **aud** or **audit**, which forms the base of the words in this section, comes from the Latin verb *audire*, meaning "to hear."

Word Building Chart
for *aud, audit*

Word	Beginning block	Middle block	End block	Quick definition
audible	none	**audi** (hear)	**-ible** (able)	able to be heard
inaudible	**in-** (not)	**audi** (hear)	**-ible** (able)	not able to be heard
audience	none	**aud-i** (hear)	**-ence** (condition)	a group of listeners; literally, the condition of hearing
audit	none	**audit** (hear)	none	an inspection of financial records; originally, a hearing (from Latin *auditus*)
audition	none	**audit** (hear)	**-ion** (act of)	act of hearing; a trial performance
auditorium	none	**audit or** (one who hears)	**-ium** (place)	place for hearing speeches, performances

audible (adj.) (AW-da-bul),
inaudible (adj.) (in-AW-da-bul)

Audible means "loud enough to be heard." **Inaudible** means "not loud enough to be heard."

Their conversation was clearly audible.
He tried to quiet the mob, but his voice was inaudible above their angry shouts.

audience (n.) (AW-dee-enss)

An **audience** is a group of people who gather to hear speeches, music, or other kinds of performances. Originally, an audience was "a hearing." The word is still sometimes used in this sense.

> The Pope granted an audience to the president.

audit (v. & n.) (AW-dit)

Like *audience*, **audit** originally meant "a hearing," but in modern usage, an **audit** is usually an inspection, especially of public or private financial records. **Audit** is both a verb and a noun.

> The government may audit your financial records if you fail to report all your income.

Audit still relates to *hearing* when it refers to the practice of attending university lectures. A student who **audits** a course takes no tests and receives no grades, but attends classes only to hear the lectures.

> I plan to audit a course in child psychology.

audition (n.) (aw-DISH-un)

The act or sense of hearing is called **audition**, but this word is frequently used to mean "a hearing given to a performer as a test or tryout." **Audition** is also used as a verb.

> You should audition for the part, because you have real talent.

auditorium (n.) (aw-da-TOR-ee-um)

An **auditorium** is a building or large room where people assemble to hear speeches, concerts, or other presentations.

> Graduation ceremonies will be held in the auditorium.

Group Two

audient (adj.) (AW-dee-ent)

listening; paying attention

> Students will be less audient if their instruction is boring.

auditory (adj.) (AWD-a-tor-ee)
relating to hearing

Auditory nerves transmit sound sensations to the brain.

auditive (adj.) (AWD-a-tiv)
relating to hearing (an alternate form of *auditory*)

The telephone developed from the auditive experiments of Alexander Graham Bell, who was trying to invent a hearing aid for deaf children.

audiometer (n.) (aw-dee-OHM-a-ter)
a device for measuring the acuteness of hearing

Audiometers detect hearing deficiencies.

audio-visual (adj.) (aw-dee-o-VIZH-yoo-ul)
relating to entertainment and instructional forms other than books; providing sensory experience that is both auditory and visual

Audio-visual teaching aids include television, film strips, photographs, and sound recordings.

Exercise 13.2

Substitute words from both groups for the parenthesized words in the sentences below.

1. Her voice was barely (able to be heard) _____ from the stage.

2. The (group of listeners) _____ applauded loudly.

3. The (large room holding an audience) _____ was full.

4. The government has ordered an (inspection of financial records) _____ of the bank.

5. Some educators fear that (communication forms other than books) _____ entertainment may entirely replace reading.

6. Watching a film is a visual experience; listening to music is an (auditory) _____ experience.

7. The (device for hearing measurement) _____ gives information about hearing ability.

8. Children who seem to be not (attentive) _____ may have hearing deficiencies.

TOUCHING

The sense of touch is called the **tactile** sense. The Latin word *tactus* means "touched." Its root **tact** forms the base of words relating to touch. Other forms of **tact** are **ting** and **tang**, from the Latin verb *tangere*, meaning "to touch."

Word Building Chart
for *tact, tang, ting*

Word	Beginning block	Middle block	End block	Quick definition
tactile	none	**tact** (touch)	**-ile** (pertaining to)	pertaining to touch;
tact	none	**tact**	none	literally, touch; speech or action that avoids offending
tactful	none	**tact** (touch)	**-ful**	full of tact; considerate
tactless	none	**tact** (touch)	**-less** (lacking)	lacking tact
contact	**con-** (together)	**tact** (touch)	none	touch together; meet
contagious	**con-** (together)	**tag** (form of *tang*, touch)	**-ious** (tending to)	tending to infect by contact
intact	**in-** (not)	**tact** (touch)	none	untouched; undamaged
tangible	none	**tang** (touch)	**-ible** (able)	able to be touched; having material substance
intangible	**in-** (not)	**tang** (touch)	**-ible** (able)	not capable of being touched; lacking material substance

tactile (adj.) (TAKT-ul)

Tactile is an adjective pertaining to the sense of touch.

Braille is a tactile method of reading used by people who are blind.

tact (n.) (TAKT)

Tact means "touch," but not in the physical sense. **Tact** implies a special kind of touch—namely, the right "touch" with words or actions. **Tact** is the skill of speaking or acting in a way that does not offend people. A person who has **tact** is in touch with the feelings of others and shows respect for their feelings.

Tact is a necessary quality for getting along with people.

tactful (adj.) (TAKT-full), tactless (adj.) (TAKT-luss)

The adjective form of *tact* is **tactful**, which literally means "full of tact." **Tactful** means "considerate; skilled in using appropriate words to avoid giving offense."

The teacher was always honest but tactful with her students.

The opposite of *tactful* is **tactless**. The suffix *-less* means "without." **Tactless** means "lacking tact; blunt in speech; speaking in an insensitive manner."

His tactless remarks embarrassed and angered me.

contact (n.) (KAHN-takt)

The prefix *con-* means "together" or "with." **Contact** means "the act of being in touch with someone or something; a meeting." **Contact** is also a verb.

We should contact the injured boy's parents immediately.

contagious (adj.) (kun-TAY-juss)

An adjective form of *contact* is **contagious**, meaning "infectious; spreading by contact," as a **contagious** disease.

Her laughter is contagious.

intact (adj.) (in-TAKT)

The prefix *in-* means "not." **Intact** means "not touched" in the sense of being undamaged or unchanged.

> The storm destroyed everything around us, but left our house intact.

tangible (adj.) (TAN-ja-bul),
intangible (adj.) (in-TAN-ja-bul)

The suffix *-ible* means "able." Something that is **tangible** is able to be touched. This adjective applies to concrete objects—things that have form and substance and can be perceived with the senses. A table, for instance, is a **tangible** object. It has a form and can be both touched and seen.

Other things exist, however, which are **intangible**; that is, they are not touchable. Ideas, for example, are **intangible** because they have no material substance.

> Painting and sculpting are satisfying hobbies because they produce tangible results.
> Happiness is an intangible quality.

Group Two

tangent (adj.) (TAN-jent)

(1) a straight line touching a curved line at one point; (2) a sharp change in direction, especially in discussion of a subject

> In geometry, *tangent* refers to a straight line that touches but doesn't intersect a curved line.
> The history teacher tends to go off on tangents about current politics.

tangential (adj.) (tan-JEN-shul)

digressing; only slightly touching upon or related to the matter at hand

> Your statements are tangential to the matter under discussion.

contingent (adj.) (kun-TIN-jent)

(1) dependent on an uncertainty; (2) happening by chance; unplanned; (3) a group representing a larger group

The project is contingent upon their signing the contract.
The schedule allows for contingent delays.
A contingent from Texas has arrived at the convention.

contingency (n.) (kun-TIN-jen-see)

a possible occurrence

When planning a camping trip, you should prepare for all contingencies.

contiguous (adj.) (kun-TIG-yoo-us)

touching; adjacent, close by

The owners of the contiguous properties engaged in a dispute about the boundary line.

Exercise 13.3

Substitute words from both groups for the words in parentheses in the following sentences:

1. Your (blunt) _____ remark hurt her feelings.

2. The earthquake caused great damage, but the school building was (untouched) _____.

3. I will (get in touch with) _____ you on Monday.

4. Money is a (touchable) _____ reward for work.

5. Pride in a job well done is an (untouchable) _____ reward.

6. The two acreages are (adjacent) _____.

7. His fingers had lost (relating to touch) _____ sensitivity.

8. We are prepared for any (possible event) _____.

9. We can't end the meeting on time if you keep going off on (digression) _____s.

10. These (barely related) _____ questions show that you lack understanding of the subject.

14
Looking

Another group of words related to seeing is based on the major Latin root **spec**, which comes from the verb *specere*, meaning "to look." Other forms of **spec** are **spect** and **spic**. The words in this chapter are based on this important root.

The Word Building Chart
for *spec, spect, spic*

Word	Beginning block	Middle block	End block	Quick definition
spectacle	none	**spect** (look)	**-acle** (that which)	something that is looked at; a sight
spectacles	none	**spect** (look)	**-acles** (that which)	plural of spectacle; eyeglasses
spectacular	none	**spectac** (spectacle)	**-ular** (like)	like a spectacle; showy
specimen	none	**speci** (look)	**-men** (something done, produced)	a sample used for examination; example
speculate	none	**spec** (look)	**-ulate** (make)	look at with the mind; make a guess; surmise
speculation	none	**specul** (surmise)	**-ation** (the act of)	the act of surmising; a guess
expect	**ex-** (out)	**(s)pect** (look)	none	look outward for something to happen; anticipate
expectation	**in-** (out)	**(s)pect** (look)	**-ion** (act of)	the act of expecting; anticipation
inspect	**in-** (into)	**spec** (look)	none	look into; examine

inspection	in- (into)	spect (look)	-ion (act of)	the act of inspecting; examination
prospect	pro- (ahead)	spect (look)	none	a look ahead; an expectation
prospective	pro- (ahead)	spect (look)	-ive (relating to)	relating to an expectation of the future
respect	re- (again)	spect (look)	none	view with esteem
suspect	su- (from *sub-*, under)	spect (look)	none	look under the surface; mistrust
suspicious	su- (under)	spic (look)	-ious (full of)	full of mistrust
suspicion	su- (under)	spic (look)	-ion (state of)	a state of mistrust
conspicuous	con- (together)	spic (look at)	-uous (having the quality of)	easily noticed; drawing attention
inconspicuous	-in + con- (not + together	spic (look at)	-uous (having the quality of)	not noticeable
despise	de- (down)	spise (look)	none	look down on; view with contempt
despicable	de- (down)	spic (look)	-able (capable)	capable of being despised; contemptible

Group One

spectacle (n.) (SPEK-ta-kul)

A **spectacle** is a showy sight or a public display—something people come to look at. A **spectacle** may be a marvelous natural scene or a large visual exhibit such as a show or a pageant.

The Rose Bowl Parade is an annual spectacle.

Spectacle also means ''an exhibition of embarrassing or deplorable behavior''—the kind that causes people to turn and look.

The couple made a spectacle of themselves in the restaurant by their loud quarreling.

spectacles (n.) (SPEK-ta-kuls)

The plural of *spectacle* is **spectacles**, which also means ''eyeglasses.''

My grandfather was always losing his spectacles.

spectacular (adj. & n.) (spek-TAK-yoo-lur)

The adjective form of *spectacle* is **spectacular**, which means ''making a great display; showy.''

The lightning from the approaching clouds was even more spectacular than the fireworks display.

As a noun, **spectacular** means ''a show, especially a television show that is a lavish musical production.''

I enjoy watching television spectaculars because of the dancing and the beautiful costumes.

spectator (n.) (SPEK-tay-tur)

A **spectator** is an onlooker, or one who watches happenings or events.

I was not involved in the riot; I was only a spectator.

specimen (n.) (SPES-a-min)

A **specimen** is a part of anything used to show the nature of the whole. In other words, a specimen is a sample.

Inspector Harris removed a specimen of soil from the victim's shoe and took it to the crime lab.

speculate (v.) (SPEK-yoo-late),
speculation (n.) (spek-yoo-LAY-shun)

Speculate relates to "looking" in the sense of looking for answers to unknowns. To **speculate** is to theorize, surmise, or guess. A **speculation** is a theory or a guess.

Some scientists speculate that there is life in other places of the universe.

The scandal caused much speculation about whether the chairman would resign.

expect (v.) (eks-SPEKT),
expectation (eks-spek-TAY-shun)

To look out for something about to happen is to anticipate or **expect**. A second definition of **expect** is "require."

I expect to graduate in June.

I expect to be paid for this work.

An **expectation** is (1) the prospect of some future good; (2) something that is expected or required.

He had expectations of fame and wealth.

inspect (v.) (in-SPEKT),
inspection (n.) (in-SPEK-shun)

The prefix *in-* means "into." **Inspect** literally means "to look into; to examine carefully." An **inspection** is the act of inspecting; an examination.

The chief of detectives was called in to inspect the scene of the crime.

Looking for clues, he made a close inspection of the room.

prospect (n.) (PRAHS-pekt),
prospective (adj.) (prahs-PEK-tiv)

The prefix *pro-* means "forward" or "ahead." **Prospect** literally means "a look forward," and relates to probabilities or possibilities for the future. A **prospect** is what is likely to happen in the future.

Prospective, the adjective form of *prospect*, relates to something that is anticipated, or still in the future. In one sense, **prospective** describes something that is almost certain to be, such as "the **prospective** bride," meaning "the woman who is engaged to marry." In another sense, **prospective** means "potential" or "possible," such as **prospective** buyers of products.

> At the party, I was introduced to several prospective clients.

prospector (n.) (PRAHS-pek-ter)

A **prospector** is a person who looks for precious minerals, metals, or oil.

> After years of searching, the old prospector finally struck a rich vein of gold ore.

auspice (n.) (AWS-pis), auspices (n.) (AWS-pa-sez)

(1) a sign foretelling the future; omen (from *avis*, bird, and *specere*, look at); a soothsayer in ancient Rome who foretold events by interpreting the movements of birds; (2) guidance; protection; patronage; sponsorship

> The sailors regarded the friendly albatross as a favorable auspice.
> The missionaries performed their work under the auspices of the church.

Note: The plural form of **auspice** is more commonly used today.

auspicious (adj.) (aw-SPISH-us)

favoring success; propitious

The highly praised performance was an auspicious beginning of her career as opera singer.

circumspect (adj.) (SIR-kum-spekt)
wary; cautious; watchful on all sides (from *circum-*, around, and **spect**, look)

In business matters, she was circumspect, thoroughly investigating everyone with whom she dealt.

introspection (n.) (in-tra-SPEK-shun)
from *intro-*, within, and **spect-**, look, the act of looking within oneself in the sense of mental self-examination; looking at one's own actions, motives, and emotions

If he would take some time for introspection, he might stop blaming everyone else for his problems.

introspective (adj.) (in-tra-SPEK-tiv)
given to introspection; preoccupied with one's own thoughts and feelings; inclined to analyze one's own mental and emotional states

She was a quiet, introspective person.

respect (v. & n.) (re-SPEKT)
As a verb, **respect** means "to view with regard or esteem." Its literal meaning, "look at again," is related to the modern term "look at twice," which implies giving due consideration to someone.

I respect my grandmother because she is very wise.

The noun **respect** means (1) honor; esteem; (2) relation; reference.

I have respect for my grandmother.
With respect to your proposal, the council wishes to review it.

suspect (v. & n.) (sa-SPEKT)
This word is built on a shortened spelling of the prefix

sub-, which means "under," and **spect**, meaning "look." The literal definition of **suspect** is "look under." One who suspects has distrust or doubt and tends to look under the surface of a situation for evidence of guilt or evidence that things are not as they seem. **Suspect**, then, means (1) to doubt; distrust (2) to guess.

> She pretends to be indifferent, but I suspect that she still cares about him.

As a noun, **suspect** means "one who is thought to be guilty, especially of a crime."

> The police have arrested a suspect in the case.

suspicious (adj.) (sa-SPISH-us),
suspicion (n.) (sa-SPISH-un)

Suspicious, the adjective form of *suspect*, means (1) distrustful; (2) arousing mistrust. **Suspicious** can refer either to the feeling of one who suspects or the person or thing that is suspected.

> The maid became suspicious of the man who claimed to be a repairman.

Suspicion, the noun form of *suspect*, means (1) mistrust; (2) the imagining of something wrong without actual proof.

> My suspicion was aroused by the odd change in her behavior.

conspicuous (adj.) (kun-SPIK-yoo-us),
inconspicuous (adj.) (in-kun-SPIK-yoo-us)

The prefix *con-* means "together." **Conspicuous** literally means "look at together." Its ordinary definitions are "drawing attention; noticeable," although it is sometimes used to mean "easily seen."

> Dressed in gaudy clothes and jewelry, she was quite conspicuous in the Sunday congregation.

Inconspicuous means "not noticeable."

> He was shy and preferred being inconspicuous.

despise (v.) (des-PIZE),
despicable (adj.) (des-PIK-a-bul)

Although the word **despise** does not fit the spelling pattern of other "look" words, its root **spise** comes from *specere*, meaning "look." The prefix *de-* means "down"; **despise** literally means "to look down," and, specifically, "to look down on someone or something with hatred or contempt." **Despicable** is the adjective form of **despise** and means "contemptible; hated; vile."

> Although most snakes are harmless, many people despise them.

> To abandon his sick wife and child was a despicable act.

Group Two

aspect (n.) (ASS-spekt)
view of a side or sides

> Her angry outburst revealed an aspect of her personality that I had not seen before.

perspective (n.) (per-SPEK-tiv)
from *per-*, through, and the root **spect**, look—literally, a look through; a view; viewpoint; the proportionate importance of a matter as seen from an individual view; in drawing, the art of making a flat surface appear to have depth

> By depending mostly on the government for information, news journalists are giving us a limited perspective of the effects of our foreign policy.

perspicacious (adj.) (per-spa-KAY-shus)
having keen understanding, insight; astute; sharp; shrewd; from *per*, through, and **spic**, see

> He is known for his perspicacious leadership.

perspicacity (v.) (per-spa-KAS-a-tee)
keen insight; mental quickness

> Because of her perspicacity, we usually sought her advice.

retrospect (n.) (RET-ra-spekt)

from *retro-*, backward, and **spect**, a look backward; a review of past events

In retrospect, I realize I should have continued my education.

respective (adj.) (ri-SPEK-tiv)

relating severally to each; particular; each to each

The council discussed the respective advantages and disadvantages of the three proposed plans.

specter (n.) (SPEK-ter) (also spelled spec*tre*)

an apparition; phantom; ghost; vision

Gliding down the staircase was the specter of a beautiful young woman.

specious (adj.) (SPEE-shus)

apparently right or good, but not really so; false; deceptive; insincere

Your argument is specious because it is based on false information.

Exercise 14.1

From both groups, choose **adjectives** that could replace the italicized words in the phrases below. Write the adjectives in the blank spaces on the right.

1. *noticeable* in that ridiculous hat _____

2. a *contemptible* liar _____

3. *possible future* customers _____

4. the *particular* benefits of the three methods _____

5. *favorable* moment for launching the ship _____

6. *distrustful* of the man claiming to be a police-
   man _____

7. a *showy* display of Christmas decorations _____

8. *deceptive* advertising claims _____

9. *cautious* when driving _____

10. *astute* reasoning _____

Exercise 14.2

Choose **nouns** from both groups to complete the sentences below. Watch for clues to guide your choices.

1. In the haunted house, I saw a _____.

2. Most fans watched the game on television. There weren't many _____ in the stadium.

3. He made an embarrassing _____ of himself at the party. Everyone was talking about him.

4. I have my _____s about him. I don't trust smooth-talking salesmen.

5. In _____, I would have done it differently, but it's useless to dwell on past mistakes.

6. This small statue is a _____ of ancient Greek sculpture.

7. The detective demonstrated his _____ by quickly exposing the crooks' clever scheme.

8. The peace talks were conducted under the _____ of the United Nations.

9. This book gives a Native American _____ of United States history.

10. Rather than focus on one _____ of the problem, we should look at it from all sides.

15

Beginnings and Endings

BEGINNINGS

Genesis means "the creation, origin, or beginning of anything." The name Eugene means "of good birth." Both words come from the Greek *genea*, meaning kind, class, race or birth. The root **gen**, or **genit**, has produced hundreds of words, including *gentry*, a land-owning, highborn class (which produced *gentleman*); *general*, relating to all kinds; and *genitals*, the reproductive organs. Attached to the ends of a root or base word, **gen** acts as a suffix meaning "produce," as in *allergen*, a substance that produces allergies, or *hallucinogen*, a drug that produces hallucinations.

The Word Building Chart
for *gen, genit*

Word	Beginning block	Middle block	End block	Quick definition
genealogy	none	**gene** (stem of *gen*, race)	**-alogy**	the study of racial, tribal, or family origins
gene(s)	none	**gene** (origin)	none	hereditary factor that determines physical characteristics
genetics	none	**gene** (origin)	**-tics** (study of)	the scientific study of heredity
generate	none	**gener** (from *generare*, originate)	**-ate** (cause)	cause to be; originate
genius	none	**geni** (stem of *gen*, birth)	**-us** (that which, Latin suffix)	extraordinary intelligence that is inborn
genial	none	**geni** (birth)	**-al** (having the quality of)	having an inborn quality of kindness
genuine	none	**genu** (stem of *gen*, origin, birth)	**-ine** (having the quality of)	having the original quality claimed; natural
generic	none	**gene** (kind, race)	**-ric** (relating to)	relating to a genus or class
genocide	none	**geno** (from *genos*, race)	**-cide** (kill)	the killing of a race

congenital	con- (with)	genit (birth)	-al (relating to)	relating to a condition occurring with birth

---

Group One

genealogy (n.) (jeen-ee-OLL-a-jee)

The study of ancestral origins or family trees is called **genealogy**. Notice that its spelling varies from the usual "-ology" spelling.

> My cousin is interested in genealogy and has traced our ancestral line back to the early 1800s.

genes (n.) (JEENS)

Genes are particles in chromosomes of reproductive cells that transmit hereditary characteristics from parents to their offspring.

> Genes inherited from the parents determine a child's physical characteristics.

genetics (n.) (ja-NET-iks)

The scientific study of inheritance in living things is called **genetics**.

> Genetics has provided important knowledge about inherited diseases.

generate (v.) (JEN-a-rate)

To **generate** is to originate; produce; or bring into being.

> Electricity generated by water power is called hydroelectricity.

genius (n.) (JEEN-yuss)

The ancient Romans believed that every person's birth was accompanied by a guardian spirit who was appointed to give guidance throughout life. The individual traits that comprised each person's nature were thought to result from the influence of this guiding spirit, or **genius**. The modern definition of **genius** is "an extraordinary inborn talent or intelligence," but in some cases, **genius** refers to the inborn nature or spirit of a person.

> Mozart, a musical genius, began writing symphonies at the age of eight.

genial (adj.) (JEEN-ee-ul)

A derivative of *genius*, the adjective **genial** means "having an inborn spirit of social enjoyment." Persons who are **genial** are friendly, kind, sympathetic, and cheerful by nature. "Comforting" and "warm" are other definitions.

> His genial personality attracts many friends.

genuine (adj.) (JEN-yoo-in)

The adjective **genuine** comes from Latin *genuinus*, meaning "inborn, natural." Other definitions are "real; authentic; true, sincere."

> This is a genuine pearl.

generic (adj.) (ja-NAIR-ik)

A *genus* is a class of animals or plants that have similar characteristics. The adjective **generic,** a derivative of *genus*, means "characteristic of a class."

> Wolves and domestic dogs belong to the same generic category.

genocide (n.) (JEN-a-side)

This word comes from the roots **gen**, race, and **cide**, kill. **Genocide** is the killing of a race.

> Raphael Lemkin introduced the word *genocide* into English in 1944, following the Nazis' attempt to annihilate the Jews in Europe.

congenital (adj.) (kun-JEN-i-tul)

Formed from *con-*, with, and **gen**, birth, **congenital** means "with birth; existing or occurring during the gestation period or birth, but not inherited."

The bone deformity was congenital.

Congenital is also used figuratively.

He is a congenital coward.

Group Two

congenial (adj.) (kun-JEEN-yul)

(1) having similar tastes; kindred; (2) suited to one's nature; agreeable; pleasant

She enjoyed congenial company in the group of young artists.

Gregarious by nature, he finds sales work more congenial than a desk job.

degenerate (v. & n.) (de-JEN-er-ate [-it])

(1) to become worse, inferior; to revert to a lower type; (2) a deteriorated, morally degraded person

The discussion degenerated into a brawl.

After losing his fortune, he became a degenerate.

heterogeneous (adj.) (het-er-a-JEEN-ee-us)

composed of dissimilar elements; mixed (from Greek *hetero*, other, and **genos**, kind)

The population is heterogeneous, consisting of many different ethnic groups.

homogeneous (adj.) (hō-ma-JEEN-ee-us)

similar throughout; uniform; consisting of the same kind (from *homo*, same, and **genos**, kind)

A homogeneous society is one without cultural diversity.

ingenious (adj.) (in-JEEN-yus)
clever; inventive, imaginative; resourceful

Her solution to the problem was ingenious.

ingenuity (n.) (in-ja-NOO-a-tee)
cleverness, inventiveness; resourcefulness

Planning the escape required great ingenuity.

ingenuous (adj.) (in-JEN-yoo-us)
(1) natural; unsophisticated; simple; (2) direct; frank; artless

Her ingenuous outlook on life contrasted with the cynical attitudes of his more sophisticated companions.
She had a childlike quality of ingenuous honesty.

indigenous (adj.) (in-DIJ-a-nus)
native; originating in a place or country

The prototype of the "teddy bear" is the koala, which is indigenous to Australia.

progenitor (n.) (prō-JEN-a-ter)
an ancestor; forefather

Abraham was the progenitor of the Hebrews.

progeny (n.) (PRAH-ja-nee)
offspring; descendants

The Hebrews were Abraham's progeny.

genre (n.) (ZHAN-ra)
(1) kind, sort; category, especially of literature and art having certain style or subject matter; (2) a style of art that depicts scenes of common life

Steinbeck's *Grapes of Wrath* is an example of social-protest literature, a genre that became popular in the 1930s.

eugenics (n.) (yoo-JEN-iks)

from *eu-*, good, and *gen*, birth, the science of improving humans by controlling hereditary factors, through controlled selection of parents

> Hitler was interested in eugenics as a means of producing a race of mentally and physically superior humans.

Exercise 15.1

From Groups One and Two, select **antonyms** for the adjectives below.

1. _____ cold, unfriendly
2. _____ foreign
3. _____ fake
4. _____ sophisticated
5. _____ homogeneous
6. _____ unimaginative
7. _____ disagreeable

Exercise 15.2

Complete the sentences below by substituting words from both groups for the words in parentheses.

1. Improvements in food production have been brought about by (science dealing with heredity) _____.

2. My sister, whose hobby is (the study of family trees) _____, has traced our family line back to an eighteenth-century Irish ancestor.

3. Stealing the closely guarded painting required great (cleverness) _____.

4. According to the Book of Genesis, Adam was the (forefather) _____ of the human race.

5. Those who interpret the Bible literally believe that all humans are the (descendants) _____ of Adam and Eve.

6. Begin organizing the collection by placing these items in (of the same kind) _____ groups.

7. Although they resemble small bears, koalas are not (pertaining to a genus) _____ ally related to bears.

8. He is such a (morally degraded person) _____ that he will do anything for money, no matter how dishonest.

9. She has always thought she was better than anyone else. She's a (from birth) _____ snob.

10. The principal's ideas for improving the school didn't (produce) _____ much enthusiasm.

A second set of words dealing with beginnings or origins is based on the root **nat**, meaning "to be born." A number of familiar words come from this root, including *nation*, which is defined as "a body of persons having the same origin and language," and *nature*, meaning (among other definitions) "the basic character of a thing." Included in Group Two are some less common words, three of which are based on **nasc**, an alternative form of **nat**.

The Word Building Chart
for *nat*

Word	Beginning block	Middle block	End block	Quick definition
natal	none	**nat** (birth)	**-al** (relating to)	relating to birth
native	none	**nat** (origin, birth)	**-ive** (pertaining to)	pertaining to the place of origin, birth
nativity	none	**nativ** (relating to birth)	**-ity** (process)	the process of birth; the circumstances relating to a birth
natural	none	**natur** (birth)	**-al** (relating)	relating to that which is created or born; pertaining to the nature of a thing
naturalize	none	**natural** (pertaining to birth)	**-ize** (make)	to make a native of
naive	none	from French *naif* (natural)	none	having natural innocence
naiveté	none	**naive** (natural)	**-té** (French suffix, quality of)	the quality of natural innocence
prenatal	**pre-** (before)	**nat** (birth)	**-al** (relating to)	relating to the time before birth
postnatal	**post-** (after)	**nat** (birth)	**-al** (relating to)	relating to the time after birth

neonatal	neo- (new)	nat (birth)	-al (pertaining to)	pertaining to the newly born

---

Group One

natal (adj.) (NATE-ul)

Natal means "relating to birth."

The word *marsupial* refers to the natal characteristics of such animals as the kangaroo, whose young are born undeveloped and carried in a pouch.

native (n. & adj.) (NATE-iv)

A **native** is a person born in a particular place.

He is a native of Kansas.

As an adjective, **native** means "born or originating in a particular place; indigenous."

He is a native Kansan.

nativity (n.) (na-TIV-a-tee)

Nativity means "birth" and also "the time, place, and circumstances surrounding a birth." Christ's birth is referred to as *the Nativity*.

The Nativity story is told each year at Christmas.

natural (adj.) (NACH-ur-ul)

Nature means "the created world" or "the essential qualities of a thing." Its adjective form, **natural**, means (1) produced by nature, not artificial; (2) belonging to one's nature; inborn

Cotton is a natural fiber.
She is a natural athlete.

naturalize (v.) (NACH-er-a-lize)

Naturalize means "give citizenship to persons from other countries," or, literally, "make natives of."

When the government naturalizes aliens, it gives them all the rights accorded to native-born citizens.

naive (adj.) (nah-EEV), naiveté (n.) (nah-eev-TAY)

A French derivative of **nat**, the adjective **naive** means "lacking worldly experience; ingenuous; having childlike innocence."

The young candidate was naive about politics.

The noun form of *naive* is **naiveté**.

His naiveté in politics was a disadvantage.

prenatal (adj.) (pree-NATE-ul)

Prenatal means "prior to birth."

Lack of good prenatal care can cause health problems for babies.

postnatal (adj.) (post-NATE-ul)

Postnatal means "after birth."

According to the postnatal checkup, both the mother and her child are in good health.

neonatal (adj.) (nee-ō-NATE-ul)

The root **neo** means "new." **Neonatal** means "newly born."

The new babies are kept in the neonatal ward.

Group Two

nascent (adj.) (NAY-sent)

beginning to exist or grow

He sensed a nascent spirit of rebellion among the people, which could eventually grow into a full-scale revolution.

renascent (adj.) (ri-NAS-ent)
reborn; revived

The team's victory gave the students a renascent sense of pride in their school.

renaissance (n.) (REN-a-sahns)
rebirth; revival; (with capital R) a revival of classical learning in Europe, lasting from the fourteenth through the sixteenth centuries.

The Renaissance was inspired by the classical writings of the early Greeks and Romans.

agnate (adj.) (AG-nate)
related on the father's side

An example of an agnate relationship would be that of two cousins who are the respective children of a father and his brother.

enate (adj.) (EE-nate)
related on the mother's side

Enate relatives are those who were born on the mother's side of the family.

cognate (adj. & n.) (KOG-nate)
originating from the same source; belonging to the same family or kind; *cog-*, together, and **nate**, birth, literally, "born together"

The term *cognate* often refers to words of different languages that have a common root and meaning, such as the English *mercy* and Spanish *merced*.

innate (adj.) (in-ATE)
inborn; natural; not acquired

He had innate musical talent.

Exercise 15.3

The phrases below are associated with words from both groups. Write the word that comes to mind as you read each phrase.

1. a hair color that is not artificial   adj. _____

2. as innocent and unknowing as a child   adj. _____

3. born in New York   n. _____

4. Christmas   n. _____

5. how immigrants become citizens   v. _____

6. a natural ability   adj. _____

7. before the baby is born   adj. _____

8. after the baby's birth   adj. _____

9. the new baby   adj. _____

10. just beginning   adj. _____

ENDINGS

Finis, a Latin word that has come into English unchanged, means "the end." Its root, **fin**, meaning "end, limit, or last," has produced some very common words such as *finish* and *final*. Most derivatives of **fin** have meanings that are plainly related to those of the root. In some, however, the relationship is not as clear. The word *fine* is one such derivative, but the connection becomes more clear with the knowledge that in earlier times *fine* meant "completed, finished, or perfected." To make something "fine" was to make it complete. For example, grain was finished being ground into flour when its particles had become very small or "fine." Garments were made complete by adding embroidery, lace, and other "finery," which is what these finishing touches came to be called. Of course, sewing these required precision, or "fine" skill.

Before the Middle Ages, *fine* meant "end or settlement."

Thus, a sum of money required as a penalty in a court case came to be called a *fine* because paying it ended the matter. The words *finance* and *financial* also came from the root **fin**. They are based on the Latin verb *finer*, which means both "to end" and "pay." A money matter could be ended by paying one's bill. To *finance* something was (and is) to pay for it.

One derivative of **fin** that seems to have lost connection is the noun *affinity*, which appears in Group Two. This is one of the few Latin-based words whose link to its root cannot be readily explained. The other words that follow are more closely associated in meaning to **fin** or "end."

The Word Building Chart
for *fin*

Word	Beginning block	Middle block	End block	Quick definition
final	none	**fin** (end)	**-al** (relating to)	relating to the end of something; last
finality	none	**final** (relating to an end)	**-ity** (state)	an ending state; conclusion
confine	**con-** (thoroughly)	**fine** (stem of *fin*, limit)	none	to thoroughly limit
define	**de-** (down)	**fine** (limit)	none	to set down or determine limits; show clearly
definite	**de-** (down)	**fin** (limit)	**-ite** (made)	defined; made clear; clearly defined
indefinite	**in-** (not)	**defin** (limit)	**-ite** (made)	not made clear; not well defined
refined	**re-** (again)	**fin** (finish)	**-ed** (made)	made finished, complete

Group One

final (adj.) (FY-nul), **finality** (n.) (fa-NAL-a-tee)
Final means "pertaining to the end; last." The state of being final is **finality**.

> She has written the final chapter.
> Some people do not believe in the finality of death.

finalize (v.) (FY-na-lize)

To **finalize** something is to put it into a complete or final form.

> We hope to finalize the wedding plans soon.

confine (v.) (kun-FINE)

Confine means "limit; restrict; keep within a boundary; shut away."

> Please confine your discussion to the matter at hand.

define (v.) (di-FINE)

To **define** is to (1) state the exact meaning of a word; (2) determine a boundary; (3) explain, interpret; (4) show clear outlines

> How does the dictionary define *apotheosis*?
> The treaty has defined the tribal territory as extending from the great river to the mountains.
> Religious leaders defined the doctrine differently, causing the church to divide.
> Certain exercises help to strengthen and define the muscles.

definite (adj.) (DEF-a-nit), indefinite (adj.) (in-DEF-a-nit)

The adjective form of *define* is **definite**, which means (1) fixed, certain; (2) exact; (3) precise; clear.

> They are making definite plans for the wedding.
> He did not give a definite reason for his action.
> Her health shows definite improvement.

Indefinite means "not limited or fixed; unknown; unexplained, not clearly stated."

> She will be gone an indefinite length of time.

refine (v.) (ri-FINE), refined (adj.) (ri-FIND)

The literal meaning of **refine** is "bring to a finished stage." Broader definitions are (1) to reduce to a fine and pure state;

remove impurities; (2) become polished, cultivated; (3) improve.

> A conversion process refines crude oil into gasoline.
> Finishing schools were established for girls in order to refine their manners and tastes.
> It will take much practice to refine your skill.

As an adjective, **refined** means (1) purified as a product; (2) polished; well bred; free of coarseness in taste and manners.

> Refined products include oil, metals, sugar, and grains.
> His refined young wife did not adjust easily to frontier life.

Group Two

finite (adj.) (FY-nite)
having an end or limit; limited

> Our knowledge of the universe is finite.

infinite (adj.) (IN-fa-nit)
endless, limitless

> Caring for children requires infinite patience.

infinity (n.) (in-FIN-a-tee)
boundlessness; eternity

> To look at the heavens is to gaze at infinity.

infinitesimal (adj.) (in-fi-na-TES-a-mul)
too small to be measured; too small to matter, insignificant

> Why complain about such infinitesimal matters?

finale (n.) (fi-NAHL-ee)
conclusion; the last part of a musical composition or production

All the performers assembled on stage for the grand finale.

finesse (n.) (fi-NESS)
delicate skill; cunning

He played the difficult composition with finesse.

definitive (di-FIN-a-tiv)
most accurate and complete; final; ending the matter; un-changeable

This book is considered the definitive work on the Civil War.

affinity (adj.) (a-FIN-a-tee)
attraction; kinship, kindred feeling

Having experienced poverty herself, she felt an affinity for the poor.

Exercise 15.4

Make derivative forms of the words from Group One by joining them to the suffixes below. The definitions on the right will indicate which words to choose. You will use some words more than once. In some cases, you will have to drop the final letter before adding the suffix. Use your dictionary if needed.

1. _____ment n.   restriction

2. _____ment n.   fineness; purification

3. _____ity n.   state of being ended, settled

4. _____ry n.   place where raw products are purified

5. _____ly adv.   lastly

6. _____ition n.   statement of a word's meaning

7. _____able adj.   can be explained

Exercise 15.5

Select the word from both groups that completes the phrase and is similar to the word in parentheses.

1. (limited) _____ understanding

2. (last) _____ warning

3. (very small) _____ objects

4. (fixed) _____ time

5. (unknown) _____ number

6. (improve) _____ his writing

7. (polished) _____ language

8. (shut) _____ him in his room

9. (kinship) _____ with the downtrodden

10. (most complete) _____ study

16
Words About Life

Viva! This lively salute, which is both Spanish and Italian, means Live! Long live! It comes from the Latin root **viv**, meaning "live." Several English words come from **viv** and a closely related root, **vit**, meaning "life." *Vitamin* is based on **vit**, along with other words in this section.

This lesson includes four groups of words whose definitions relate to "life," the first of which is based on **viv** and **vit**.

The Word Building Chart
for *viv, vit*

Word	Beginning block	Middle block	End block	Quick definition
vivid	none	**viv** (life)	**-id** (like)	lifelike, sharp, clear, as an image
revive	**re-** (back)	**vive** (life)	none	bring back to life
revival	**re-** (back)	**viv** (life)	**-al** (act of)	the act of bringing back to life
survive	**sur-** (from *super-*, beyond)	**vive** (live)	none	live beyond
survival	**sur-** (beyond)	**viv** (live)	**-al** (act, state of)	state of living beyond
vital	none	**vit** (life)	**-al** (relating to)	relating to life; necessary for life
vitality	none	**vital** (relating to life)	**-ity** (state)	a state of being alive; liveliness
vitalize	none	**vital** (life)	**-ize** (give)	give life to; enliven
revitalize	**re-** (again)	**vital** (life)	**-ize** (give)	give life to again; renew
devitalize	**de-** (away, down)	**vital** (life)	**-ize** (make)	make less vital; take away energy

Group One

vivid (adj.) (VIV-id)

Vivid means (1) realistic; lifelike; (2) lively; active; (3) clearly seen in the mind; (4) bright, intense, as a color; (5) graphic; very detailed; presenting an exact picture.

> I had a vivid dream last night.
> A writer of good fiction must have a vivid imagination.
> My most vivid childhood memories are of the summers I spent on my grandfather's farm.
> The sea and sky were painted in vivid shades of blue.
> She gave a vivid description of the accident.

revive (v.) (ri-VIVE), revival (n.) (ri-VIVE-ul)

To **revive** means "to bring back to life" or "to enliven again." **Revive** also means "to refresh; reawaken; renew."

> They are trying to revive the drowning victim.
> The trip to the museum revived my interest in history.

Revival is (1) the act of being brought back to life; (2) recovery, as from illness; (3) a renewal of interest after neglect.

> New life-saving methods have been successful in the revival of some patients.
> Exercise is necessary for the revival of her health.
> A revival of learning known as the Renaissance took place in Europe at the end of the Middle Ages.

survive (v.) (sur-VIVE), survival (n.) (sur-VIVE-ul)

The verb **survive** is formed from the prefix *sur-*, which is a form of the prefix *super-*, and the root **viv**. *Super-* means "above" or "beyond." **Survive** means "to live beyond" in the sense of remaining alive, particularly after a life-threatening experience. Another meaning of **survive** is "to live through whatever difficulties or obstacles are encountered." Other meanings of **survive** are "to outlast; outlive; live beyond another; remain in existence in spite of time and change."

Millions of Africans did not survive the famine.

He survived his wife by only a year.

The custom of parentally arranged marriages survives in some parts of the world.

Survival, the noun form of *survive*, means "the state of remaining alive or in existence."

The survival of our planet depends on how wisely we treat it.

vital (adj.) (VITE-ul), **vitality** (n.) (vy-TAL-a-tee)

Vital means (1) necessary for life; (2) necessary for existence; (3) of immediate importance; (4) pertaining to facts related to life.

The heart is a vital organ of the body.

It is vital to democracy that all citizens be well educated.

The growing illiteracy problem is one of the most vital issues this nation faces.

Each state has an office of vital records where birth and death certificates are kept.

Vitality, the noun form of *vital*, is most often used to mean "energy; health; vigor; liveliness."

Kittens are appealing because they have so much vitality.

vitalize (v.) (VITE-a-lize)

Vitalize means "to enliven; energize."

Exercise can vitalize both the body and mind.

devitalize (v.) (dee-VITE-a-lize)

The prefix *de-* in this verb means "away." **Devitalize** means "take away vitality; deprive of strength, energy."

Lack of recreation can devitalize a person.

revitalize (v.) (ree-VITE-a-lize)

Revitalize means "revive; put energy back into someone or something; to give new life to something."

I needed time away from my work to revitalize my health and spirits.

Group Two

vivacious (adj.) (va-VAY-shus)
lively, especially in temperament or personality; cheerful; animated; full of spirit

> She is well liked because of her friendly, vivacious personality.

vivacity (n.) (va-VAS-a-tee)
liveliness; vitality

> His humor and vivacity cheered us.

convivial (adj.) (kun-VIV-ee-ul)
sociable; gregarious; fond of feasting and good fellowship

> A convivial person loves being surrounded by good company.

vivisection (n.) (VIV-a-sek-shun)
from *viv*, life, and *sect*, cut, the practice of operating or experimenting on live animals

> Medical discoveries have been made through vivisection.

antivivisectionist (n.)
(an-ty [or -ee]-viv-a-SEK-shun-ist)
one who opposes experiments on live animals

> An antivivisectionist believes that the use of animals in medical research is unnecessary and inhumane.

viviparous (adj.) (vy-VIP-er-us)
from *viv*, live, and *par*, parent, bearing live young, not eggs

> Most mammals are viviparous.

The Greek word **bios** means "life." Numerous words related to natural science come from the root **bio**. Except for *biography* and *autobiography*, the words in the following two groups are scientific terms.

The Word Building Chart
for *bio*

Word	Beginning block	Middle block	End block	Quick definition
biography	**bio** (life)	**graph** (write)	**-y** (something done)	a writing about someone's life
autobiography	**auto-** (self)	**bio + graph** (life + write)	**-ive** (something made)	a self-written story of one's life
biology	none	**bio** (life)	**-logy** (study of)	the scientific study of living things
antibiotic	**anti-** (against)	**bio** (life)	**-tic** (that which)	a substance that works against harmful bacterial life

Group One

biography (n.) (by-OG-ra-fee)
The written story of someone's life is called a **biography**.

The Life of Samuel Johnson, by James Boswell, is a well-known biography about the writer and poet who compiled one of the first English dictionaries.

autobiography (n.) (aw-tō-by-OG-ra-fee)
A self-written story of one's own life is called an **autobiography**.

Benjamin Franklin's *Autobiography* was popular reading in Franklin's time and is still widely read.

biology (n.) (by-OL-a-jee)
The scientific study of living things is called **biology**.

Botany, the science of plant life, and zoology, the study of animal life, are branches of biology.

antibiotic (n.) (an-ta-by-OT-ik)
An **antibiotic** is a substance that destroys harmful bacteria in the body.

Penicillin is a powerful antibiotic prescribed in the treatment of many infectious diseases.

Group Two

biodegradable (adj.) (by-ō-di-GRADE-a-bul)
capable of being absorbed by the organic environment, when disposed of; naturally decaying, decomposing

According to environmentalists, the earth is being overfilled with trash because of so many disposable products that are not biodegradable.

biogenesis (n.) (by-ō-JEN-a-sis)
the doctrine that life originated from living organisms only; the generation and development of life from preexisting organisms

Those who interpret literally the Genesis story in the Bible disagree with the doctrine of biogenesis.

amphibious (adj.) (am-FIB-ee-us)
from *amphi-*, both, and *bio*, life, relating to *amphibians*, (1) life-forms that can live both on land and in water; (2) a craft that can operate on water and land

Frogs are classified as amphibious animals because they live under water as tadpoles during the developmental stage.
The fuselage of an amphibious aircraft, when in water, functions like a boat's hull by keeping the craft stable and afloat.

Exercise 16.1

This exercise involves all four word groups you have just studied. Complete the sentences below, using the **verbs** and **adjectives** from the groups. Study the sentences for clues to guide your choices.

1. The doctors worked quickly to _____ the patient after she stopped breathing.

2. An infant cannot _____ without good care.

3. Losing sleep will soon _____ you. To have energy you need more rest.

4. Great writers know how to give life to their characters. To learn how to _____ your stories' characters, you should study examples of good writing.

5. I have _____ memories of that house. In my mind, I can still see every detail.

6. Our _____ friend greatly enjoyed the dinner party.

7. The refugees desperately need food and medicine. It is _____ that we send these supplies immediately.

8. She's full of pep and good cheer. We enjoy her _____ personality.

9. The opposite of _____ is oviparous, which means producing eggs, rather than live young.

10. Disposable items made of plastic are not _____.

Exercise 16.2

Write a **noun** from the four groups you've just studied that can be associated with each phrase below.

1. amazing alertness and vigor for his age _____

2. Carl Sandburg's account of Lincoln's life _____.

3. regarded at first as miracle drugs for treating infections _____

4. her lively personality _____

5. theory that various life forms evolved from organisms that had formed in primeval waters and mud _____

6. operating on live animals _____

7. views the experiments as unnecessary cruelty to animals _____

8. a book she's writing about herself _____

9. includes the study of marine life _____

The root **anim** comes from the Latin word *anima*, which means "life; the life source; breath; mind; soul; spirit." The word *animal*, meaning "a living, moving organism," was derived from the root **anim**, as are the words in the following groups. Each word pertains in some way to life or spirit.

The Word Building Chart
for *anim*

Word	Beginning block	Middle block	End block	Quick definition
animate	none	anim (life)	-ate (give)	give life to
inanimate	in- (not)	anim (life)	-ate (give)	not given life; lifeless
animated	none	anim (spirit)	-ated (given)	given spirit; spirited
animation	none	anim (life)	-ation (the act of)	the act of giving lifelike qualities
unanimous	un- (from *uni-*, one)	anim (mind)	-ous (being)	being all of one mind; agreeing
unanimity	un- (one)	anim (mind)	-ity (state of)	state of agreement by all

Group One

animate (v. & adj.) (AN-a-mate [-mut]),
inanimate (adj.) (in-AN-a-mut)

As a verb, **animate** literally means "to breathe life into."
Other definitions of **animate** are (1) to put life into; make
alive; (2) to produce activity or motion in; (3) to energize;
enliven; inspire.

An actor must know how to animate a script's character.
Puppetry is the art of animating puppets and marionettes.
His energy and enthusiasm animated the audience.

As an adjective, **animate** means "having life; living."

Animals are animate beings.

Inanimate means "not having life; not possessing the essential qualities of living animals; lifeless."

A rock is an inanimate object.

animated (adj.) (AN-a-mate-ud)

Animated means (1) lively; (2) vivacious; spirited; (3) seeming to move as if alive.

They were having a very animated discussion about politics.

The speaker's animated style held his listeners' attention.

On Saturdays, the children watch animated cartoons on television.

animation (n.) (an-a-MAY-shun)

Animation means (1) liveliness; vivacity; (2) the art of making movie cartoons.

His speeches lack animation.

Walt Disney, the creator of Mickey Mouse and Donald Duck, made many technical advances in the art of animation.

unanimous (adj.) (yoo-NAN-a-mus),
unanimity (n.) (yoo-na-NIM-a-tee)

In the word **unanimous**, the prefix *un-* is a shortened spelling of *uni-*, which means "one." **Unanimous** means "of one mind; being in total agreement; without dissent; sharing the same opinion by all concerned."

The members were unanimous in their decision to ask for the treasurer's resignation.

Unanimity, the noun form of *unanimous*, means "complete agreement in opinion; harmony in sentiment."

A jury that has failed to reach unanimity in its verdict is called a hung jury.

Group Two

animosity (n.) (an-a-MAHS-a-tee)
a spirit of ill will; enmity; hostility; hatred

> Because of a misunderstanding, their friendship has been replaced by animosity.

magnanimous (adj.) (mag-NAN-a-mus)
from Latin *magnus*, great, and the root **anim**, spirit, "great in spirit; high-minded; generous, especially in forgiveness"

> To forgive is not only magnanimous but healthy for the mind.

magnanimity (n.) (mag-na-NIM-a-tee)
greatness of soul or heart

> In a gesture of magnanimity, he gave back the land to his former enemies.

pusillanimous (adj.) (pyoo-sa-LAN-a-mus)
from Latin *pusilla*, very little, and the root **anim**, spirit, literally "having very little spirit; lacking courage; cowardly"

> The newspaper columnist called the antiwar demonstrators "pusillanimous traitors."

equanimity (n.) (ee-kwa-NIM-a-tee)
from *equa*, equal or even, and the root **anim**, mind, evenness of temperament; calmness; composure

> She handled the troublesome situation with equanimity.

Ancient Romans believed that since humans must breathe in order to live, breath and spirit were the same life force. The root **spir**, meaning "breath," forms the base of the word *spirit* and several other words related to life, breath, or spirit. The ancient Greeks and Romans also related the entering of thoughts into the mind to the breathing of air into the body. In their view, the mind "breathed in" ideas just as the body breathed air, which accounts for such derivatives as *aspire*, *conspire*, and *inspire*.

The Word Building Chart
for *spir*

Word	Beginning block	Middle block	End block	Quick definition
spirited	none	**spir** (spirit)	**-ed** (having)	having spirit; lively
spiritual	none	**spirit** (soul)	**-ual** (pertaining)	pertaining to the soul, as opposed to the body
conspire	**con-** (together)	**spire** (stem of *spir*, breathe)	none	literally, breathe together; plan together in secret something unlawful
conspiracy	**con-** (together)	**spir** (breathe)	**-acy** (that which)	unlawful scheme; literally, that which is breathed together in secret
expire	**ex-** (out)	**(s)pire** (breathe)	none	breathe out; die
expiration	**ex-** (out)	**(s)pir** (breathe)	**-ation** (act of)	act of breathing out; coming to an end
inspire	**in-** (in)	**spire** (breathe)	none	breathe in; infuse with thought, feeling
inspiration	**in-** (in)	**spir** (breathe)	**-ation** (act of)	act of inspiring, influencing
perspire	**per-** (through)	**spire** (breathe)	none	literally, "breathe" through the pores; sweat
perspiration	**per-** (through)	**spir** (breathe)	**-ation** (result)	sweat; result of perspiring

| respire | re-
(again) | spire
(breathe) | none | to breathe (inhale and exhale again and again) |
| respiration | re-
(again) | spir
(breathe) | -ation
(action of) | the action of breathing |

Group One

spirited (adj.) (SPIR-a-ted)

Spirited means "animated; lively."

> They were having a spirited conversation.

spiritual (adj.) (SPIR-i-choo-ul)

Spiritual means pertaining to the soul or spirit; not material; pertaining to sacred things; relating to the mind's highest qualities.

> Most religions promote spiritual rather than material values.

conspire (v.) (kun-SPIRE),
conspiracy (n.) (kun-SPIR-a-see)

The literal meaning of this verb, "to breathe together," paints a picture of the action that it implies—two or more persons whispering together about something evil or unlawful that they plan to do, a plot that they must not mention to anyone else. To **conspire** is to plan together in secret to commit an unlawful act.

> A memorable scene is that in which Lady Macbeth conspires with her husband to murder the king.

A **conspiracy** is a plot or secret plan by two or more persons to commit a wrong.

> He was sentenced to prison for his part in the conspiracy to defraud investors of their money.

expire (v.) (eks-SPIRE),
expiration (n.) (eks-PER-ā-shun)

Expire means "breathe out" or "exhale," especially in the sense of breathing out one's last breath. In other words, **expire** means "die," but not always in the sense of physical death. Something that comes to an end, such as a contract, can be said to **expire**.

My magazine subscription is about to expire.

Expiration literally means "the exhalation of air from the lungs," but it frequently refers to the end of a period of time, a termination, or the close of something.

What is the date of expiration of your driver's license?

inspire (v.) (in-SPIRE),
inspiration (n.) (ins-per-Ā-shun)

Inspire means "to breathe into" in the sense of infusing with spirit or feeling. To **inspire** is "to put spirit into, influence; stir feelings; move a person to an idea or action."

The sight of so much misery inspired him to devote his life to relieving suffering.

Inspiration means (1) someone or something that acts as an inspiring influence; (2) someone or something that inspires creative action; (3) divine influence; (4) a bright or clever idea.

His courage was an inspiration to all of his classmates.
His experiences in India provided the inspiration for his book.
He drew inspiration from reading the Psalms.
He was trying to think of a way to raise funds when he had a sudden inspiration.

perspire (v.) (per-SPIRE),
perspiration (n.) (pers-per-Ā-shun)

Perspire comes from the Latin prefix *per-*, meaning "through," and the root **spir**, meaning "breathe." Literally,

perspire means "to breathe through the pores of the skin," but the actual meaning of **perspire** is "to give off fluid through the pores; to sweat."

The witness was very nervous and began to perspire.

Perspiration is the process of emitting through the pores the saline fluid secreted by the sweat glands.

The athletes were covered with perspiration.

respire (v.) (re-SPIRE),
respiration (n.) (res-per-A-shun)

Used more as a medical term, **respire** means "inhale and exhale," or, in other words, "breathe."

To inspire and expire repeatedly is to respire.

Respiration is the act of breathing.

His respiration has improved, and he is out of the oxygen tent.

Group Two

aspire (v.) (a-SPIRE),
aspiration (n.) (as-per-A-shun)

from the Latin *adspirare*, "to breathe upon, or attempt to reach, to have desire or ambition for something high and good; to reach or strive toward something higher"

She aspired to fame as an opera singer.

aspiration: an exalted desire, a high or noble ambition

His aspiration was to be an Olympic champion.

spirituality (n.) (spir-a-choo-AL-a-tee)

the quality of being spiritual; concern with matters of the soul or intellect, which are apart from material concerns

A society whose values lack spirituality is in the process of decay.

spiritualism (n.) (SPIR-a-choo-lizm)
belief that disembodied spirits can communicate with living persons

> Participants in the practice of spiritualism attempt to contact the spirits of dead relatives or acquaintances.

spiritous (adj.) (SPIR-a-tus)
containing intoxicating spirits, alcohol

> Some religions forbid the consumption of spirituous beverages.

Exercise 16.3

Write the **noun** forms of the verbs below in the space provided. Then, in the parentheses to the right of each space, write the letter of each noun's definition.

1. conspire   _____ (_____) a. termination

2. inspire   _____ (_____) b. sweat

3. unanimous   _____ (_____) c. the act of breathing

4. expire   _____ (_____) d. vivacity

5. perspire   _____ (_____) e. clever idea; divine influence

6. animate   _____ (_____) f. agreement by all

7. respire   _____ (_____) g. a plot

Exercise 16.4

Using Group Two of the **anim** and **spir** groups, supply the missing words in the sentences below.

1. She forgave all those who had mistreated her and offered them her help. I have never known a more _____ person.

2. To run away and leave your friends in danger was a _____ act. You should be ashamed of such cowardice.

3. I told my friend I didn't believe in (communication with the dead) _____, but she insisted that I go with her to the seance.

4. A disagreement shouldn't lead to (hostility) _____ between friends.

5. He had no ill will toward anyone. Always kind and caring, he was a friend to any person in need. We will always remember his (generosity) _____.

6. He preached that we should give less attention to acquiring material things and more to developing _____.

7. In their zeal to rid the town of evil, the pious ladies of the Temperance Society invaded the tavern and smashed several bottles of the Devil's _____ brew.

8. He _____d to a career in acting.

9. Her _____ was to render service to the needy.

10. His faith gave him peace of mind and enabled him to endure trouble and sorrow with _____.

...nsen. They naturally be interested by the ...and felt in
the heart. Only figures ...... been literal, male, but are
related to matters of the mind and heart. Matters the sight-
less senses ...personal be the such as love.... hate, fear,
and despair.

17
Words About Feelings

The words in ... section ... from the roots of..., which
means... belief, trust.

A devotee ...se of religious beliefs or other... but
a devotee simply ...ver...of belief...

In previous chapters you studied word-building charts, which
were provided primarily to accustom you to analyzing words.
Word analysis, an important step to full understanding of
words, is a habit you should acquire in vocabulary building
now that you know the meanings of so many word parts. As
you study this chapter, begin analyzing the words on your
own. As soon as you pronounce each word, try to break it
down into its parts so that you will have some idea of the
meaning even before you read its definition. This should be
part of your approach to learning any new word. Remember
that, with some exceptions, the key to a word's definition lies
within the word itself.

The work that you have just completed involved words
from roots that, for the most part, expressed physical action.
The material showed how words grew in number and com-
plexity from roots symbolizing concrete actions—that is,
those actions that could be observed by the physical senses.
You've seen how the simple concept of following something
or someone, as expressed by the root **sequ**, could eventuate
in various concepts of following, such as those expressed by
obsequious and *consequence*.

Far fewer roots express abstractions, things such as justice,
wisdom, peace, love, which cannot be perceived by the

senses. They can only be perceived by the mind and felt in the heart. This chapter examines some abstract roots that are related to matters of the mind and heart. Most of the derivatives pertain to emotional feelings such as love and hate, trust and distrust.

BELIEF AND TRUST

The words in this section are based on the root **cred**, which means "belief; trust."

creed (n.) (KREED), credo (n.) (KREE-do)

A **creed** is a set of religious beliefs or other principles that people believe and follow as a code of behavior. The Latin word *credo*, literally meaning "I believe," has the same definition as *creed*.

> The Apostles' Creed, a traditional confession of faith, is a summary of Christian beliefs.
> The Golden Rule was her simple credo.

credit (n. & v.) (KRED-it), creditor (n.) (KRED-a-ter)

Credit means "belief, trust; trustworthiness; honor, a source of honor; acknowledgment of something done." To buy on **credit** is to make purchases and pay for them at a later time. **Credit**, in this case, is the seller's trust that the buyer will pay the money owed. In commerce, **credit** is the reputation for being trustworthy in paying debts. To be a **credit** to something such as one's family or school is to bring it honor. To give **credit** is to acknowledge that someone has done something worthy.

> I give him credit for saving my life.
> The teacher gives us extra credit for book reports.

As a verb, **credit** means (1) to give credit for, (2) to accept as true; to believe.

> I credit him with savings my life.
> I don't credit anything she says.

A **creditor** is someone to whom money is owed.

His creditors are demanding full payment of his debts.

discredit (v.) (dis-KRED-it)
The prefix *dis-* means "not"; *credit* means "belief; honor." **Discredit** means (1) not to believe; (2) cause to doubt; (3) harm one's reputation or honor.

The police discredited the suspect's statements.
The witness's testimony discredited the suspect's story.
The senator's involvement in the illegal scheme discredited him.

credence (n.) (KREED-enss)
Like *credit*, **credence** means "belief," especially belief based on evidence.

These pictures give his story credence.

credential (n.) (kri-DEN-chul)
A **credential** is evidence that one is qualified to do something and therefore entitled to the confidence of others. **Credentials** are letters, certificates, or anything that gives evidence of someone's identity or qualifications for a profession.

Applicants for this position will be asked to show their credentials.

credible (adj.) (KRED-a-bul),
credibility (n.) (kred-a-BIL-a-tee)
The suffix *-ible* means "able to be." **Credible** means (1) able to be believed; (2) reliable; deserving confidence.

He told a credible story.
That gangster is not a credible witness.

Credibility is believability; the ability to be believed, credence.

False rumors spread by her opponents damaged the candidate's credibility.

incredible (adj.) (in-KRED-a-bul)

Incredible means (1) unbelievable; (2) hard to believe; amazing.

That story he told was incredible.
The Grand Canyon is an incredible sight.

credulous (adj.) (KRED-yoo-lus),
incredulous (adj.) (in-KRED-yoo-lus)

Credulous means "gullible; believing on slight evidence; easily fooled." **Incredulous** means "unbelieving; not inclined to believe; skeptical."

Unaware that they had been swindled, the credulous investors expected to make a fortune.
Before he could finish his campaign speech, the incredulous listeners began to jeer.

credenza (n.) (kri-DEN-za)

During the Renaissance in Italy, leaders feared being murdered by poison, and it became customary to test food from a special table, called a **credenza**, before it was served. Today, **credenza** means "a side table, a buffet."

The dinner guests served themselves from the credenza.

Exercise 17.1

Complete these sentences with words from the group you have just studied.

1. You're too _____. You shouldn't believe everything you read in those silly magazines.

2. On her office wall, the doctor displays a diploma from medical school and her license to practice medicine. These are her _____s.

3. I believe that happiness comes from helping others to be happy. This is my simple _____. (Two possible answers.)

4. There is no evidence to give her story any
   _____.

5. They are trying to _____ me by their lies.

6. Without a job, I don't know how I'll pay my
   _____s.

7. No one gives me any _____ for all the work I
   do around here.

8. That story is a wild exaggeration. How can you expect
   anyone to believe something so _____?

9. She has a grudge against him and would do anything
   to get even. I don't think her accusations against him
   are _____.

10. The farmer stood transfixed, staring _____ly at
    the strange, glowing object. He could not believe what
    his eyes told him—a saucer-shaped ship in his field!

FAITH AND TRUST

Semper fidelis, the motto of the United States Marine
Corps, means "always faithful." Another Latin phrase used
by Americans is *bona fide*, which implies that something is
genuine because it is presented "in good faith." The connection between these phrases and the words in the following
group is the root **fid**, which means "faith, trust."

fidelity (n.)
(fa-DEL-a-tee)

(1) faithfulness; unswerving loyalty; allegiance
(2) adherence to factual trust: the fidelity of the news report
(3) exactness of reproduction: a high-fidelity sound recording

infidelity (n.)
(in-fa-DEL-a-tee)

faithlessness; disloyalty

infidel (n.)
(IN-fa-del)

one who rejects religious belief; term used by some
Christians and Muslims to label one who is not of
their respective faiths

fiducial (adj.)
(fi-DOO-shul)

based on faith

confide (v.)
(kun-FIDE)

literally, "with trust," to entrust private information or secrets to someone

confidential (adj.)
(kon-fa-DEN-chul)

relating to information that is private or secret

confidant (n.)
(KON-fa-dahnt)

a person in whom one confides (note that the spelling is different from that of the adjective *confident*)

confidence (adj.)
(KON-fa-denss)

(1) faith, trust; (2) a secret; a piece of confidential information

confident (n.)
(KON-fa-dent)

having assurance, faith

diffident (adj.)
(DIF-a-dent)

from *dif-* (form of *dis-*), away, and *fid*, faith, literally away from faith, lacking faith, confidence in oneself; shy, timid

perfidious (adj.)
(per-FID-ee-us)

from *per-*, through, and *fid*, faith, "through faith," operating under the pretext of being loyal while betraying someone; treacherous; basely false

perfidy (n.)
(PER-fa-dee)

treachery; the violation of a trust (Note that *perfidy* is a stronger term than *infidelity*. It implies a very base kind of disloyalty.)

Exercise 17.2

Write the appropriate words to complete the meanings of the sentences.

1. Even though both believe in God, a narrow-minded Christian and an intolerant Muslim might label each other an _____, because they each believe that the other does not possess the true faith.

2. She saw her husband at the restaurant with another woman and accused him of marital _____.

3. I have faith in your abilities, and I'm _____ that you can handle this job.

4. Lacking self-assurance, the _____ young man felt very uncomfortable in the presence of the party guests.

5. That is _____ information which I have sworn never to reveal.

6. The movie is remarkable for its _____ to the actual facts of the historical event it portrays. The representation is accurate in every detail.

7. I know that she would never reveal any secret I shared with her. She's my best friend and _____.

8. She is the one who has spread these _____ rumors about me, while pretending to be my friend.

9. I am outraged that he has betrayed me in this vicious manner, and I will never forgive his _____.

10. No one has proved the existence of a Supreme Being, but, although belief in such a being is purely _____, many find strength in their faith that a loving God truly exists.

LOVE

Some words require two roots to give them full meaning. Among them are Greek words that have to do with love and hate. Their common roots are **miso-** or **mis-**, meaning "hatred," and **philo-** or **phil-**, which means "love." Philadelphia, the largest city in Pennsylvania and birthplace of the United States, took its name from a Greek word meaning "brotherly love." Following are words that combine the root **phil-** with other roots. Practice pronouncing each word.

philander (v.) (fil-AN-der),
philanderer (n.) (fil-AN-der-er)
The verb **philander** comes from *phil-*, meaning "love," and *andros*, meaning "man." Originally, **philander** meant

"a loving man." Today, **philander** means "to flirt with or pursue women without having serious intentions."

A **philanderer** is a man who doesn't stay faithful to one woman for any length of time.

> She could not change his wanton ways, and he continued to philander.
> His wife was apparently unaware of his reputation as a philanderer.

philanthropy (n.) (fil-ANTH-rup-ee), philanthropist (n.) (fil-ANTH-ra-pist), philanthropic (adj.) (fil-an-THROP-ik)

Both **philanthropy** and *anthropology*, meaning "the study of people and their various cultures," come from the root **anthropo**, which means "people." **Philanthropy** means "love of people in general; the practice of promoting the happiness and well-being of people through charitable works or large donations to charitable organizations."

A **philanthropist** is one who actively promotes people's welfare, but today the term more often refers to a wealthy person who donates large sums of money to charitable causes.

Philanthropic means "pertaining to charitable works."

> Feeling a great sympathy for the needy, he devoted himself entirely to philanthropy.
> The philanthropist Andrew Carnegie donated money to build libraries all across America.
> The Red Cross is a well known philanthropic organization, serving disaster victims throughout the world.

philatelist (n.) (fi-LAT-a-list)

The Greek word *ateles* meant "prepaid postage as indicated by a stamp." A **philatelist**, literally "a lover of stamps," is a stamp collector.

> General Rommel, the brilliant military strategist, was also a noted philatelist and considered a leading expert on rare stamps.

philology (n.) (fil-OL-a-jee)

The root word **logos** means both "knowledge" and "word." Literally, **philology** means "love of words," but in actual usage means "linguistics; the scientific study of the origin and development of languages."

> Through comparative philology, scholars have found that most European and many Asian languages are related.

philosophy (n.) (fil-OSS-a-fee)

The literal meaning of **philosophy** is "love of wisdom." Dictionaries define **philosophy** as (1) the search for wisdom; (2) practical wisdom that helps one endure suffering or live more happily; (3) the underlying principles that explain how something works: the *philosophy* of economics; the *philosophy* of education, etc.

> The philosophy of a culture is expressed through its arts and customs.

bibliophile (n.) (bib-lee-O-file)

The root **biblio** means "book"; a **bibliophile** is a book lover.

> My friend has read countless books. She's a true bibliophile.

HATE

misanthrope (n.) (MIS-an-thrope)

The root **mis** means "hatred"; *anthropos* means "people." A **misanthrope** is a person who distrusts and hates people.

> The title character of Molière's play *The Misanthrope* views the entire human race as a corrupt, detestable lot.

misogamy (n.) (mis-OG-a-mee),
misogamist (n.) (mis-OG-a-must)

The root **gam**, from the Greek word *gamos*, means "marriage"; *miso*- means "hatred." **Misogamy** is hatred of marriage. A **misogamist** is a person who hates marriage.

Misogamy was not an uncommon attitude among intellectuals of that time, who believed that marriage enslaved women.

misogyny (n.) (mis-OJ-a-nee),
misogynist (n.) (mis-OJ-a-nust)

The Greek word *gyne* means "woman." **Misogyny** is hatred of women. A **misogynist** is one who hates or distrusts women.

Feminists claimed that women, having been denied equal rights, were victims of misogyny.

His arrogant manner toward women marked him as a misogynist.

Latin roots that mean "hate" have produced a few words but not enough to comprise groups. The small group below comes from the Latin root **am**, which means "love," including love of the romantic kind.

amorous (adj.)   relating to romantic love, sexual desire
(AM-a-rus)

enamor (v.)   to inflame with love; to charm, fascinate, captivate
(en-AM-er)

enamored   infatuated; in love
(adj.)
(en-AM-erd)

amiable (adj.)   friendly, kind, warmhearted, lovable
(AIM-ee-a-bul)

amicable (adj.)   friendly, peaceable (used often in relation to situations in
(AM-ik-a-bul)   which hostility might be expected: *an amicable divorce*)

inimical (adj.)   from *inamicus*, "not a friend," hostile, antagonistic; op-
(in-IM-a-kul)   posed in a harmful way; behaving as an enemy

amateur (n.)   someone who engages in an occupation such as art or
(AM-a-chur)   science purely for the love of it; one who enjoys an occu-
    pation as a hobby rather than a profession

paramour (n.)   from French *amour*, love affair, a lover of a married person;
(PAR-a-moor)   a partner in an illicit love affair

Exercise 17.3

Complete the following sentences.

1. *Lingua* is the Latin word for *tongue*, or *language*. *Linguistics*, the science of language, is a synonym of _____.

2. My friend, who loves reading, has a large collection of books. He is a _____.

3. Stamp collecting is the hobby of a _____.

4. A charitable organization such as the Salvation Army might also be described as a _____ organization.

5. Ebenezer Scrooge had no use for people, except to work them long hours for little pay. Scrooge was a _____.

6. Hoping he would fall madly in love with her, she tried to _____ him with her seductive wiles.

7. He was not _____ed by her charms. His heart belonged to another.

8. His _____ advances were not in vain. She finally agreed to marry him.

9. Although they strongly disagreed on policy, the meeting between the two leaders was _____.

10. He denied ever having an extramarital affair and said that he never even knew the woman who claimed to be his _____.

OTHER FEELINGS

Some roots have more than one meaning. The Greek root **path** means "feeling," "suffering," and "disease." The following words are based on **path**.

pathos (n.) (PAY-thahs),
pathetic (adj.) (pa-THET-ik)

Pathos is a quality that arouses pity, sorrow, or sympathy, especially in stories or drama. **Pathetic**, the adjective form of *pathos*, means "arousing sadness, tenderness; pitiful."

The story of the mother's search for her child is filled with pathos.
The pathetic little boy was shivering from the cold.

sympathy (n.) (SIMP-a-thee)

The prefix *sym-* means "with" or "same." **Sympathy** means "feeling with another person in the sense of sharing sorrow, pain, disappointment, etc." **Sympathy** is pity, or a sharing of emotion.

I feel sympathy for anyone in pain.

empathy (n.) (EMP-a-thee)

Empathy is the ability to put oneself in the place of another and imagine how that person feels.

A teacher should have empathy for students.

antipathy (n.) (an-TIP-a-thee)

Antipathy is the antonym of *sympathy*. The prefix *anti-* means "against." **Antipathy** is a feeling against someone—that is, a feeling of dislike, hostility, or hatred toward another.

Antipathy between the two men led to a duel.

apathy (n.) (AP-a-thee)

The prefix *a-* means "without"; **apathy** means "without feeling; unconcerned, indifferent."

Democracy declined because the citizens felt apathy toward their government.

telepathy (n.) (ta-LEP-a-thee)

Tele- means "from a distance"; **telepathy** means "the communication of feelings or impressions from one mind to another at a distance without the use of the senses; extrasensory perception."

Many do not believe that thoughts can be transmitted through mental telepathy.

pathology (n.) (path-OL-a-jee)
Pathology is the scientific study of the cause, nature, development, and effects of disease.

The medical students decided to specialize in pathology.

psychopath (n.) (SY-ka-path)
A **psychopath** is one who has mental illness that shows itself in a criminal or antisocial way.

Jack the Ripper must have been a psychopath.

Another spelling of **path** is **pass**, which forms the base of **passion, compassion**, and **dispassionate. Passion** is intense emotion, as of love, anger, grief, or desire. **Compassion** is formed from the prefix *com-*, meaning "with," and the root **pass**, meaning "suffering." Like *sympathy*, **compassion** means "feeling with another," especially in the sense of sharing suffering. In usage, however, the word *compassion* also implies mercy, or a strong desire to relieve another's suffering. **Dispassionate**, literally meaning "apart from emotion," is used to mean "unemotional; impartial; calmly objective in thinking."

He had a passion for flying.
St. Francis had great compassion for animals.
In considering court cases, juries must remain dispassionate.

A second set of words relating to feeling is based on the root **sens** or **sent**. Pronounce each word before studying its definition.

sensation (n.) (sen-SAY-shun)	(1) what is felt or learned through the bodily senses of hearing, touch, taste, smell, or sight; (2) that which causes great interest and excitement

sensible (adj.) (SEN-sa-bul)	(1) showing good understanding and judgment; reasonable; (2) able to perceive with the senses; conscious; aware
insensible (adj.) (in-SEN-sa-bul)	unconscious; unaware; indifferent to
sensitive (adj.) (SEN-sa-tiv)	(1) readily reacting to external forces, such as light, touch, etc.; (2) easily hurt emotionally; (3) keenly aware of others' feelings
sensory (adj.) (SEN-sa-ree)	relating to the senses; pertaining to sensation
sensual (adj.) (SEN-shoo-ul)	lewd; relating to overindulgence of the physical appetites
sensuous (adj.) (SEN-shoo-us)	appealing to the senses; keenly enjoying luxury and beauty (Note: *sensuous* describes an appreciation of pleasure beyond the satisfaction of bodily appetites; *sensual* refers only to indulgence of physical desires.)
sentient (adj.) (SEN-chent)	having the power of sense perception; having feeling, as opposed to lifeless objects
sentimental (adj.) (sent-a-MENT-ul)	(1) having tender emotions; romantic; foolishly tender
dissent (v.) (dis-SENT)	the prefix *dis-* means "apart"; *sent* means "feel" in the sense of holding an opinion. *Dissent* means "feel apart," or in other words "disagree; differ in opinion"
dissension (n.) (di-SEN-shun)	quarreling; strife; discord; angry disagreement

Exercise 17.4

True or false:

_____ 1. *Apathetic* means "indifferent; uncaring."

_____ 2. *Antipathy* is the opposite of apathy.

_____ 3. *Antipathy* means "a feeling of friendship and sympathy."

_____ 4. *Pathetic* means "arousing pity."

_____ 5. In drama, *pathos* is an element of comedy.

_____ 6. To be in *sympathy* with an idea is to feel the same.

_____ 7. *Pathologists* are skilled in tracing the causes of diseases.

_____ 8. A telephone message is a form of *telepathic* communication.

_____ 9. A rock is a *sentient* being.

_____ 10. *Dissent* means "agree."

18

Words About Words

Ventriloquism is the act of speaking so that the voice seems to come from another person or source. This word, from *venter*, "abdomen," and *loquor*, "to speak," belongs to a word group based on **loqu** or **locut**, which means "speak." Some of the words from this group are included in this section.

circumlocution (n.) (sir-kum-low-KUE-shun)
Circum- means "around." **Circumlocution** means (1) indirect, roundabout expression, such as "passed away" or "departed this life," in place of "died"; (2) the use of excessive words to communicate a thought—that is, talking in circles rather than coming directly to the point.

> Please stop your tiresome circumlocution, and get to the point.

colloquial (adj.) (ka-LOW-kwee-ul),
colloquialism (n.) (ka-LOW-kwee-ul-iz-um)
The prefix *col-* is a changed spelling of *com-*, meaning "together." **Colloquial** describes informal, conversational speech used when people speak together. A **colloquialism** is a word or phrase that is acceptable for conversation but would not be used in formal speech.

The popular speaker preferred to address his audiences in a relaxed, colloquial style.

"What's up?" is a colloquialism that means "What is happening?"

elocution (n.) (el-ō-KUE-shun)

The prefix *e-*, as you know, means "out." **Elocution** is the art of public speaking. One trained in **elocution** knows how to speak outward to an audience by effective use of language, voice, and gestures.

The Greek orator Demosthenes trained himself in elocution by placing pebbles in his mouth and speaking to the roaring sea.

eloquence (n.) (EL-a-kwenss),
eloquent (adj.) (EL-a-kwent)

Eloquence is effective, persuasive use of language, especially in public speaking. **Eloquent** speech is fluent, polished, and persuasive.

The missionary spoke with eloquence about the harsh conditions suffered by the native inhabitants.

Thousands gathered to hear Dr. King's eloquent plea for just treatment of all citizens.

grandiloquent (adj.) (gran-DIL-a-kwent)

Grand, of course, means "big"; **grandiloquent** means "talking big," using pompous, bombastic, flowing speech.

In those days, politicians customarily spoke in grandiloquent tones.

loquacious (adj.) (low-KWAY-shus)

A very talkative person can be described as **loquacious**, which means "inclined to talk; talkative."

Even after the teacher's reprimand, the loquacious child continued to chatter.

soliloquy (n.) (sa-LIL-a-kwee)

The Latin word *solus* means "alone." **Soliloquy** means "talking to oneself" and refers especially to speech by an actor alone on stage.

The soliloquy was an important element of Shakespeare's plays.

somniloquy (n.) (som-NIL-a-kwee)

Somnus means sleep. **Somniloquy** is the act of talking while asleep.

Her nightly somniloquies revealed guilty secrets.

The Greek root **log** comes from *logos*, which means "science, knowledge" (as in the *-ology* suffix) and also "word." Below are words related to speech and writing that were derived from **log**.

eulogy (n.) (YOO-la-jee)

From the prefix *eu-*, "good," and the root **log**, "word," **eulogy** literally means "good words." In common usage, a **eulogy** is "a speech praising someone, especially after death; a speech given at a funeral or memorial service."

In the eulogy he recalled his friend's selfless courage.

dialogue (n.) (DIE-a-log)

From *dia-*, "between," and **log**, "word," **dialogue** means "words exchanged between speakers, in a discussion; conversation in a play or novel" (also spelled *dialog*).

The film had too much dialogue and not enough action.

monologue (n.) (MON-a-log)

From the prefix *mono-*, meaning "one," and **log**, meaning "word," a **monologue** is "a speech uttered by one person or a solo performer" (also spelled *monolog*).

The comedian's monologue lacked original humor.

prologue (n.) (PRŌ-log)

From the prefix *pro-*, "before," and the root **logue**, "word," a **prologue** is a foreword in a book, poem, or play.

Chaucer's introduction to *Canterbury Tales* is a famous prologue.

A **dictionary** is a book containing the words of a language. The root **dict** comes from the Latin verb *dicere*, meaning "to say." The words in this section are based on the root **dict**.

edict (n.) (EE-dikt)

An **edict** is a public decree or command, an order.

According to the edict, anyone found guilty of speaking against the emperor would be severely punished.

contradict (v.) (kon-tra-DIKT),
contradiction (n.) (kon-tra-DIK-shun)

The prefix *contra-*means "against; opposite; contrary." **Contradict** means "deny or say the opposite of what has been said." A **contradiction** is a statement that denies another statement.

dictate (v.) (DIK-tate)

Dictate means (1) to say aloud words for another to write down; (2) give orders; to tell others what to do.

She dictated a message over the telephone.

dictator (n.) (DIK-tate-er)

A **dictator** is one who, like an autocrat, has absolute power to govern. A **dictator** is usually considered a tyrant or an oppressor. What he says is law, and no one is allowed to challenge his authority.

The dictator was both feared and despised.

diction (n.) (DIK-shun)

Diction is (1) the choice of words used to communicate ideas; (2) enunciation; the manner of uttering speech sounds.

Her diction indicated that she was highly educated.

predict (v.) (pre-DIKT),
prediction (n.) (pre-DIK-shun)

Literally, **predict** means "to say before." To **predict** is to foretell, tell beforehand, prophesy. A **prediction** is a forecast or prophecy.

> The weather forecast predicted rain.
> None of the fortune-teller's predictions came true.

verdict (n.) (VER-dikt)

Verdict means "the finding or decision of a jury; a jury's expressed conclusion or judgment." The root **ver** means "true." Literally, **verdict** means "truly said."

> The case was dismissed when the jury failed to reach a verdict.

Exercise 18.1

Find the word from the preceding group that best fits each statement below, and write it in the blank space. Some words may be repeated. Watch for clues within the statements to guide your choices.

1. A euphemism (YOO-pha-miz-um) is an indirect, less blunt way of saying something. For example, an employer might tell an employee "I think it is best to let you go," rather than say, "You're fired." The phrase "let you go" is less direct or blunt than "fired" and is therefore a euphemism. A word from the preceding group that is close in meaning to *euphemism* is _____.

2. Shakespeare's play *Macbeth* is a story about the murder of a king. Macbeth, the murderer, feels so guilty that he becomes despondent and slowly goes mad. Reflecting on his life, he makes a speech to himself. This famous speech by Macbeth is a _____.

3. In *Macbeth*, it is Lady Macbeth who persuaded her husband to kill the king. Her conscience, too, troubles her,

and she becomes a somnambulist—that is, a sleep-walker. She also speaks during her sleepwalking. Speech given in sleep is called a _____.

4. "Good evening, ladies and gentlemen" is a formal greeting. "Hi, everybody" is a _____ style of greeting.

5. *Soliloquy* is close in meaning to _____. Both mean "a speech given by an actor alone on stage."

6. Our _____ guest talked so much at dinner that no one else had a chance to speak.

7. I have trouble taking notes from that professor. He talks around and around and never seems to get to the point. His _____ confuses me.

8. The two world leaders met to discuss the problems between their countries. Both realized that _____ was preferable to war.

9. The government has just issued an _____ saying that all persons must be off the streets by sunset.

10. My brother gave the _____ at our father's funeral.

We usually think of a **verb** as a part of speech that indicates the action part of a sentence. Actually, **verb** comes from the Latin word *verbum*, meaning "word." The words below are based on the root **verb**.

verbal (n.) (VUR-bul), **verbalize** (v.) (VUR-ba-lize)
Verbal means "expressed in words, especially spoken words; expressed orally, not written." To **verbalize** is to put thoughts and feelings into words, to express oneself verbally.

We made a verbal agreement to share the expenses equally.
She finds it difficult to verbalize her feelings.

verbatim (adj. & adv.) (vur-BATE-um)
Verbatim means "in the exact words; word for word."

I repeated the message verbatim.

verbiage (n.) (VUR-bee-ij), **verbose** (adj.) (vur-BOSE)
Verbiage means "an excess of words; wordiness." **Verbose** means "wordy; using an unnecessary number of words; repetitious in words."

Good writers avoid verbiage.
This article is too verbose to be interesting.

The words below come from the root **voc** or **vok**, which means "voice" or "call." Pronounce each before studying its meaning.

vocabulary (n.) (vō-KAB-yoo-lair-ee)	(1) an alphabetically arranged list of words and their definitions; (2) the sum of all the words known and used or recognized by a person
vocal (adj.) (VŌ-kul)	(1) pertaining to voice, speech; uttered by voice, oral; (2) freely and readily voicing one's opinions; (3) relating to use of the voice in music; singing
vociferous (adj.) (vō-SIF-er-us)	loud-voiced, noisy; clamorous; characterized by shouting, loud outcries
vocation (n.) (vō-KAY-shun)	(1) divine call to a religious career; (2) occupation; profession; a calling to one's life's work
avocation (n.) (AV-ō-kay-shun)	hobby; diversion; literally, away from one's vocation or main occupation. (The prefix *a-* is a shortened spelling of *abs-*, meaning "away.")
advocate (v.) (AD-vō-kate)	to speak in favor of something or someone; to speak in someone's behalf (originally, to call on someone for help). An **advocate** (n., AD-vō-kut) is a person who defends an idea, a cause, or another person.

equivocate
(v.) (e-KWIV-a-kate)

literally, to speak with equal voice; to deliberately mislead by making ambiguous statements—that is, statements that can have double meanings; to avoid giving direct answers by making vague, indefinite statements

evoke
(v.) (e-VOKE)

to call out, or draw out, a response, emotion, memory, etc.

invoke
(v.) (in-VOKE)

(1) to call upon someone, especially God or a divinity, for protection, assistance, or a blessing; (2) to quote a law for support or protection

invocation
(n.) (in-vō-KAY-shun)

a prayer; an appeal for help or protection

provoke
(v.) (pra-VOKE)

from *pro-*, "forth," and **vok**, "call," to call forth strong emotion, especially anger; to stir or arouse to action

provocation
(n.) (prah-va-KAY-shun)

the act of arousing anger, hostility

revoke
(v.) (re-VOKE)

to call back in the sense of canceling or repealing something

revocation
(n.) (rev-a-KAY-shun)

cancellation; reversal; repeal

Exercise 18.2

Substitute words from the two groups you have just studied for the parenthesized words in the phrases below.

1. _____ (to call out) pity for the poor little child

2. _____ (oral, not written) agreement

3. _____ (call back) certain privileges

4. _____ (to call upon) the gods for victory over enemies

5. _____ a statement quoted (word for word)

6. _____ (noisy, clamorous) complaints of the students

7. _____ (to speak in favor of) freezing the production of nuclear weapons

8. _____ (readily voicing opinions) about politics

9. _____ a religious (divine calling)

10. _____ (put into words) her feelings

WRITTEN WORDS

The root **litera** means "letter" and forms the base of a group of words related to reading.

alliteration (n.) (a-lit-er-Ā-shun)

Alliteration is the beginning of several words in a series with the same letter. For example, *Susie sells sea shells*.

A well-known example of alliteration is the phrase "nattering nabobs of negativism."

literacy (n.) (LIT-er-a-see),
illiteracy (n.) (il-LIT-er-a-see)

The condition of being able to read is called **literacy**. The prefix *il-* is a changed spelling of *in-*, meaning "not." **Illiteracy** is the state of not being able to read.

Because of the system of writing invented by Sequoya, literacy was high among the Cherokee Indians.
When the Roman empire fell, illiteracy had become so widespread that few Romans could read their own names.

literate (adj.) (LIT-er-ut),
illiterate (adj.) (il-LIT-er-ut)

Literate means "able to read"; **illiterate** means "not able to read."

> It has been estimated that twenty-seven million adult Americans are illiterate.
>
> According to Thomas Jefferson, democracy depended on a literate and informed citizenry.

literal (adj.) (LIT-er-ul)

Literal means "translating word for word; interpreting words in their most exact sense; real, not figurative."

> A figure of speech is an expression that is not meant to be interpreted in a literal sense.

literature (n.) (LIT-er-a-chur)

Literature is written work, such as poetry or fiction, that lasts through time because of the force and beauty of its style and because it deals with universal themes of love, hatred, death, and so on.

> Geoffrey Chaucer is considered the father of English literature.

literary (adj.) (LIT-er-air-ee)

Literary means "relating to literature."

> *Beowulf* was the first major literary work to be written in English.

obliterate (v.) (a-BLIT-er-ate)

Obliterate means "blot out; destroy completely or 'to the letter.' "

> The explosion obliterated the factory.

Earlier you learned that the Greek root **graph** means "write." A Latin root that means "write" is **script** or **scribe**, as in the word *scribble*. Below are other words based on this root.

scribe
(n.) (SKRYB)
> in earlier times, one who copied manuscripts or kept accounts; in biblical references, a teacher and writer of Jewish law; one paid to write letters

script
(n.) (SKRIPT)
> (1) cursive handwriting; (2) the written words memorized by actors for a play

scripture
(n.) (SKRIP-chur)
> (1) sacred writing (when capitalized); (2) anything written

circumscribe
(v.) (SIR-kum-skryb)
> to encircle with boundaries or limits, especially in the form of laws or customs; to place limits on behavior by understood or written rules

describe
(v.) (di-SKRYB)
> to give an account of; give a mental picture of in words; literally, to write down

inscribe
(v.) (in-SKRYB)
> to write or engrave names, words, or characters, especially on solid objects; to autograph a book, photograph, or document

manuscript
(n.) (MAN-yoo-skript)
> a handwritten book (from *manus*, meaning "hand"); an author's typewritten article or book that is submitted to a publisher

prescribe
(v.) (pre-SKRYB)
> to recommend as a remedy; to order treatment or medicine for a patient

proscribe
(v.) (pro-SKRYB)
> to prohibit; forbid; outlaw. (From an ancient Roman practice of writing down and posting in public places the names of those condemned to death or banishment, *proscribe* originally meant "to publish the names of outlaws.")

postcript
(n.) (POST-skript)
> a note added after the close of a letter; a paragraph added to a document

subscribe
(v.) (sub-SKRYB)
> (1) to agree with, endorse, support an idea or theory; originally, to sign one's name underneath a document to show agreement with the ideas contained; (2) to order and receive a newspaper or other periodical

transcribe
(v.) (tran-SKRYB)

(1) to put spoken words into written words; (2) to reproduce in type or longhand words written in shorthand; (3) to copy from an original, duplicate; to write over again

transcript
(n.) (TRAN-skript)

(1) a copy of a student's academic courses and grades; (2) a written copy of a trial or other legal proceeding; (3) a copy of a television or radio broadcast; (4) a copy of an original manuscript

Exercise 18.3

Choose the appropriate words from the preceding section to complete these sentences:

1. In the Middle Ages, many monks spent their lives as _____s, copying ancient manuscripts and translating Scriptures.

2. He cannot read or write. He is _____.

3. After a slave rebellion in 1831, most southern states passed literacy laws making it a crime to teach Blacks to read. Slaveholders knew that _____ people were more inclined to demand fair treatment and freedom.

4. The rate of _____ in this country is dangerously high. According to statistics, one out of every five adult Americans is semiliterate or cannot read at all.

5. *Don Quixote*, a novel composed nearly four centuries ago, is still considered one of the greatest works of _____ ever written.

6. Cervantes, the author of *Don Quixote*, was a _____ genius.

7. The following is an example of _____: "Peter Piper picked a peck of pickled peppers."

8. These sentences cannot be interpreted in a _____ way: It's raining cats and dogs. She is heartbroken.

9. My father's name is _____d on a monument dedicated to the town's soldiers who died in World War II.

10. Before the invention of the printing press, all books were written by hand. Some of these old _____s have survived and are very valuable.

19
Every Word Has a History

Every word you speak, even your name, has its own history, one that may have begun centuries ago. If, for example, your name is Christopher or any of its forms—Chris, Christine, Tina, Kristen—you bear the name of a third-century martyr whose job as a ferryman was to carry travelers across a river that had no bridge. According to legend, one day the ferryman was asked to carry a child across. By the time he reached the shore, the child had grown so heavy that the ferryman remarked, "It felt as if I carried the weight of the world on my back." A voice replied, "You have carried the weight of the world and the One who made it." Then the ferryman realized that the child he had carried was Christ. Thereafter, the ferryman was called Christopher, meaning "Christ-bearer."

Most names have special meanings. The name *John* or any of its forms—*Joan, Jack, Jean, Janet, Jane*—means "God's gracious gift," according to its Hebrew origin. *Mark*, from the Latin name Marcus, means "the warlike one." Both names relate to Mars, the god of war. The Hebrew name *Jesse* and its feminine form *Jessica* mean "the wealthy one." *Angela* means "angel" or "messenger." Your own name probably has an interesting meaning that you can trace through books of name origins.

The English language contains words derived from every imaginable source—from people, places, things, customs, happenings, and historical events. The twenty-three words that follow are among the many that have interesting origins.

bedlam
(n.) (BED-lum)

This word refers to an uproar; a scene of noisy, wild confusion. (From "St. Mary of Bethlehem," a London hospital for the insane, Bethlehem was mispronounced "Bedlam.")

boycott
(n.) (BOY-kot)

A **boycott** is a form of protest in which a group refuses to buy from or deal with a person or an organization. In the 1800s, Captain Charles Boycott was an English landlord's agent in charge of collecting rents from poor Irish tenants. Captain Boycott was considered so cruel and ruthless that, in protest, the people living in the area refused to associate in any way with him or his family.

carnival
(n.) (KAR-na-vul)

This word relates to the centuries-old Christian observance of Lent, the forty-day period preceding Easter. The Lenten period, which commemorates Christ's crucifixion, is devoted to fasting and denial of worldly pleasures. Traditionally, Roman Catholics give up eating meat on certain weekdays in remembrance of Christ's sacrifice of his own flesh on the cross. The days just before Lent, however, are celebrated in some countries with carnivals. The word **carnival** comes from the Latin *carnis*, meaning "meat; flesh." Although **carnival** literally means "to take away flesh," it is actually a festival with music, parades, and feasting. This celebration is the last chance before Lent for the faithful to enjoy meat-eating and other pleasures. The most famous carnival of this kind in the United States is the Mardi Gras, held annually in New Orleans; however, **carnival** more often refers to a traveling amusement show.

cavalier
(adj.) (kav-a-LEER)

This word describes a person who is disdainful; arrogant, overbearing; high-handed; discourteous; supercilious. **Cavalier** was derived from the Latin word for "horse"—*caballus*. Originally, a **cavalier** was a knight or horseman. In those days, no one from the lower economic class owned or rode a horse. In both a literal and figurative sense, the peasants were "looked down on" by the rich nobles who rode horses. Thus, **cavalier** describes a haughty, inconsiderate attitude.

chauvinism
(n.) (SHŌ-va-niz-um)

Chauvinism is blind, foolish patriotism. Nicolas Chauvin was a French soldier whose devotion to Napoleon was so extreme that he was widely ridiculed. His name became associated with an exaggerated belief in the superiority of one's country. In recent history, the term **male chauvinism** has been associated with the women's movement for equality. This term expresses the idea that males regard themselves as naturally superior to women.

dexterous
(adj.) (DEKS-trus)

The Latin word *dexter* means "right hand." **Dexterous** means "having physical skill, especially of the hands; mental quickness, cleverness." It comes from *ambi*, meaning "both," and *dexter*, meaning "able to use both hands equally well," or literally, "having two right hands."

adroit
(adj.) (a-DROIT)

This word refers to one who is dexterous; expert with the hands; mentally quick; clever. **Adroit**, a synonym for *dexterous*, is from French and literally means "to the right" or "right-handed." Apparently, it was once believed that left-handed people were less capable of performing actions requiring skill.

ambidextrous
(adj.) (am-bi-DEKS-trus)

From *ambi*, meaning "both," and *dexter*, meaning "right hand," **ambidextrous** means "able to use both hands equally well," or literally, "having two right hands."

sinister
(adj.) (SIN-a-stir)

Sinister was the Latin word that meant "left hand," but because left-handed people were considered abnormal and viewed with suspicion, the definition of **sinister** had changed to "evil; underhanded; threatening" by the time the word entered the English language.

jingoism
(n.) (JIN-gō-iz-um)

This word refers to warlike patriotism; an inclination toward military action in foreign policy rather than negotiation. *Jingo* was a nonsense word used by magicians. The phrase "by jingo" became an exclamation of surprise or strong belief, and in the 1870s this phrase was often repeated in war songs to add emphasis and spirit.

laconic
(adj.) (la-KAHN-ik)

To be **laconic** is to be terse; concise; curt; brief in speech. This adjective came from Laconia, an area of Greece inhabited by the Spartans, a warrior society. Devoted to fighting, the Spartans valued physical action more than words and were noted for their terseness of speech. According to legend, when the great conqueror Philip of Macedonia was about to attack the gates of Sparta, Laconia's capital, he sent this message to the Spartan king: "If we capture your city, we will burn it to the ground." The Spartans replied with one word—"If."

maudlin
(adj.) (MAWD-lun)

Originally, **maudlin** referred to Mary Magdalene, a biblical figure usually depicted weeping or having red, swollen eyes. In England, *Magdalene* was pronounced "maudlin." The word came to mean "weepy; excessively tearful; overly sentimental or emotional."

profane
(adj.) (prō-FANE)

This word comes from the Latin prefix *pro-*, meaning "before" or "in front of," and the root **fanum**, meaning "temple." In a literal sense, something that is in front of the temple is not inside it and therefore is not sacred. Thus, **profane** meant "unsacred; irreverent; vulgar." **Profane** language contains cursing or obscenities. As a verb, to **profane** something sacred is to treat it with irreverence.

radical
(adj.) (RAD-a-kul)

As a political term, **radical** means "changing a government from the root; making extreme changes and reforms in an existing government." As a general term, **radical** means "extreme." The words **radical** and **radish** share the same root, *rad* (from Latin *radix*), which in fact means "root."

eradicate
(v.) (ee-RAD-a-kate)

From *e-*, meaning "out," and *radix*, meaning "root," **eradicate** means "to rid; pull out by the root; destroy totally."

sabotage
(n. & v.) (SAB-a-tahj)

Sabotage is damage or destruction intended to hinder or stop the production or shipment of war supplies by the enemy. A **saboteur** (sab-a-TOOR) is one who commits sabotage. These words came from the French word *sabot*, meaning "shoe." At one time, factory workers were little more than slaves, forbidden to unionize or strike. Occasionally, a rebellious worker would throw a shoe, or *sabot*, into a factory machine in order to damage or stop it. Being wooden, workers' shoes could cause considerable damage to machinery.

sadistic
(adj.) (sa-DIS-tik)

This word means "taking delight in cruelty; enjoying inflicting pain." It originated with the Marquis de Sade, a French nobleman who invited unsuspecting guests to his home for the purpose of torturing them. A **sadist** is a person who enjoys being cruel.

salary
(n.) (SAL-a-ree)

In the time of the Roman Empire, soldiers often fought in places where salt was scarce, so a part of their wages was paid in salt. The Latin word for *salt* is *sal*; payment in salt was called *salarium*. This is the origin of the word **salary**, which means "periodic, fixed payment for work, especially nonmanual work." The expression "worth his salt," meaning "worth his pay," originated from this custom also.

sandwich
(n.) (SAND-wich)

This word came from an eighteenth-century nobleman, the Earl of Sandwich, who was so fond of gambling that, rather than stop his game for supper, he ordered his servant to bring him two slices of bread with meat in between. By this invention, soon known as the sandwich, the earl could continue playing cards while he ate.

supercilious
(adj.) (soo-per-SIL-ee-us)

This word, meaning "disdainful; snobbish; arrogant; showing haughty contempt," is a synonym for *cavalier*. **Supercilious** comes from *supercilium*, meaning "eyebrow" (*super*, "above," and *cilium*, "eyelid"). A **supercilious** person is snobbish and haughty. If you were to assume a haughty pose, you would probably lift your chin, point your nose higher, and raise your eyebrows slightly. This pose seems to characterize someone who feels superior to others and is probably the origin of this word.

trivial
(adj.) (TRIV-ee-ul)

Trivial derives from the Latin words *tri*, meaning "three," and *via*, meaning "road." In ancient times, **trivial** referred to any place where three roads met. At such busy intersections, people could pause long enough only for a bit of small talk. Thus, **trivial** came to mean "of little importance; insignificant."

vandalism
(n.) (VAN-da-liz-um)

Meaning "pillage; senseless destruction or damage to property," **vandalism** came from the Vandals, a Germanic tribe that raided and looted cities of the Roman Empire. In the fifth century, the vandals overran and pillaged Rome.

sycophant
(n.) (SIK-a-fant)

This servile flatterer bows and scrapes before higher-ups in order to gain favor. A **sycophant** is like the student who brings the teacher shiny apples in the hope of getting good grades. However, this word comes from figs, not apples. It means literally a "fig-shower," from *sykon*, "fig," and *phan*, "show." In ancient Greece, a **sycophant** was an informer who reported the names of those who had not paid the tariff on figs. He also informed officials when figs were being taken from the sacred groves. Then, as now, **sycophant** was a contemptuous term referring to someone who ingratiated himself by insincere flattery or other means.

Exercise 19.1

Mark the following statements either true or false.

_____ 1. The word *sandwich* came from a popular food served in the Sandwich Islands.

_____ 2. The following statement shows a *jingoistic* attitude:
"We're the greatest country on earth, and it's time we showed the world who's boss, even if it means war."

_____ 3. This statement is an example of *chauvinism*: "Our nation is superior to all others. We were chosen by God to be the greatest nation in the world."

_____ 4. This is an example of *laconic* narration: "I saw
Jim last Monday, or maybe it was Tuesday. Any-
way, I just sort of bumped into him at the mall.
He said 'Hi' and I said 'Hi' and he said, 'What
have you been doing lately?' and I said, 'Not
much.' "

_____ 5. *Bedlam* is a state of calmness and order.

_____ 6. A *maudlin* speech is one that is lighthearted and
full of jokes.

_____ 7. A magician must have *dexterity*.

_____ 8. An *ambidextrous* person with a broken right hand
would be unable to write.

_____ 9. An *adroit* person is skillful.

_____ 10. A *sadist* enjoys doing kind, thoughtful deeds.

Exercise 19.2

Complete these sentences by using the appropriate words
from the preceding group.

1. I can't stand soap opera characters who are always sob-
bing about something. They're so _____.

2. The police are trying to restore order. It's just
_____ in there.

3. Someone has abused this poor animal. How could anyone
be so _____.

4. If that company does not stop polluting the river, our
group is going to _____ their products.

5. I don't believe that _____ and jingoism have
anything to do with true patriotism.

6. He's so overbearing and arrogant. I hate his
_____ way of ordering everyone around. (two
possible answers)

7. She thinks she's better than any of us. I really resent her _____ attitude. (two possible answers)

8. Those boys smashed the windows of the library and sprayed paint all over the books. The police caught and arrested them for _____.

9. The bridge collapsed under the weight of the train. The investigators suspect it was a case of _____.

10. He's adroit at chess but not as _____ at athletic games.

Becoming truly word conscious requires that we become interested in our language as a whole. We usually take for granted the language we speak every day, giving little thought to why we speak as we do. But, like everything else, English has its own story. The English language of a thousand years ago was very different from that of today. It reached its present form through centuries of development. The history of English is divided into three periods: Old English, Middle English, and Modern English.

THE OLD ENGLISH PERIOD
A.D. 449–1066

English is a Germanic language. This becomes apparent by comparing a number of German and English words:

English	German
mother	mutter
father	vater
land	land
blood	blut
folks	volks
ghost	geist

These are just a few examples of the many English and German words that are similar. The Angles and Saxons, who conquered Britain in the fifth century, were Germanic tribes whose language was closely related to those of other tribes occupying northern Europe. Britain, named for its inhabitants, the Bretons, acquired its second name, Angleland, from the Anglo-Saxon conquerors. Their language was Angleish.

In the eighth century, the fierce warriors known as Vikings began invading England. These Norsemen ("men of the North") terrorized the English by their coastal raids in which they looted and burned villages and murdered the inhabitants. But after the Vikings settled in England, they enlarged the native vocabulary, especially with words containing the letter *k*. *Dark*, *skirt*, *sky*, *take*, along with numerous other words including *k* are of Old Norse origin. The Vikings also added many words with the hard *g* sound, such as *egg*, *leg*, and *get*.

Norse words replaced many Old English words, but some remained in use along with English words of the same meaning. This accounts for some of the synonyms that we use. (Remember, synonyms are words whose meanings are the same.) Here are examples:

Old Norse	Old English
sick	ill
skill	craft
shriek	screech
skin	hide

Below is an example of Old English dating from the ninth century. See if you can translate the lines. They are part of a well-known prayer.

> Faeder, ure, thu the eart on heofonum, si thin nama
> gehalgod. Tobecume thin rice. Gewurthe thin villa
> on earthan swa swa on heofonum . . .

THE MIDDLE ENGLISH PERIOD
1066–1500

The next major change in the English language began in 1066, when the Norman French conquered England. Because the French won the decisive Battle of Hastings, we speak a very different kind of English today from that spoken by England's early inhabitants. During the period of Middle English, thousands of French words came into the language. French, a Latin-based tongue, was spoken by the new ruling and upper classes, while English became a peasant language. Literature was written in French, but ordinary words that applied to English daily life were not displaced by French words. Most remain, such as *house, cook, sweep, work*. The French, however, introduced hundreds of words we now think of as commonplace. *Jewel, river, village, jealous*, and *revenge* are examples.

Latin was the official language of law, the Church, and scholars. The Church in Rome had Christianized most of Europe by the sixth century, setting up monasteries that became centers of learning. During the Middle English period, French and Latin words coexisted with several remaining English words, adding to English more synonyms such as these:

English	French	Latin
kingly	royal	regal
hate	detest	abhor
bind	join	unite

The language of the Middle English period is much more recognizable to the modern reader. You should have little difficulty figuring out the meaning of these lines, which were translated from a biblical passage (see p. 306 for translation):

> The kyngdom of heuenes is lijc to an housbond man that wente out first bi the morewe to hire werk men in to his vynegerd. And whanne the couenant was maad, of a peny for the dia, he sent him in to his vynegerd.

MODERN ENGLISH

If you were transported back to the England of a thousand years ago, you would not be able to speak or understand your own language. If you landed there in, say, 1350, you would probably be able to read English, but you would have trouble understanding spoken English, because pronunciation was very different from that of today. By the year 1600, however, you would have a much easier time with the language. These are Shakespeare's famous lines from Hamlet:

> To be or not to be, that is the question. Whether 'tis nobler in the mind to suffer the slings and arrows of outrageous fortune, or to take arms against a sea of troubles . . .

Shakespeare wrote in modern English, and although his plays can be difficult to understand, the difficulty lies more with the speech style of that time rather than the words themselves. Most of Shakespeare's language has survived.

Many English words have gradually changed in meaning. Where there have been changes, the changes reveal a great deal about the development of social values. For instance, the adjectives *courteous, gentle*, and *noble* describe people who are polite, kind, and brave, but centuries ago, these words were associated only with the rich, land-owning class of people. *Courteous* described the manners of those connected with the royal courts. The word *gentle* came from "gentry," a class of landholders, and meant "well born; of good family and breeding." The adjective *noble*, meaning "brave; distinguished by lofty deed," was also associated only with the wealthy—the *nobility*.

Such adjectives were not used to describe common working people, nor were people of this class ever addressed as "ladies and gentlemen." In fact, some very negative words came to be related to the working class. The word *vulgar*, originally meaning "relating to the common people," came to mean "offensive; gross in manners; obscene." In the Middle Ages,

a villain was a farm worker, but later *villain* was defined as
"an evil person; a criminal." *Churlish* and *boorish* mean
"surly; ill mannered; rude," although originally a churl or a
boor (from the Dutch word *boer*) was simply a farm laborer.
The word *common*, however, is still used to mark someone
as inferior or coarse in manner and taste. The landless, common class was thought incapable of cultivating the virtues
attributed to the upper classes.

Slowly English society became more democratic. A large
merchant class had arisen by the sixteenth century, and more
people could afford to be educated. In 1475, William Caxton,
a printer, developed an improved printing process that made
books cheaper and available to more people.

During the fifteenth century, the biggest change since the
Norman-French conquest had begun to take place in the English language. This change was brought about by the Renaissance (REN-a-sahns), which means "rebirth," specifically
the rebirth of learning. Europeans had become fascinated with
the culture of the ancient Greeks and Romans. Their art and
architecture were copied everywhere, and educated people
learned both Greek and Latin in order to read classical writings. This brought about a huge influx into English of Latin
and a considerable amount of Greek.

A time of exploration and conquest also began during the
Renaissance. The American colonies were established under
British rule, and by the twentieth century England had built
an empire, ruling countries and colonies all over the world.
As the British Empire grew, so did the English language,
which absorbed words from every place.

Today, English is the most widely spoken language on
earth. With around 800,000 words (a million, by some esti-
mates), English has the largest vocabulary ever assembled in
the history of the world. Over 60 percent of English words
are based on Latin and Greek roots.

The next chapter introduces you to some of these roots,
but first let's talk a little more about the development of
English. You probably figured out that the Old English passage quoted earlier in this chapter is from the Lord's Prayer.

The Middle English writing is part of the biblical parable of the workers. Translation:

> The kingdom of heaven is like a householder who went out early in the morning to hire workers for his vineyard. And when the covenant was made of a penny (a denarius) for the day, he sent them into his vineyard. . . .

The word *housbond*, from the Old English *husbonda*, is the origin of *husband*, which meant, originally, "householder" or "owner of an estate."

The exercise below pertains to the three periods of English. You should have no difficulty answering the questions.

Exercise 19.3

1. These writings are from three different periods of the development of English:

   A. "Poor girl! She weeps . . . meddle not with her. For shame, thou hilding of a devilish spirit."

   B. Men ne cunnou secgan to soth . . . haeleth under heofenum, hwa thaem hlaeste onfeng.

   C. So the laste schulen be the firste, and the firste the laste.

   List the three English periods, matching the letters in front of the writings to the periods in which they fit.

   A. _____

   B. _____

   C. _____

2. A. From Example A above, what word means "good-for-nothing"? _____

   B. What phrase in Example B means "heroes under heaven"? _____

C. Example C is a biblical quotation about Paradise. Rewrite the words in modern style. You will probably be able to guess the meaning of "schulen." _____

3. Before Christianity came to England, the Anglo-Saxons worshiped some of the same gods worshiped by the Norse people. The chief Norse god was Odin. The Anglo-Saxons called him Woden. Woden's wife was Frigga, whom the Norsemen called Freya. Tiu (TEE-oo), or Tiw, was the god of war. Thor was the god of thunder. Which days of the week are named after Woden, Frigga, Tiu, and Thor? _____

4. Keeping in mind what you read about the Middle English period, list the words from these nine pairs of synonyms that came from English. Then list those that came from French: A. infant—baby; B. eternal—forever; C. shake—tremble; D. big—large; E. perspire—sweat; F. glad—joyous; G. employ—hire; H. shiny—lustrous; I. buy—purchase. Remember which must have been the more plain and ordinary of the two languages.

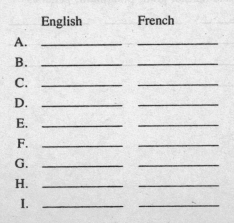

	English	French
A.	_____	_____
B.	_____	_____
C.	_____	_____
D.	_____	_____
E.	_____	_____
F.	_____	_____
G.	_____	_____
H.	_____	_____
I.	_____	_____

5. A. Some words change or narrow in meaning through time and usage. For instance, when people in past centuries used the word *awful*, they were not always describing something bad. What do you think the older definition of *awful* might be? _____

   B. *Conceit* once referred to things conceived in the mind—thoughts and ideas. What does *conceit* usually mean now? _____

   C. *The Quick and the Dead* is the title of a famous novel. In this title, *quick* is not used to mean "rapid." From the context of the title, what do you think it is used to mean? _____

6. From this group of seventeen words, ten entered the language during the period of Modern English. During this time, the Americas, Australia, and parts of Africa and Asia were explored and conquered. This period also brought in scientific advancement. Keeping this in mind, choose and list the ten words:

   apple, banana, chili, roast, ship, kayak, canoe, wolf, giraffe, kangaroo, wagon, telegram, mariner, submarine, gold, plutonium, genetics

   _____   _____   _____

   _____   _____   _____

   _____   _____   _____

   _____

20
Words from Mythology

Through learning some of the Greek and Roman myths, you will learn derivatives of mythological names. Some derivatives are common words; others will be less familiar. Associating the words with their related myths is a simple way to understand and remember them.

Because the ancient Romans had originated from a part of Italy known as the plain of Latium, their ancestors were called Latinz and their language, Latin. The Roman Empire grew from the city of Rome to include much of the known world. When the Romans conquered the Greeks, they recognized the superiority of Greek learning. Wealthy Romans often used Greek slaves to teach their children. The Romans absorbed a great deal of the Greek language into their own and copied much of the Greek culture, including Greek mythology. Most of the major Roman deities (gods and goddesses) were actually Greek in origin. The Romans told the same myths about them, simply substituting Roman names for their Greek names. Venus, for instance, was the Roman name given to Aphrodite (af-ra-DĪT-ee), the goddess of love. Jupiter was the Roman name of Zeus, the chief Greek god.

Throughout history, societies have felt a need to explain the mysteries of nature. Mythology was an imaginative attempt to satisfy human curiosity about life's mysteries.

THE MYTH OF CERES AND PROSERPINA

Ceres was the Roman goddess of grain and the harvest. Her Greek name was Demeter. Ceres had a beautiful daughter named Proserpina (Persephone), who loved to walk in the meadows and forests. Everywhere her feet touched, flowers sprang from the ground.

Proserpina (prō-SUR-pa-nuh) was so lovely that Pluto, the god of the Underworld, fell in love with her. Pluto was usually cold and uncaring toward everyone, human or divine, but his love for Proserpina was deep and passionate. One day as she was walking, Pluto captured her and carried her down into the Underworld. There, he offered her all the gold, silver, and gems that lay under the earth if she would be his wife. But Proserpina, preferring flowers and the other simple beauties of nature, refused them.

Ceres, in the meantime, searched the earth for her beloved daughter. When the earth produced no clues, Ceres became distraught and scorched the earth, vowing that no seed would grow until her daughter was returned to her.

Finally, the river Arthemus, which came from underground, told Ceres that he had seen a girl there bearing Proserpina's description. Ceres then pleaded with the chief god, Jupiter (Zeus), to force his brother Pluto to release Proserpina, but Jupiter told her that the three goddesses of destiny, the Fates, had decided that Proserpina would become queen of the Underworld by marrying Pluto. Not even the king of gods could change destiny.

At last, Ceres persuaded the Fates to relent. Proserpina was allowed to spend six months each year above ground with her mother. When Proserpina emerged, the air grew warm and fresh. Plants and flowers again sprang up where she walked. Each year when she descended to the Underworld, Ceres mourned and the earth became cold and barren. This is how the ancient Romans and Greeks explained the annual occurrences of the seasons.

Related Words

Ceres

Ceres was the goddess of agriculture. She was associated especially with the growing of grain. The word derived from Ceres, as you may have guessed, is **cereal** (n.) (SEER-ee-ul).

Jupiter

Except for Earth, each planet in our solar system has been given the name of an ancient deity. The largest planet was named for Jupiter, the king of the gods. Jupiter was the Roman name for Zeus. Sometimes the Romans called him Jove. This is the origin of the expression "By Jove," an exclamation used to give emphasis or convey surprise. Jove was a mischievous, fun-loving god. **Jovial** (adj.) (JOE-vee-ul), derived from his name, means "fun-loving; jolly; good-natured, convivial."

Pluto

Jupiter's brother was Pluto, whose personality was quite different from that of Jupiter. Caring little for other gods or mortals, Pluto was known for being cold and distant. For this reason, the planet Pluto was named for him. Pluto is the farthest planet from the sun and very cold.

Pluto's Underworld, also called the Lower World, held the earth's minerals. The word **plutonium** (n.) (ploo-TŌ-nee-um), a derivative of *Pluto*, is the name of a highly poisonous metal made from uranium and used to produce nuclear energy.

The Lower World also contained the dead. In Greek mythology, Pluto was sometimes called Hades (HAY-deez), which was also the name of the Underworld, which he ruled. The word *hades* meant "the unseen." The Greeks believed that souls of the dead were carried by the river Styx to Hades. In Hades were various regions to which people were assigned according to how they had led their lives on earth. Good souls were carried to the Elysian Fields, a beautiful part of Hades, where they could continue the occupations of their mortal lives. Wicked souls were sent to the lowest regions of Hades, where they suffered eternal torment.

Later in history, Christians adopted the word *hades*. The writers of the New Testament in the Bible used it to mean "hell; a place of eternal punishment."

The Fates

The Greeks believed that fate was the force that ruled human life, and nothing could change one's destiny, not even the gods. In mythology, fate was represented by three goddesses called the Fates. Their individual names were Clotho, Lachesis, and Atropos. Clotho spun the thread of life; Lachesis determined its length; Atropos cut the thread, thereby ending life. According to the Greeks, the Fates decided what would happen to each human life from the hour of birth to the moment of death. Usually depicted as elderly, stern-faced women, the Fates almost never changed their decisions.

The following words are related to the myth of the Fates.

fate (n.) (FATE)	(1) destiny; a force that determines what happens; (2) outcome; final result
fateful (adj.) (FATE-ful)	relating to an event that affects what happens afterward; relating to an occurrence that changes the course of history
fatalism (n.) (FATE-a-liz-um)	a belief that events or conditions are predestined and cannot be changed.
fatalistic (adj.) (fate-a-LISS-tik)	accepting whatever happens; resigned to fate
fatal (adj.) (FATE-ul)	resulting in death
fatality (n.) (fay-TAL-a-tee)	death caused by disaster or calamity; a victim whose death is a result of a disaster or calamity

All ancient peoples devised stories to explain the mysteries of creation. The following shows how the Greeks explained the origin of the world.

THE CREATION MYTH

Before any material thing existed, the universe was only a vast black hole, or void—a state of nothingness, which the Greeks called *Chaos* (KĀ-ahs). Chaos was the unformed universe. No plan, purpose, or order existed then. There was only darkness.

Out of the blackness arose a powerful spirit of Love. This spirit created Mother Earth, whom the Greeks called *Gaea* (JEE-a), or *Ge*. Then the heavens were created. The heavens contained the spirit of Uranus (yoo-RĀ-nus), who became Gaea's husband and ruler of earth.

Chaos shared its darkness with the earth in order to give it night. This darkness was ruled by Nox, goddess of night. Nox then gave birth to light, so that day would always follow night.

From Gaea and Uranus, the god of time, Cronos, was born. His name came from the Greek word *chronos* (KRŌ-nōs), meaning "time." Cronos later became ruler of the universe and fathered six sons, including Zeus (Jupiter), who when grown took Cronos's place as chief god.

According to the myth, an oracle had warned Cronos that one of his children would try to overthrow him. To prevent this, Cronos swallowed all of his children except Zeus, for whom his mother had substituted a stone wrapped in a blanket. This was unnoticed by Cronos. When Zeus grew up, he overthrew his father and became king of the gods.

The Greeks used the myth of Cronos swallowing his children to show how time destroys its own creations.

Related Words
Chaos

From the original idea of Chaos as an unformed universe without plan or order, the word **chaos** (n.) (KAY-oss) became a descriptive term meaning "complete disorder and confusion."

Gaea (Ge)

Gaea is from *ge*, which meant "earth." These words are derivatives of *ge*:

geography (n.) (jee-OG-ra-fee)	formed from *ge* and *graph*, meaning "writing," literally "to describe the earth"; broader meaning is "the scientific study of the earth's features—mountains, plains, rivers, soil, crops, etc."
geology (n.) (jee-OL-a-jee)	from *ge* and *logos*, meaning "science; knowledge," specifically the science of the earth's structure and the formation of its rocks, minerals, and soil
geometry (n.) (jee-OM-a-tree)	from *ge* and *metry*, meaning "measurement," originally a branch of mathematics used to measure land, now a necessary tool of navigation, engineering, and architecture, to determine the position, size, shape, or volume of anything

Uranus

Uranus, the third-largest planet in the solar system, is named for the god of the heavens. The word **uranium** (n.) (yoo-RAY-nee-um) was derived from *Uranus* and is the name of a radioactive metal used to produce atomic energy.

Nox

The word **equinox** (n.) (EE-kwa-nox) comes from *equi*, meaning "equal," and *nox*, meaning "night." **Equinox** refers to the two times of the year when the night is equal in length to the day. The vernal equinox, occurring on or about March 21, is the first day of spring; the autumnal equinox, around September 21, is the first day of autumn.

The word **nocturnal** (adj.) (nok-TUR-nul) means "relating to the night."

Cronos (chronos)

The Greek word *chronos*, meaning "time," forms the base of these words:

chronic (adj.) (KRON-ik)	relating to a habit, condition, or disease that continues over a long period of time
chronicle (n.) (KRON-a-kul)	a record of events in the order of time
chronology (n.) (kron-OL-a-jee)	a record of events arranged in the order of time; a chronicle
anachronism (n.) (a-nak-ra-niz-um)	from the prefix *ana,* "against"; something that goes against time (For example, a knight on horseback in the midst of a twentieth-century battlefield would be an anachronism.)
synchronize (v.) (SIN-kra-nize)	from the root **syn**, "same" or "together"; specifically, "to operate together at exactly the same time; to set clocks or watches at precisely the same time"

In Roman mythology, Gaea was called Terra. The following words were derived from Terra and relate to the earth.

terrain (n.) (ta-RANE)	an area of land, refers mainly to features of the earth's surface: rocky **terrain**; mountainous **terrain**, etc.
territory (n.) (TAIR-a-tor-ee)	a region of earth usually having man-made boundaries
terrace (v.) (TER-ess)	to make raised levels of earth, as on hilly land, to keep soil from washing away
terrestrial (adj.) (ta-RES-tree-ul)	relating to life on earth; relating to life on land as opposed to water
extraterrestrial (adj.) (eks-tra-ta-RES-tree-ul)	with the prefix *extra*, "outside; beyond," means "beyond the earth"
inter (v.) (in-TUR)	"to bury in the earth"; noun form, **interment**, means "burial in the earth"

subterranean
(adj.) (sub-ta-RAY-ne-un)

with the prefix *sub*, "under," means "under the earth's surface"

Saturn

Cronos's Roman name was Saturn. The ringed planet, Saturn, was named for him. His day of honor was called Saturn's Day, which became *Saturday*.

In Italy, Saturn was worshiped as the god of both time and agriculture. He was usually depicted as a sad-faced, bent old man holding a scythe. This may be the origin of our New Year's Eve symbol for the old year, a bent and weary Old Father Time.

In his other hand, Saturn held a snake biting its own tail. This represented the cyclical nature of the seasons. Like a wheel, the seasons turn in a never-ending circle.

Saturn was noted for his sad, gloomy expression. **Saturnine** (adj.) (SAT-ur-nine) means "morose; gloomy-natured."

Exercise 20.1

Mark the following statements true or false.

_____ 1. A jovial person is gloomy.

_____ 2. A saturnine person is cheerful.

_____ 3. Pluto's kingdom was subterranean.

_____ 4. A Martian is a terrestrial creature.

_____ 5. A Martian is an extraterrestrial creature.

_____ 6. A terrain always has legal boundaries.

_____ 7. A territorial agreement would have something to do with land boundaries.

_____ 8. Interment is burial at sea.

_____ 9. A fateful occurrence is one that ends in death.

_____ 10. A person with a fatalistic belief works to change conditions.

Exercise 20.2

Complete these sentences with the appropriate words.

1. If you're going to become an architect, you will have to work harder at math, especially _____.

2. Finding oil in the earth requires knowledge of _____.

3. What a mess! Nothing is where it belongs. I can't find a thing. The baby is crying, and the children are fighting. This house is in a state of _____.

4. A written history is a _____. (two possible answers)

5. She has a habit of being deceitful. She has been that way as long as I've known her, and I don't think she will ever change. She's a _____ liar.

6. The horse-drawn wagon rumbling along the modern city street is certainly an _____.

7. Whales are marine animals; elephants are _____.

8. A visitor from the planet Venus would be an _____ creature.

9. Coal mining is a _____ occupation.

10. We all have to meet here at the exact same time because the bus won't wait. Please _____ your watches.

GODS AND MORTALS

The religion of the ancient Greeks was in some ways very different from those of other early cultures. Other peoples in ancient times worshiped the sun for its power, certain animals for their strength, or other strange, fanciful divinities. The Greeks gave human forms to their major deities, depicting them as muscular, handsome men and graceful women. The gods and goddesses had human personality traits as well, including human faults. Zeus, their king, had a weakness for attractive women, both divine and mortal. His wife, Hera, was a jealous, bad-tempered queen who caused her faithless husband a great deal of trouble as punishment for his amorous adventures. The Greeks admired their gods as superhumans—human in form and character, yet far more powerful than mortals.

Mortals, on the other hand, were at first regarded as lesser animals by the deities. According to one myth, the god Prometheus created humans from earth and water and then was taunted by the other gods for making such inferior, helpless creatures. Another myth says that Prometheus was assigned the task of giving the animals gifts for their survival. After the animals had received their powers, there were no gifts left for humans, so Prometheus stole the secret of fire from Zeus and gave it to them. This enraged Zeus, and he punished Prometheus severely.

Later in mythological history, the gods and goddesses began to intervene in mortal affairs, even opposing one another in men's wars in order to help their favorite mortals. In folklore, mortal lives were intertwined with those of divinities. Some deities fell in love with mortals and married them. The stories in this section tell of interactions between human and divine beings. The first story tells of a god's love for a mortal woman.

Psyche and Eros

Psyche (pronounced SY-kee) was a beautiful mortal princess—more beautiful even than Aphrodite, the goddess of love. Envious of Psyche's beauty, Aphrodite ordered her son Eros (ER-ose) to make Psyche fall in love with someone unattractive. Eros was the god of love, and it was believed that when he wounded someone with his arrow, that person fell in love. When Eros saw Psyche, he was so stunned by her beauty that, instead of wounding her, he accidentally wounded himself and fell deeply in love with her. One dark night he captured and married Psyche. He then carried her to his palace, where he visited her only by night, warning her that she was never to see his face. One night as Eros lay sleeping, Psyche, no longer able to contain her curiosity, lighted a lamp and saw his handsome face, but a drop of the lamp's hot oil fell on his shoulder, awakening him. Angered by Psyche's disobedience, Eros disappeared. Psyche searched everywhere for him and finally came upon Aphrodite's temple. Aphrodite, out of spite, then subjected Psyche to a series of trials that caused her great suffering. Eros, feeling deep love and pity, secretly came to Psyche's aid. Finally Aphrodite forgave them both, and after much pleading by Eros, Zeus made Psyche immortal so that she and Eros could live together forever.

This story had much meaning for the Greeks. Eros symbolized the heart, or human emotions. Eros wanted Psyche to love him not for his appearance but for his heart, which was filled with love. *Psyche* was the Greek word for "soul" or "mind." Psyche's suffering represented the trials of life which humans must endure. The marriage of Eros and Psyche symbolized the union of heart and mind that makes human beings complete persons. The Greeks valued both feelings and the intellect. Their great respect for the powers of the mind was symbolized by Psyche's beauty. The following words are based on the word **psyche**, meaning "mind."

psychiatry
(n.) (SY-KY-a-tree)

the branch of medicine that deals with the treatment of mental or emotional disorders

psychology
(n.) (sy-KOL-a-jee)

the scientific study of the mind and the mental activities of both humans and animals (**Psychology** includes research into child development, mental and emotional disorders, social behavior, and learning. Clinical *psychologists*, like psychiatrists, treat people with mental or emotional difficulties, but, unlike psychiatrists, psychologists are not medical doctors.)

psychic
(adj.) (SYK-ik)

having supernatural mental powers; having clairvoyance or extrasensory perception, the ability to perceive things in the mind without the use of physical senses

psychosis   a severe mental disorder
(n.) (sy-KŌ-sis); (plural,
psychoses [sy-KŌ-seez])

psychotic   relating to severe mental illness
(adj.) (sy-KOT-ic)

Eros was the god of love and fertility. His Roman name was Cupid. Two words that are associated with Eros, or Cupid, are *erotic* (i-ROT-ik), meaning "pertaining to sexual desire; amorous," and *cupidity* (kyoo-PID-a-tee), which originally meant "sexual desire" but now means "greed for riches; avarice."

Tantalus

Tantalus, a Greek king fathered by Zeus, was punished in Hades for crimes against the gods. This myth has various versions. According to one, Tantalus stole the gods' secrets. Another version is that he stole ambrosia and nectar, their special food and drink. Tantalus's punishment was to stand with a rope around his neck in water up to his chin. Unbearably thirsty and hungry, Tantalus tried to drink, but with every attempt, the water receded. Just above him were fruit-laden branches, but each time Tantalus reached for the fruit, the wind swept away the branches.

This myth was the origin of the verb **tantalize** (TAN-ta-lize), which means "to tempt unbearably" or "to torment or tease by temptation." **Tantalum** (n.) (TAN-ta-lum), another derivative of *Tantalus*, is the name of a dense metal incapable of absorbing water.

Narcissus

Narcissus was an exceedingly handsome mortal youth who, on seeing his face reflected in a pool of water, fell in love with his image. But whenever he reached into the water to touch the image, it dissolved in the ripples. Heartbroken because he could not grasp his reflection, Narcissus pined away beside the pool until he died. Upon his death, he was transformed into a flower that came to be called the narcissus. As a noun, **narcissism** (NAR-si-siz-um) means "excessive self-love; self-admiration." As an adjective, **narcissistic** (nar-sis-SIS-tik) means "full of self-love; excessively interested in oneself."

Nemesis

Nemesis was the Greek goddess of justice. It was she who had cast a spell on Narcissus that caused him to fall in love with his reflection and die beside the pool. The vain and coldhearted Narcissus had been loved by a beautiful nymph named Echo, but he had rejected her love. Echo had been happy, lively, and so full of chatter that she had once been assigned as Hera's companion to keep Hera's mind off the love affairs of her husband, Zeus. But after Narcissus's rejection, Echo was so heartbroken that she faded away until only her voice was left. This greatly angered Nemesis and she avenged Echo's sorrow by bringing about Narcissus's death.

Nemesis was known to the Greeks as "she whom none can escape." The word **nemesis** (n.) (nem-A-sis) means "a relentless enemy; an unusually persistent and vengeful opponent."

Mars

Mars was the Roman name of Ares, the god of war. He was the son of Jupiter and Juno (Zeus and Hera). The Greeks did not like the war god, and supposedly he was despised by most of the other deities because of his terrible temper and his love for violence and bloodshed. He was especially hated by Athena, the goddess of wisdom, for whom Athens is named. As defender of cities, Athena sometimes fought against Ares (Mars) in the wars of mortals.

Unlike the Greeks, the Romans honored Mars highly, placing him next in importance to Jupiter. Military conquests were important to Rome. Its armies conquered much of the known world, and Romans paid great homage to Mars because of their victories. The planet Mars and the month of March were named for him. The adjective **martial** (MAR-shul), a derivative of *Mars*, means "military; relating to war or the armed services." The following terms are associated with war or armed service.

court-martial　trial by a military court; a court composed of military officers for the trial of persons in the armed services

martial arts　the arts of war or self-defense

martial law　rule by a military force rather than a civil government

Exercise 20.3

Mark the following statements true or false.

_____ 1. A *psychologist* is a medical doctor.

_____ 2. *Psychiatrists* are licensed to prescribe medicine.

_____ 3. *Psychotic* means "nervous."

_____ 4. *Psychoses* are mild mental disorders.

_____ 5. One of the functions of *psychology* is to find out how people learn.

_____ 6. *Psychiatry* is a branch of medicine.

_____ 7. A *psychic* person is one who is mentally ill.

_____ 8. Karate is a *martial* art.

_____ 9. A soldier's uniform is *martial* attire.

_____ 10. Under *martial* law, citizens govern themselves by democratic processes.

Exercise 20.4

Choose the appropriate words to complete these sentences.

1. The man had once suffered from a severe mental illness, but he was cured of his _____ and now leads a normal life.

2. Educational _____ is the study of various theories about how learning takes place.

3. My sister and I lived several hundred miles apart. One evening I suddenly had a feeling that something was very wrong with my sister. Later, I learned that she had been seriously injured in a car accident that happened at the same moment in which I had sensed fear about her safety. I'm convinced that this was a _____ experience.

4. Certain drugs can cause hallucinations and other _____ symptoms.

5. My cousin has always been interested in helping people who have mental illness. After medical school, she intends to train in _____.

6. She's a _____ person. She doesn't care about anyone except herself. I've never known anyone so conceited and self-centered.

7. Some writers call these times the age of _____, and they warn that this "me first" way of thinking is harming our society. We have become obsessed with ourselves and uncaring about others.

8. The soldier faces a _____-_____ for striking an officer.

9. _____ _____ is rule by military force and it does away with people's right to govern themselves.

10. _____ sciences teach methods of warfare.

GIFTS FROM THE GODS

The ancients believed that the deities had great influence over their lives and that they gave or withheld such gifts as wealth, talent, and wisdom. Persons who received these and other gifts were thought to have found special favor with the gods and goddesses. This section presents a few of the divine gift-givers and the words associated with their names.

The Muses

The nine goddesses of the arts, music, literature, and science were called the Muses (myoozes). The word *music* means literally "the art of the Muse." It was believed that the Muses inspired persons to create melody, drama, poetry, and art and to pursue knowledge. Before beginning their work, writers and artists prayed to the Muse who represented their art form in the hope that they would be given inspiration to produce great works.

These words come from *muse*:

amuse (v.) (a-MYOOZ)	(1) to entertain; to occupy pleasingly; (2) to cause to laugh or smile
museum (n.) (myoo-ZEE-um)	a place housing art collections, scientific exhibits, or historical artifacts

---

Terpsichore

The muse of dancing and singing was Terpsichore (terp-SIK-er-ee). Her name, from the Greek words *terpsis*, meaning "enjoyment," and *choros*, meaning "dance," literally means "enjoyment of the dance." In ancient Greece, a chorus was originally a ceremonial dance accompanied by singing. Later, *chorus* came to refer to a group who danced together as in a chorus line, or sang together as in a choral group or a choir.

Derivatives:

chorus (n.) (KOR-us)	(1) a group of persons who sing together; (2) a musical composition performed by a large body of singers; a group of singers and dancers who perform in musical productions
choreography (n.) (kor-ee-OG-ra-fee)	dance arrangement; from *choros*, "dance," and *graph*, "writing," a written dance arrangement

terpsichorean relating to dance
(adj.) (terp-si-
KORE-ee-un)

Polyhymnia

Polyhymnia (pol-i-HIM-nē-ah) was the Muse of sacred music. Her name literally means "many hymns." A **hymn** (n.) (him) is a sacred song or a song of praise.

Mnemosyne

The Muses were the daughters of Zeus and Mnemosyne (ne-MOS-a-nee), the goddess of memory. Words related to Mnemosyne are **amnesia** (n.) (am-NEE-zha), meaning "loss of memory," **amnesty** (n.) (AM-nes-tee), a pardon for an offense (literally, a forgetting), and **mnemonics** (ni-MAH-niks), the science of memory improvement.

Fortuna

The Roman goddess of fortune was Fortuna (for-TOO-nah), who brought good or bad luck according to her whims. Like our modern-day "Lady Luck," she was not concerned about what people deserved. To the Romans, this explained why good things happened to bad people, while good people often suffered misfortunes. Fortuna was usually pictured holding a cornucopia, or horn of plenty, which is a symbol of abundance.

Derivatives:

fortune (1) what happens, good or bad; fate; destiny; luck or chance
(n.) (FOR- (2) an amount of wealth
chun)

fortunate lucky; having good fortune
(adj.) (FOR-
cha-nut)

fortuitous
(adj.) (for-
TOO-a-tus)

happening by chance; accidental

Terminus

Terminus (TUR-ma-nus) was the Roman god of boundaries and limits. It was believed that he protected the properties of those he favored from invasion and loss. Terminus was honored annually in ceremonies during which a stone post was placed in the ground. This was to acknowledge Terminus as protector of property boundaries.

The following words are related to the name *Terminus*.

term
(n.) (term)

(1) a period of time having fixed limits; (2) a word used to designate a specific thing; a technical word; (3) a condition of an agreement

terminal
(n. & adj.)
(TER-ma-nul)

(1) the point at which something ends; the point at which a journey ends;
(2) pertaining to a limit or an end;
(3) fatal; ending in death

terminate
(v.) (TER-ma-
nate)

to finish; to end something

exterminate
(v.) (eks-TER-
ma-nate)

literally, to drive out (from *ex-*, "out," and *terminus*, "boundary"); to abolish; annihilate; destroy entirely

interminable
(adj.) (in-TERM-
in-a-bul)

endless; unlimited; not ending

Plutus

The Greek god of riches was Plutus, whom Zeus blinded at birth so that he would not be able to distinguish between good and bad people when he bestowed wealth. This explained to the Greeks why underserving people had riches, while many good people were not as blessed. Plutus was often depicted as lame or having wings to show that wealth came slowly and could fly away quickly. **Plutocracy** (ploo-TOK-ra-see), a word related to the myth of Plutus, means "a class of rich people who rule by means of their wealth." A **plutocrat** (PLOO-ta-krat) is a member of this class, but the term can denote any rich person.

Exercise 20.5

Mark the following statements true or false.

_____ 1. Ballet dancers are *terpsichorean* performers.

_____ 2. A *choreographer* is a choir director.

_____ 3. The word *amnesia* is from the base **mnesia**, meaning "remember," plus *a-*, meaning "not." Its literal meaning is "not remembering."

_____ 4. A *hymnal* is a book of sacred songs.

_____ 5. *Amusing* always means "funny."

_____ 6. A *museum* might contain a famous painting, an arrow, or a dinosaur's bones.

_____ 7. The prefix *a-* means "not"; *amnesty* means "not forgetting."

_____ 8. To *exterminate* something is to get rid of it.

_____ 9. *Terminal* can mean "having a limited time to live."

_____ 10. *Interminable* means "having a limited amount of time."

Exercise 20.6

Supply the missing words.

1. Under the Constitution, a president's _____ of office is limited to four years.

2. A person who doesn't remember his or her own name has _____.

3. _____ is a general pardon granted to political offenders.

4. An airport or train station is a _____.

5. Those two are constantly squabbling about something. Their _____ quarreling is really getting on my nerves.

6. This chemical spray, used to _____ garden pests, also gets rid of insects that infest houses, but it is unsafe to breathe.

7. Her boss has threatened to _____ her employment. She has been late every day.

8. We were _____ not to have been injured when the car brakes failed.

9. She tried to convince her jealous husband that she had not planned to meet her former sweetheart at the restaurant. According to her story, their meeting had been entirely _____.

SPELLS OF THE GODS

Early in human history, primitive peoples sought answers to the mysteries of natural phenomena. Mythology supplied simple answers: All of nature was ruled by supernatural beings, spirits who caused the winds to blow and the rivers to run, and who gave the earth rain and sunlight for its crops. Angry spirits caused earthquakes, volcanoes, and violent storms. Kinder spirits granted more favorable conditions for human survival.

Mythology also solved the mysteries surrounding the nature of humans and their common experiences—mysteries such as sleep and dreams, sickness and health. These and other phenomena were attributed to spells and tricks performed by divine beings. The sting of Cupid's arrow, for instance, explained to the Romans and Greeks the mystery of romantic love, why people fell in love with certain persons and not with others equally attractive. In this section, you will learn about more gods and the spells they cast.

Pan

Pan, the Greek god of forests and meadows, was regarded as the protector of goatherds' flocks. He was one of the lesser divinities whose bodies were not fully human in form. His body was half-human and half-goat. Pan was a playful, mischievous god. Whenever he would suddenly appear to people, his strange form would cause great terror. His name is the origin of the noun **panic** (PAN-ik), which means "intense, unreasoning fear." The verb **panic** means "to lose control of the ability to think because of extreme fear." It was believed that this kind of fear had first been introduced to humans by Pan.

Luna

Luna was the Latin word for "moon." The first Roman moon goddess was Diana, who was also the goddess of hunting. Later, the Romans came to believe that the moon itself was a goddess, whom they called Luna. They thought that Luna cast spells that caused certain illnesses and that she drove people insane when they offended her. **Lunatic** (n.) (LOON-a-tik) literally means "moonstruck" and refers to a person who is insane. **Lunacy** (n.) (LOON-a-see) means "madness, insanity." **Lunar** (adj.) (LOON-ur) means "relating to the moon."

The Furies

According to the Greeks, it was the Furies who drove people mad. The Furies were the three terrible goddesses of angry vengeance. Terrifying in appearance, they had wings of brass scales, snakes for hair, and eyes dripping with blood. Their hands carried whips, sickles, and torches. The Furies relentlessly pursued and tormented those whose crimes had gone unpunished. They avenged the ghosts of those in Hades who had been treated wrongly in their mortal lives. Although guilty persons sometimes escaped punishment from their fellow mortals, they never escaped the vengeance of the Furies, whose terrible spells tortured their minds until they went insane. The following words are associated with the Furies.

fury
(n.) (FYOOR-ee)

(1) violent anger, rage; (2) violent action; agitation

furious
(adj.) (FYOOR-ee-us)

extremely angry, enraged

furor
(n.) (FYOOR-or)

a great stir, commotion; wild excitement, frenzy

infuriate
(v.) (in-FYOOR-ee-ate)

to enrage, to cause extreme anger

Somnus

Somnus was the Roman god of sleep. His Greek name was Hypnos. He and his twin brother Mors were the sons of Nox, goddess of the night. Somnus and Mors lived together in a cave beside the river Lethe, the river of forgetfulness. The soft sound of the river brought sleep to everything in the cave. When night came, Somnus cast his spell of sleep over the earth so that mortals could forget their troubles and rest their bodies and minds from labor. The following words come from *Somnus*.

somniferous
(adj.) (som-NIF-er-us)

from *somnus*, meaning "sleep," and *fer*, meaning "bear" or "carry"; "sleep-bearing" or "sleep-producing"; anything that causes sleep; also, "soporific"

somnolence
(n.) (SOM-na-lens)

sleepiness; drowsiness

somnolent
(adj.) (SOM-na-lunt)

sleepy; drowsy

somnambulism
(n.) (som-NAM-byoo-liz-um)
the act of sleep-walking; from *somnus*, meaning "sleep," and *ambulate*, meaning "walk"

insomnia
(n.) (in-SOM-nee-a)
a state of sleeplessness, usually chronic

The Greeks believed that Hypnos (Somnus) sometimes caused persons to sleep with their eyes open. This is the origin of the word *hypnosis*, which is not actually sleep, but a state of deep relaxation in which the mind seems to function in a different way. Persons in a *hypnotic* trance respond readily to suggestions made by *hypnotists*. Under hypnosis, persons may be able to remember incidents long repressed in their subconscious minds. This is sometimes helpful in curing emotional problems. Hypnosis has also been used as a substitute for anesthesia in dental or surgical procedures. Under deep hypnosis, patients responding to suggestions by doctors feel no sensation of pain. Although hypnosis has been known of for many centuries, scientists have found it difficult to explain or even define. Following are some of the definitions of *hypnosis* and its derivatives.

hypnosis
(n.) (hip-NŌ-sis)
a sleeplike condition caused by artificial means; a trance; a deeply relaxed mental state that causes a greater responsiveness to suggestions; a changed state of consciousness

hypnotic
(adj.) (hip-NOT-ik)
relating to hypnosis; relating to something that causes hypnosis

hypnotize
(v.) (HIP-na-tize)
to produce hypnosis; to entrance

Mors

Mors was the twin brother of Somnus (Hypnos). His name came from the Latin word *mors*, which means "death." Unlike his kind and gentle brother, Mors was cold and merciless. As the god of death, his spells caused eternal sleep. The words below are related to *mors*.

moribund (adj.) (MORE-a-bund)	at the point of death; in a dying stage; at the point of passing from existence
mortal (adj.) (MORE-tul)	*noun*: "one who is subject to death; a human being"; *adjective*: (1) subject to death; (2) fatal, causing death; (3) dire, pertaining to a life-or-death situation
immortal (adj.) (im-MORE-tul)	lasting forever; deathless; having eternal life
mortician (n.) (more-TISH-un)	one who prepares bodies for last rites and burial

Morpheus

The son of Somnus (Hypnos) was Morpheus, the god of dreams. Morpheus, it was believed, created the forms that people see in their dreams. His name is the origin of the word **morphine** (n.) (MORE-feen), which is a pain-relieving narcotic drug, so named because of its pleasant, dreamlike effects. Other words based on the name Morpheus usually relate to forms or shapes. The adjective *anthropomorphic* is a combination of the Greek word *anthropos*, meaning "human," and *morph*, meaning "form." **Anthropomorphic** (an-thra-pō-MORE-fik) means "ascribing human form or human characteristics to something not human." **Metamorphosis** (n.) (met-a-MORE-fa-sis) means "a transformation; a change from one form or substance to another."

Athena

Athens, the most important city of ancient Greece, was a center of learning and the arts. Athena, the goddess of wisdom, was its patroness and protectress. It was believed that, in time of war, Athena used the shield of her father, Zeus, to protect the Athenians. The shield was called an *aegis*. According to a myth, Athena once gave her brother Perseus the aegis, after he had been ordered to kill the Gorgon, Medusa. The Gorgons were three sisters whose appearance was so terrifyingly ugly that anyone who looked in their faces was turned to stone. Perseus used the aegis as a mirror to see Medusa so that he could cut off her head. The word **aegis** (n.) (EE-jis) came to mean "protection; sponsorship."

Exercise 20.7

Mark these statements true or false.

_____ 1. Caterpillars change into moths or butterflies. This change is called a *metamorphosis*.

_____ 2. The major gods and goddesses were *anthropomorphic*. In other words, the Greeks imagined them as having human forms.

_____ 3. The word *morphine* was derived from *mors* and means "death."

_____ 4. A person feeling *panic* can think clearly and act wisely in dangerous situations.

_____ 5. The rate of infant *mortality* is much lower than it was at the beginning of this century. This means that in modern times, fewer humans die in infancy.

_____ 6. Something that is *immortal* soon passes out of existence.

_____ 7. Something that is *moribund* soon passes out of existence.

_____ 8. Someone in *mortal* danger is in a life-threatening situation.

_____ 9. *Morticians* are scientists who try to find cures for fatal diseases.

Exercise 20.8

Complete the following sentences with words from this section.

1. Shakespeare has been dead nearly four centuries, but his plays will live forever. They are _____ masterpieces.

2. Gods are immortal; humans are _____.

3. _____s in ancient Egypt mummified the bodies of dead kings and placed them in splendid tombs filled with gold treasures.

4. We must save the few animals that are left of this _____ species. Without our help, the species will soon become extinct.

5. His rudeness _____s me. I'm so angry that I feel like quitting this job right now.

6. The rock star's surprise appearance created a _____ in the audience.

7. My father is going to be _____ when he finds out that I wrecked his new car.

8. Under the _____ of the National Geographic Society, the explorers set out on an expedition to the Arctic. The Society had sponsored several such expeditions.

9. The king was in a state of _____, and everyone was afraid of him. He could be very cruel when angry.

10. There is a fire in the next room. Everyone must leave the building through the emergency exit. Please stay calm. There is no reason to _____.

21
Words from Ancient Philosophy

Not all the ancient Greeks believed in an array of magical gods who by supernatural powers created and controlled the universe. The Greek philosophers were not interested in superstitious tales. *Philosophy* literally means "love of wisdom." These wise men wanted to learn as much as possible about the nature of the world and the life it contained. They believed that knowledge could be gained by observing and reasoning. Some philosophers were interested in scientific knowledge. Others speculated about the meaning of life and the principles of conduct that, if followed, could bring happiness and peace to people's lives. These philosophers were concerned with *ethics*.

This chapter will acquaint you with some groups of ancient philosophers and English words that are related to their names.

The Cynics

The Cynics believed that goodness was the only thing in life that had true value. Material possessions did not bring happiness, and striving to own things made life complicated

335

and less free. The most famous of the Cynics was the philosopher Diogenes, who preached that the simple life was the happiest kind. Diogenes went to extremes of simplicity in his life. He preferred eating coarse bread and walking barefooted. A tub, rather than a house, served as his shelter. Once, when he saw a child drinking water from his cupped hands, Diogenes threw away the cup he had been carrying, commenting that the child had been wiser than he.

Other Cynics followed this eccentric way of life. The word *cynic* meant "dog." The Cynics chose to live, in a sense, like dogs by rejecting the values of their society. They did not care about the things that occupied most people's lives—comforts, possessions, and acceptance by society.

When Diogenes had become famous for his teachings, Alexander the Great went to see him out of curiosity. Diogenes, who was sunning himself, barely acknowledged the presence of the powerful emperor. When Alexander asked what he might do for him, Diogenes replied, "Please move out of my sunlight." Diogenes shunned riches and fame, believing that people wasted their lives trying to acquire more than they needed in order to impress others.

It was said of Diogenes that he sometimes walked the streets of Athens carrying a lamp in broad daylight, and that he would startle strangers by shining the lamp in their faces, declaring that he was searching for an honest man. Supposedly, this was his way of calling attention to the need for people to take an honest look at themselves and the motives for their actions—actions that he believed should be motivated by goodness rather than personal gain or society's approval.

Cynics of later times became noted for their contemptuous attitude toward society and their distrust of people's motives. Today, the word **cynic** (n.) (SIN-ik) refers to one who believes that people are motivated by self-interest. A **cynic** has a sneering, distrustful attitude toward others' intentions. **Cynicism** (n.) (SIN-a-siz-um) is the belief that selfish motives underlie people's actions, no matter how good such actions may appear. **Cynical** (adj.) (SIN-a-kul) means "sneering; distrusting others' virtues."

The Skeptics

Led by a philosopher named Pyrrho, the Skeptics thought that it was impossible to have absolute knowledge about anything. Humans could know only how things appeared to be, and because the senses were limited, things might not be as they appeared.

The Skeptics believed it was foolish to trust claims of knowledge. Some knowledge could be gained by observing and reasoning, but never by relying solely on someone's statements. Doubt, to the Skeptics, was a necessary element of learning.

In a sense, all philosophers were Skeptics. They doubted the supernatural explanations given for things not understood. Their doubts brought about the beginning of science, and science showed that, as the Skeptics said, things are not always as they seem. The moon, for example, seems to produce light, but astronomers, by observing and reasoning, found that moonlight is reflected light from the sun. Supposedly learned men for centuries believed the earth to be flat. Had Columbus not doubted this he would never have set out on his fateful voyage that ended in the New World and the discovery that the earth is round.

The word **skeptic** (n.) (SKEP-tik) is commonly used to mean "a doubter"; **skeptical** (adj.) (SKEP-ta-kul) means "having doubt." **Skepticism** (n.) (SKEP-ta-siz-um) means "doubt of accepted belief and doctrines" or simply "doubt."

The Stoics

The Stoics followed the teachings of Zeno, a Greek philosopher who lived around 300 B.C. Because Zeno taught from his porch, or *stoa* in Greek, his students were called *Stoics*. Zeno believed that there was only one God, and every created thing was made from God's substance. Since every living creature shared in one divine life, kindness was very important. If people realized that they were each a part of the same life, they would not want to harm others any more than they would wish to hurt themselves.

Epictetus, a later Stoic philosopher who had once been a slave, taught that fortune and misfortune alike were part of a divine plan. All suffering would eventually end in happiness. The way to have peace of mind was to accept God's will without complaint, no matter how much trouble or sorrow came about. The Stoics were best known for their belief in being calm, cheerful, and uncomplaining under all circumstances.

The word **stoic** (n.) (STO-ik) today refers to someone who has an uncomplaining nature. **Stoical** (adj.) (STO-a-kul) means "indifferent to pleasure or pain; uncomplaining." **Stoicism** (n.) (STŌ-a-siz-um) means "endurance of hardship, pain, or sorrow without complaint; calm acceptance of misfortune."

The Sophists

The Greek word *sophist* means "wise man." Sophists believed that people should develop their powers of reasoning. Like the Skeptics, they questioned accepted beliefs. They challenged people to think for themselves rather than blindly follow traditional teachings.

The Sophists later became paid teachers who gave instruction in grammar, fine speech, and the use of logic. These Sophists were not highly regarded as philosophers because they took pay for their teaching. Known for their ability to reason and think well, Sophists were eventually hired to argue cases before courts, much like modern lawyers. Some were so clever that they could argue convincingly for either side, and they usually represented the side that offered the most money. By their skilled and tricky use of the language, they could make simple issues seem complicated and confusing. By juggling words, they could make bad seem good and good seem bad. These dishonest tactics of persuasion became known as **sophistry** (n.) (SAHF-us-tree), a word still used today to mean "clever, false reasoning."

The Greek word *sophos* means "wise." Following are more English words based on *sophos*:

sophomore
(n.) (SAHF-a-more)

a combination of *sophos*, meaning "wise," and *moros*, meaning "fool"; literally, "a wise fool," or "one who is half-wise and half-ignorant"; modern definition: "a second-year student in a four-year course of study."

sophomoric
(adj.) (sahf-a-MORE-ik)

having limited, shallow knowledge of a subject, but presuming to know a great deal

sophisticated
(adj.) (sa-FIST-a-kate-id)

(1) worldly-wise; losing one's natural simplicity; (2) made complicated, complex; technologically advanced

The Hedonists

The root **hedon** came from a Greek word meaning "pleasure." Hedonists believed that there was no life after death, and since there was no hope for happiness in an afterlife, the chief goal of earthly life should be to have pleasure.

Today, **hedonism** (n.) (HEED-un-iz-um) means "gross self-indulgence; devotion to pleasure, especially physical pleasure." A **hedonist** (n.) (HEED-un-ist) or a **hedonistic** (adj.) (HEED-un-ist-ik) person is one who is wholly devoted to pleasure, especially bodily pleasure.

The Epicureans

The philosopher Epicurus was of the Hedonist school of thought. He believed in the theory of the Atomists, who thought that all matter was made of varying combinations of invisible particles called atoms. Epicurus reasoned that if such beings as gods existed, they were made of atoms the same as humans and therefore could have no power over human life. Death was simply the dispersion of atoms. There was no afterlife of punishment or reward. If people could not look forward to happiness in eternity, then their aim should be to find pleasure on earth.

According to Epicurus, mental pleasures were as important as bodily pleasures. These could be found in enjoyment of the arts, literature, and conversation with good friends. The Epicureans enjoyed fine food and drink but stressed moderation. Too much food or wine led to discomfort or illness, which was the opposite of pleasure. Although the Epicureans pursued intellectual pleasures, the word **epicurean** (ep-a-KYOOR-ee-un) became an adjective usually associated with fine food and drink. An **epicure** (n.) (EP-a-kyoor) is a gourmand (goor-MAHND)—that is, a person who has refined taste in food and drink. Occasionally, **epicure** refers to someone with discriminating taste in art. The words **epicure** and **epicurean** relate to refinement of taste and are no longer associated with *hedonism*.

The Gnostics

The Gnostics took their name from the Greek word *gnosis* (NŌ-sis), which means "knowledge." Gnosticism, existing in the first and second centuries A.D., was a blend of Oriental, Greek, and Christian philosophy. The Gnostics believed that through meditation, they could experience God's presence. Unlike mere faith, this experience gave direct knowledge of the reality of God. Such knowledge was superior to that given by Scriptures or the Church. This claim caused the early Christian Church to denounce the Gnostics as heretics—that is, those who spread false ideas. Gnosticism disappeared as the Church grew more powerful.

The literal meaning of **gnostic** (n.) (NAH-stik) is "one who knows." This word is no longer common, but today there are people who call themselves **agnostics**. The prefix *a* means "without." Literally, **agnostic** (adj.) (ag-NAHS-tik) means "without knowing." In contrast to Gnostic beliefs, *agnostics* are those who say they do not know if God exists. They are neither believers nor disbelievers, but claim that it is impossible to know what is not revealed by experience.

Two common words based on *gnosis* are not related to spiritual knowledge. They are **diagnosis** and **prognosis**. A **diagnosis** (n.) (die-ag-NŌ-sis) is the identification of a problem or disease. A **prognosis** (n.) (prahg-NŌ-sis) is a prediction, especially about the outcome of a disease. The prefix *pro* means "before"; **prognosis** literally means "foreknowl-edge."

Two other derivatives of *gnosis* are the familiar words **recognize**, literally "to know again," and **cognizant** (adj.) (KAHG-na-zunt), meaning "aware, knowing."

Exercise 21.1

The words from this chapter denote persons who have certain attitudes toward life: cynic; skeptic; stoic; hedonist; agnostic; epicure. Match each statement below to the type of person who would most likely express it.

_____ 1. "Life is short, so we might as well have fun. As the saying goes, 'Eat, drink, and be merry, for tomorrow we may die.'"

_____ 2. "Politicians make fine speeches, but I believe in the old saying, 'Everyone has his price.' There's no such thing as an honest politician."

_____ 3. "I don't say there's a God; I don't say there isn't. How can anyone really know?"

_____ 4. "I think there are logical explanations for UFOs. I doubt that they are alien spaceships."

_____ 5. "We should bear our burdens patiently and not complain."

_____ 6. "I would never serve inferior wine to my dinner guests."

Exercise 21.2

Complete the sentences below with the correct adjectives from this group: sophisticated; hedonistic; epicurean; cynical; skeptical; sophomoric; stoical; cognizant.

1. My mother suffered a long, painful illness, but I never once heard her complain. She was _____.

2. She thinks she's an expert in psychology just because she read a few articles on the subject. Her knowledge of psychology is _____.

3. Hippocrates, the famous Greek physician, doubted that disease had supernatural causes. He was _____.

4. He has been bitter ever since the girl he was going to marry ran away with another man. He says that women can't be trusted. His attitude toward women is _____.

5. After graduating from the university, she traveled in Europe. Her education and her travels have taught her a great deal about the world. She isn't the simple country girl that she once was. She has become _____.

6. He turns up his nose at the plain, simple meals we eat. His taste in food is _____.

7. The Roman Empire weakened when the upper classes became corrupt. Rich Romans began to indulge themselves in lavish feasting, drunkenness, and every sort of immorality. They were _____.

8. She doesn't seem to be _____ of her husband's philandering, but everyone else knows about it.

Exercise 21.3

True or false:

_____ 1. This is a *prognosis*: "The patient has pneumonia."

_____ 2. This is a *diagnosis*: "The patient will probably recover in a few days."

_____ 3. This statement shows *cynicism*: "I doubt what that lawyer said, because all lawyers are crooks."

_____ 4. This statement shows *skepticism*: "I doubt what that lawyer says because he hasn't presented enough evidence."

_____ 5. This statement reflects *stoicism*: "I'm getting tired of doing all the work around here and not getting any credit for it."

_____ 6. *Hedonism* is total devotion to pleasures of the senses.

_____ 7. A *hedonistic* person cares deeply about spiritual matters and has a firm belief in life after death.

_____ 8. *Sophistry* is a deliberate attempt to mislead listeners by arguments that sound reasonable on the surface.

_____ 9. *Sophisticated* people know very little about the larger world outside their own community.

_____ 10. A *sophisticated* machine is crude or simply designed.

22
On Your Own

So far in this book, you have studied approximately one thousand words, not counting their derivative forms. Not only have you substantially increased your vocabulary, but you have learned more about the words you already know, that they are linked to other words that share a common source, and that they are made of different parts, each with their own definitions.

You have learned to look at words in a new way. You have not merely memorized a thousand words. You have dissected them, studied their parts, and put them back together. With this method, you have gained not only words but word wisdom. You have learned how to learn so that your vocabulary can rapidly enlarge.

Exercise 22.1

This exercise will show you just how word-wise you have become. The words below are made of parts that you've already learned. Match them to their definitions by writing their letters in the numbered spaces beside the definitions.

a. perspicuous (per-SPIK-yoo-us)

b. symbiotic (sim-by-OT-ik)

c. octogenarian (ok-ta-ja-NAIR-ee-un)

d. magniloquent (mag-NIL-a-kwent)

e. convoke (kun-VOKE)

f. obloquy (OB-la-kwee)

g. erogenous (i-RAHJ-a-nus)

h. neologism (ne-ŌL-a-jizm)

i. presentiment (pree-SEN-ta-ment)

j. insensate (in-SEN-sate)

k. amatory (AM-a-tor-ee)

l. maladroit (mal-a-DROIT)

m. androgynous (an-DRAHJ-a-nus)

n. euphonious (yoo-FONE-ee-us)

o. amorphous (a-MORE-fus)

p. suffuse (sa-FYOOZ)

q. precognition (pree-kog-NISH-un)

r. affidavit (af-a-DAY-vit)

s. bankrupt (BANK-rupt)

1. _____ high-flown, grandiose in speech

2. _____ a speech against someone; abusive, defamatory speech

3. _____ a person born between 80 and 90 years ago

4. _____ pleasing in sound

5. _____ a written statement sworn to before a magistrate; literal meaning, *He has pledged his faith*

6. _____ pertaining to love, especially in literature

7. _____ without form, shapeless

8. _____ having both male and female characteristics

9. _____ to call together; convene; assemble

10. _____ producing sexual pleasure

Exercise 22.2

This exercise combines word elements that you already know with these new elements: *vor*, eat; *apo-*, away, from; *epi-*, upon, outside, added to; *endo-*, within; *later*, side; *chrom*, color. Place each word's letter beside the numbered definition that fits the word.

a. carnivorous (kar-NIV-er-us)
b. herbivorous (er-BIV-er-us)
c. omnivorous (om-NIV-er-us)
d. voracious (vor-Ā-shus)
e. apotheosis (ap-ah-thee-Ō-sis)
f. epilogue (EP-a-log)
g. epigraph (EP-a-graf)
h. epidemic (ep-a-DEM-ik)
i. pandemic (pan-DEM-ik)

j. endemic (en-DEM-ik)
k. monochrome (MON-a-krome)
l. polychromatic (pah-lee-krō-MAT-ik)
m. endogamy (en-DOG-a-mee)
n. exogamy (ex-OG-a-mee)
o. unilateral (yoo-na-LAT-er-ul)
p. bilateral (by-LAT-er-ul)
q. equilateral (e-kwa-LAT-er-ul)

1. _____ within a people or locality; pertaining to disease confined to a certain people or place

2. _____ affecting people outside a group; pertaining to disease that spreads over a community

3. _____ pertaining to something such as a disease that affects all the people or is spread over a wide area

4. _____ a painting in different shades of one color

5. _____ many-colored

6. _____ marriage within a tribe or clan, especially as a compulsory custom

7. _____ the custom of marriage outside of a tribe, clan

8. _____ having equal sides

9. _____ meat-eating

10. _____ plant-eating

Exercise 22.3

This exercise focuses on two roots that you have come across in earlier lessons. The first is the Latin root for hand, *manu*, which appears in *manufacture*, *manuscript*, *manage*, and words listed below. The second is the Latin *ped* and its Greek form, *pod*, both meaning "foot." Another meaning of *ped* is "child."

Three new roots you will see in these lists are *ortho*, meaning "straight," *cura*, "care," and *dat* (from *dare*), "to give."

manu—hand
manual (MAN-yoo-ul)
manicure (MAN-a-kyoor)
manacle (MAN-a-kul)
emancipate (ee-MAN-su-pate)
manipulate (ma-NIP-yoo-late)
mandate (MAN-date)

ped, pod—foot
pedal (PED-ul)
pedestal (PED-a-stul)
pedestrian (pa-DES-tree-un)
pedicure (PED-a-kyoor)
impede (im-PEED)
impediment (im-PED-a-ment)
expedite (EX-pa-dite)
podiatrist (pa-DY-a-trist)
podium (PO-dee-um)
tripod (TRY-pod)
megapod (MEG-a-pod)

ped—child
pediatrician (pee-dee-a-TRISH-un)
pedant (PED-unt)
pedantic (pi-DANT-ik)
pedophile (PED-a-file)
orthopedic (orth-a-PEE-dik)

1. _____ means pertaining to the hand or done by hand.

2. _____ means pertaining to the foot or a lever that is pushed by the foot.

3. A _____ is a child doctor; a _____ is a foot doctor.

4. A _____ is a walker or one who travels on foot.

5. A _____ is a cosmetic treatment of the hands and nails; a _____ is a cosmetic treatment of the feet.

6. A biped has _____ feet, a quadruped has _____ feet; something that has three feet (like a stand for holding things) is called a _____.

7. The base or foot of a column or statue is a _____.

8. A _____ is a shackle or handcuff that restrains the hands.

9. The verb *manumit*, which means "allow a slave to go free," is a synonym of _____, meaning "to *free*," or literally, "let the hands out of their shackles."

10. _____ means "to speed up" or, literally, "free the feet."

Exercise 22.4

The root *corp* means "body" or "flesh." You have learned the roots that mean hand and foot. These roots stand for other body parts: *cord, card*—heart; *capit*—head, chief; *hema* and *sanguin*—blood; *op* and *ophthalm*—eye, vision; *derm*—skin; **dent, dont**—tooth. Three new suffixes appearing in the list are -*itis*—inflammation; -*oid*—like, resembling; -*rrhea*—flow. You will recognize some derivatives from these roots in the word list below. Try matching the words to the definitions that follow.

a. corpse (KORPS)

b. incorporate (in-KORE-pa-rate)

c. corpulent (KORP-ya-lent)

d. cardiac (KAR-dee-ak)

e. cardiologist (kar-dee-OL-a-jist)

f. cordial (KORD-jul)

g. accord (a-KORD)

h. discord (DIS-kord)

i. per capita (per-KAP-a-ta)

j. decapitate (dee-KAP-a-tate)

k. sanguine (SANG-gwin)

l. consanguine (kon-SANG-gwin)

m. hematology (hee-ma-TOL-a-jee)

n. hemorrhage (HEM-rij)

o. hemophilia (hee-ma-FIL-ee-a)

p. optometrist (op-TOM-a-trist)

q. ophthalmologist (ahf-tha-MOL-a-jist)

r. ophthalmitis (ahf-thal-MITE-us)

s. epidermis (ep-a-DER-mus)

t. dermatologist (der-ma-TOL-a-jist)

u. dermatitis (der-ma-TY-tus)

v. pachyderm (PAK-a-derm)

w. dentoid (DEN-toid)

x. orthodontist (OR-tha-don-tist)

1. _____ the outermost layer of skin

2. _____ resembling a tooth

3. _____ a skin doctor

4. _____ a dentist who straightens irregular teeth

5. _____ a thick-skinned animal, like an elephant

6. _____ an eye doctor

7. _____ an inflammation of the eye

8. _____ an inflammation of the skin

9. _____   one who measures vision and
                     prescribes corrective lenses

10. _____   the scientific study of blood

The next two exercises involve word families from four
new roots. The first two are *pend*, meaning "hang," and
rect, meaning "right." The verbs *depend*, meaning "hang
on for support," and *suspend*, "hang from underneath,"
belong to the *pend* family. The word *correct*, meaning "thoroughly right," is from the *rect* group. Notice that these roots
have other meanings. See how many words you already know
or can define by knowing the root meanings.

Exercise 22.5

pend, pens—hang, weigh, pay
pendant (PEN-dunt)
pendulous (PEN-dyoo-lus)
appendage (a-PEN-dij)
appendix (a-PEN-dix)
interdependent (in-ter-de-PEN-
dent)
pensive (PEN-siv)
compensate (KOM-pen-sate)
suspense (sus-PENSS)

rect—right, straight
rectangle (REK-tang-ul)
rectify (REK-ta-fy)
rectitude (REK-ta-tood)
director (da-REK-ter)
rector (REK-ter)
directive (da-REK-tiv)
erect (e-REKT)

Choose and write the word that fits each definition below.

1. _____   literally, to straighten out; place a
                     monument, building, or statue
                     upright; (as an adjective) straight

2. _____   a hanging ornament or piece of
                     jewelry

3. _____   a right-angled parallelogram

4. _____   hanging, drooping

5. _____ a chief supervisor, one who shows the right way

6. _____ a clergyman, one who shows the right spiritual way

7. _____ an extra part added to a book, or the body part that hangs from the cecum of the large intestine

8. _____ to make right, correct a wrong or error

9. _____ moral uprightness, righteousness

10. _____ mutual reliance between persons or things; a hanging on to each other for support

Derivations of the roots below include *doctor*, originally "a teacher," and *alter*, "to change." The prefix *para-*, appearing in the *dox* list, means "alongside, beside."

Exercise 22.6

doc, dox—teach
doctrine (DOK-trin)
indoctrinate (in-DOK-trin-ate)
document (DOK-yoo-ment)
docile (DOS-ul)
orthodox (OR-tha-dox)
unorthodox (un-OR-tha-dox)
paradox (PAIR-a-dox)

alter; ali—other, another
alter ego (all-ter EE-go)
alteration (all-ter-Ā-shun)
altercation (all-ter-KAY-shun)
alternate (ALL-ter-nāte)
alternative (all-TER-na-tiv)
altruist (AL-troo-ist)
alien (Ā-lee-un)
alienate (ALE-ee-a-nate)
alibi (AL-a-by)

1. A person or animal that is submissive and easily taught or trained is _____.

2. A _____ is a teaching, especially of a religion or philosophy.

3. To _____ is to instill with a teaching.

4. _____ means one's ''other self'' or a very close friend.

5. _____ means from another country or distant place; foreign; different in nature.

6. To _____ is to estrange, make unfriendly, turn away.

7. _____ means proof of being in some other place during the time a crime was committed.

8. _____ is the act of changing or modifying something.

9. An _____ is a fight or heated dispute with another.

10. _____ means to change from one place or condition to another repeatedly, or by turns.

MORE ROOTS

In addition to the roots you have studied, your root vocabulary should include the twenty roots listed here along with some of their derivatives.

ac, acri—sharp, bitter

acid	caustic substance
acerbic	sharp-tongued, harsh
acumen	mental sharpness, keenness
acrid	bitter, stinging, as *acrid smoke*
acrimonious	bitter in feeling, sarcastic

ag—act, do, move

agent	a doer, person or thing with the power to act
agenda	schedule of work to be done
agile	quick, active, keen

| agitate | stir up, disturb, excite |
| antagonize | act against, oppose, make an enemy of |

capt, cept, ceive—take, seize, receive

capture	seize
captivate	capture attention, fascinate, as *captivate with charm*
accept	receive, take
receptacle	container
susceptible	impressionable, vulnerable, easily receiving
intercept	seize something before its arrival at an intended place
conceive	take into the mind as an idea; become pregnant
contraception	something that works against conception or impregnation

cad, cid—fall, happen

decadent	falling to ruin, decay
incident	a happening, occurrence
coincide	to happen together

cise—cut

incise	cut into
incisive	penetrating, cutting to the heart of a matter
excise	cut out
precise	exact; cut exactly

flu, flux—flow

fluid	a flowing substance, liquid
fluent	flowing freely in speech
influence	to flow in, affect, as *influence the mind*
influenza	viral, contagious disease; flu (once thought caused by unfavorable influence of the stars)
influx	a continuous flowing in of people or things

grat, gratis—pleased, thankful, free

| grateful | thankful, appreciative |
| ingrate | person who is unappreciative |

gratify	to please
gratuity	money given to show appreciation; a tip
gratuitous	freely given, uncalled for, as *a gratuitous insult*
congratulate	to express pleasure in an accomplishment shared

grav—heavy

grave	serious, weighty
gravity	weight, seriousness
aggravate	make heavy; make worse

hydro (-a)—water

hydrogen	a gas that in combination with oxygen produces water
hydrant	large water pipe to which hoses can be connected
hydraulic	operated by water or fluid pressure
dehydrate	suffer loss of water; dry up

judic—judge

judicial	relating to the administering of justice
judicious	wise, showing good judgment
adjudicate	settle by judicial decision
prejudice	judgment made beforehand without knowledge of the facts

join, junct, jug, jux—connect, join

joint	place where two parts are joined
adjoin	to be next to and connected, as *rooms that are adjoined*
junction	place where lines or roads connect
injunction	a court order, especially one forbidding an action; the act of enjoining or legally joining in to halt something
conjugal	joined in marriage; pertaining to marriage
juxtapose	to place side by side

leg, lect—read, choose

legible	readable

lectern	stand for speaker's papers, books
select	to choose
elect	to choose by voting
neglect	literally, not to choose; choose to ignore; disregard

mon—warn

admonish	to warn
monitor	person or thing that watches and warns
premonition	forewarning; foreboding

nom—name

nominate	to name a candidate for elected office
nominal	in name only, as *a nominal ruler*
cognomen	family name
misnomer	an incorrect name for something
nomenclature	system of names used in a branch of learning

polis—city, citizen

political	pertaining to the activities of government, originally government of cities
cosmopolitan	literally, a citizen of the world; broad in taste and knowledge; at home in any part of the world
acropolis	in ancient Greece, the high part of the city on which fortresses were built (the Acropolis, ancient citadel of Athens)
megalopolis	huge city
metropolitan	pertaining to a large city

tempor—time

temporal	pertaining to earthly life; limited by time
temporary	for the time being; not permanent
contemporary	one who lives in the same time period as another
extemporaneous	unplanned
improvised	literally, without time to prepare

urb—city

| urban | pertaining to a city |

| suburban | outlying areas of a city |
| urbane | refined, suave, "citified"; elegant in manner |

ver—truth

veracious	truthful
veracity	truthfulness
verify	to prove true, confirm
verisimilitude	similarity to the truth; likelihood

volv—turn, roll

revolve	to roll repeatedly
evolve	to roll outward; unfold; develop
involve	to "roll into," include necessarily
convoluted	rolled up together, coiled

Answers

CHAPTER 1: HOW WORDS WORK

EXERCISE 1.1

1. symphony
2. telephone
3. perimeter
4. photograph
5. telegraph
6. television
7. telescope
8. microscope
9. periscope

EXERCISE 1.2

1. patronymic
2. anonym
3. anonymous
4. antonym
5. synonym
6. synonymous
7. metonymy
8. homonym
9. acronym

EXERCISE 1.3

1. anonymous
2. acronym
3. synonym
4. antonym
5. synonymous
6. metonymy
7. pseudonym
8. patronymic
9. homonyms

EXERCISE 1.4

1. exclusive
2. conclusive
3. conclusion
4. reclusive
5. occlude
6. secluded
7. preclusion
8. seclusion

EXERCISE 1.5

1. father
2. paternal
3. mother
4. sister
5. fratricide
6. patricide
7. matricide
8. expatriated
9. fraternal
10. matrix
11. matrimony; patrimony

EXERCISE 1.6

1. matriarch
2. matron
3. patronize
4. paternalism
5. patriarch
6. fraternize
7. patriots
8. repatriated

EXERCISE 1.7

1. bureaucracy
2. autocracy
3. oligarchy
4. hierarchy
5. democracy; monarchy
6. theocracy
7. aristocracy

EXERCISE 1.8

1. autocrat
2. aristocracy
3. monarch; democracy; hierarchy
4. oligarchy
5. theocracy
6. anarchy

CHAPTER 2: ROOTS AND BRANCHES

EXERCISE 2.1

1. antebellum
2. pacifist
3. bellicose
4. repugnant
5. pugnacious
6. pacific
7. impugn
8. rebellion
9. oppugn
10. belligerent

EXERCISE 2.2

1. segregate
2. pedagogues
3. Senate
4. senators
5. congregation
6. egregious
7. juvenile
8. senescent
9. demagogue
10. synagogue

EXERCISE 2.3

1. archives
2. archaeologist
3. astrology
4. novel
5. novice
6. astral
7. astronomical
8. novelty
9. archaic
10. renovate

CHAPTER 3: HOW PREFIXES WORK

EXERCISE 3.1

1. disperse
2. dissect
3. sever
4. abrogated
5. deviate
6. abrasive
7. abject
8. absent
9. depart; abscond
10. dissipate

EXERCISE 3.2

1. immerse
2. immigrate
3. imbibe
4. infuse
5. embrace
6. intrinsic
7. inject
8. incipient
9. envelop

EXERCISE 3.3

1. evanescent
2. exonerate
3. extrinsic
4. exterior
5. exculpate

EXERCISE 3.4

1. collusion
2. syllable
3. cohere
4. syndrome
5. collaborate
6. confluence
7. confuse
8. combine
9. coalesce
10. symmetrical

EXERCISE 3.5

1. obviate
2. contrasted

3. counterstrike
4. obdurate
5. Antarctic
6. antidote
7. countermanded
8. controvert; objected
9. antagonized
10. obstacles

EXERCISE 3.6

1. transparent
2. transfuse
3. transient
4. diameter
5. transform
6. diaphanous
7. transact
8. transfer

EXERCISE 3.7

1. permeated
2. perdition

3. persuade
4. perforated
5. perpetual
6. perennial

5. circumference
6. perimeter
7. periphery
8. amphitheaters

EXERCISE 3.8

1. interrogate
2. interstate
3. intrastate
4. interval
5. interfere
6. intravenously
7. interject

EXERCISE 3.9

1. subterfuge
2. hypothermia
3. hypodermic
4. submerged
5. suffix
6. subtle
7. subway
8. subpoena

EXERCISE 3.10

1. supernatural
2. hyperbole
3. superfluous
4. surpass
5. hyperactive
6. surmount
7. extraordinary
8. extraneous

EXERCISE 3.11

1. circumnavigate
2. ambivalent
3. ambiguous
4. circuitous

EXERCISE 3.12

1. derided
2. deprived
3. derogatory
4. derived
5. descend
6. deteriorated
7. declined;
   declined
8. dejected
9. deciduous
10. decadent

EXERCISE 3.13

1. retaliate
2. remunerate
3. reiterate
4. redundant
5. recalcitrant
6. propensity
7. progress
8. reject
9. prolific
10. profuse

EXERCISE 3.14

1. posthumous
2. post meridiem
3. premonition
4. previous
5. preposterous
6. ancient
7. posterity
8. antedate
9. prejudice

EXERCISE 3.15

1. abbreviate
2. annihilate
3. appreciate
4. affluent
5. aggravate
6. incarnate
7. impoverish
8. imbue
9. indiscriminate
10. irreparable
11. irrelevant
12. illicit
13. immutable
14. insuperable
15. enslave
16. embody
17. enlarge
18. empower

EXERCISE 3.16

1. disconnect
2. misfortune
3. mistake
4. disassemble
5. disenchant
6. dissuade
7. misapprehend
8. mistreat
9. misdeed
10. disentangle
11. atypical
12. apolitical
13. anomaly
14. asymmetric
15. amnesia
16. amnesty

EXERCISE 3.17

1. unicorn—one horn

2. monoplane—one pair of wings; biplane—two pairs

3. tricycle

4. duel—two people

5. quadruple—four

6. decade—ten years

7. quintuplets—five; sextuplets—six

8. quartet—four; sextet—six

9. decimate—literally, kill one of every ten

10. December—tenth month; September—seventh; October—eighth; November—ninth

11. Pentagon—five sides

12. hexagon—six sides

13. octopus—eight legs

14. centipede—a hundred feet; millipede—a thousand

15. a century and a half (150 years); bicentennial—1976

EXERCISE 3.18

1. polygamy—many spouses

2. bigamy—having two spouses at the same time

3. monogamy

4. atheism

5. monotheism

6. polytheism—many gods

7. Pantheon—all the gods

8. pantheism

9. Trinity—three persons

10. oneness

11. pandemonium—place of all demons

12. all-powerful

13. everywhere, in all places

14. all-knowing

15. millennium—a thousand years

EXERCISE 3.19

1. megaliths
2. megaphone
3. microorganism
4. microcosm;
   macrocosm
5. megalomaniac

EXERCISE 3.20

1. malady—a disease; illness
   malaise—physical discomfort, fatigue, or lack of energy. Malaise may be a symptom of an oncoming illness, but it is not a disease in itself.

2. malice

3. benign—kind, gentle; malicious—spiteful; desirous of injuring another

4. In reference to tumors, benign means "harmless"; malignant means "causing great harm; cancerous."

5. To malign is to slander, spread harmful rumors.

6. malevolent—benevolent

7. formal blessing—benediction; curse—malediction

8. evil-doer—malefactor; person who does good for another—benefactor

9. doing good works; kind—beneficent; doing evil—maleficent

CHAPTER 4: COMBINING PREFIXES AND ROOTS

EXERCISE 4.1

1. c. avert
2. i. adverse
3. f. controversy
4. b. convert
5. e. divert
6. j. extrovert
7. g. introvert
8. a. pervert
9. h. reverse
10. d. revert

EXERCISE 4.2

1. convert
2. perverted
3. reverted
4. converse
5. reverse
6. introvert
7. extrovert
8. controversy
9. adverse
10. diverted
11. diverts
12. avert
13. divert
14. averted

EXERCISE 4.3

1. h. compose
2. g. depose
3. f. deposit
4. j. dispose
5. a. expose
6. c. impose
7. i. oppose
8. d. postpone
9. e. propose
10. b. suppose

EXERCISE 4.4

1. dispose
2. dispose
3. disposed
4. exposed
5. expose
6. expose
7. postpone
8. impose
9. imposed
10. imposed

EXERCISE 4.5

1. dismiss
2. commit
3. transmit
4. remit
5. emit
6. permit
7. submit
8. omit

EXERCISE 4.6

1. commit
2. commit
3. commit
4. transmit
5. transmit
6. submit
7. submit
8. submit
9. omit
10. remit

CHAPTER 5: SUFFIXES

EXERCISE 5.1

1. conversion
2. diversion
3. perversion
4. subversion
5. composition
6. deposition
7. disposition
8. exposition
9. imposition
10. opposition
11. proposition
12. supposition
13. commission
14. emission
15. intermission
16. omission
17. permission
18. remission
19. submission
20. transmission

EXERCISE 5.2

1. g
2. e
3. f
4. b
5. j
6. i
7. a
8. h
9. d
10. c

EXERCISE 5.3

1. a. commission
   b. commitment
2. a. composure
   b. composition
3. a. disposal
   b. disposition
4. a. exposure
   b. exposition
5. a. remission
   b. remittance

EXERCISE 5.4

1. adversary
2. adversity
3. impostor
4. composure
5. component
6. depositions
7. admission
8. admittance
9. disposal
10. disposition
11. exposure
12. exposition
13. transmission
14. remission
15. emission
16. emissary
17. imposition
18. omission
19. conversion
20. proponent
21. opposition
22. diversion
23. commitment
24. commission
25. dismissal

EXERCISE 5.5

1. submissive
2. versatile
3. reversible
4. irreversible
5. intermittent
6. unremitting
7. permissible
8. opposite
9. subversive

EXERCISE 5.6

1. permissively
2. unremittingly
3. intermittently
4. submissively
5. irreversibly

EXERCISE 5.7

1. unremitting
2. advertise
3. intermittent
4. unremittingly
5. reversible
6. submissive
7. versatile
8. irreversibly
9. diversify
10. opposite

CHAPTER 6: LANGUAGE TREES

EXERCISE 6.1

1. retain
2. pertain
3. sustain
4. obtain
5. detain
6. continue
7. abstain
8. maintain

EXERCISE 6.2

1. maintenance
2. sustain
3. tenet
4. abstemious
5. pertinent
6. abstinence
7. retaining
8. tenement
9. tenacity
10. untenable

CHAPTER 7: MAKING AND BREAKING

EXERCISE 7.1

1. facilitate
2. affects
3. effect
4. defect
5. affected
6. infect

EXERCISE 7.2

1. facility(ies)
2. faction
3. defect
4. factotum
5. artifice
6. deification
7. affectation
8. artifacts
9. facsimile
10. effect

EXERCISE 7.3

1. effective
2. efficacious
3. efficient
4. infectious
5. fictitious
6. facile
7. de facto
8. factitious
9. factious

EXERCISE 7.4

1. de facto
2. effective
3. facsimile
4. factotum
5. reification
6. artifice
7. infectious
8. defect
9. faction

EXERCISE 7.5

1. facility
2. factious
3. fictitious
4. efficient
5. effective; efficacious
6. facilitate

EXERCISE 7.6

1. fracture
2. fragment
3. infraction
4. fragile
5. abrupt
6. fraction
7. rupture
8. erupt
9. disrupt
10. corruption

CHAPTER 8: COMING AND GOING

EXERCISE 8.1

1. intervene
2. convene
3. convenient
4. eventful
5. prevent
6. inventive
7. preventive
8. invention
9. advent
10. event
11. revenue

EXERCISE 8.2

1. eventuated
2. venue
3. adventitious
4. supervened
5. covenant
6. conventional
7. circumvent
8. venturesome
9. eventual

EXERCISE 8.3

1. recede
2. succeed
3. successor
4. success
5. secede
6. excess
7. ancestor
8. cede
9. access

EXERCISE 8.4

1. concede
2. accede
3. precedent
4. accession
5. succession
6. predecessor
7. accessory
8. intercession
9. concession
10. successive

EXERCISE 8.5

1. False
2. True
3. True
4. False
5. True
6. True
7. True
8. True
9. False
10. False

CHAPTER 9: MORE WORDS THAT MEAN "GO"

EXERCISE 9.1

1. ingredient
2. aggression
3. digression
4. transgression
5. transgressors
6. aggressors
7. aggressive
8. progress
9. degrading
10. progression

EXERCISE 9.2

1. retrogress
2. gradient
3. gradation
4. ingress
5. egress
6. retrogression
7. degradation

EXERCISE 9.3

1. ingress
2. egress
3. digress
4. degrade
5. transgress
6. regress
7. retrogress
8. progress
9. aggress
10. congress

CHAPTER 10: LEADING AND FOLLOWING

EXERCISE 10.1

1. abduct
2. reduce
3. conduct
4. induce
5. produce
6. educate
7. deduct
8. introduce

EXERCISE 10.2

1. educe
2. seduce
3. adduce
4. deduce
5. traduce
6. seductive
7. inductive
8. deductive
9. counterproductive

EXERCISE 10.3

1. adduced
2. deduced
3. educe
4. conduct
5. abduct
6. reduce
7. deduct
8. seduce
9. induce
10. traduce

EXERCISE 10.4

1. deductive
2. conductive
3. productive
4. counterproductive
5. seductive
6. inductive

EXERCISE 10.5

1. execution
2. obsequious
3. secondary
4. subsequent, prosecution
5. subsequently, consecutive
6. consequent
7. consequence
8. persecution
9. inconsequential
10. obsequy

CHAPTER 11: PUSHING AND PULLING

EXERCISE 11.1

1. ex-
2. dis-
3. com-
4. im-
5. re-
6. pro-

EXERCISE 11.2

1. compulsive
2. impulsive
3. compulsion
4. expulsion
5. propulsive
6. repulsive
7. repulse
8. repulsion
9. propulsion
10. compulsory

EXERCISE 11.3

1. con-
2. re-
3. sub-
4. at-
5. abs-
6. dis-
7. ex-
8. de-
9. pro-
10. in-, -able

CHAPTER 12: MOVING AND SETTLING

EXERCISE 12.1

1. mobilize
2. demobilize
3. mobocracy
4. remote
5. emotive
6. emote

EXERCISE 12.2

1. motion
2. motivated
3. promoted
4. demoted
5. emote
6. mobilize
7. demobilized

EXERCISE 12.3

1. unmoved
2. emotional
3. mobile
4. moving
5. remote
6. emotive

EXERCISE 12.4

1. session
2. possess
3. assess
4. subsided
5. subsidiary
6. subsidize
7. supersede
8. sedate
9. residue
10. sedentary

CHAPTER 13: SEEING, HEARING, TOUCHING

EXERCISE 13.1

1. revision
2. revise
3. Providence
4. advise
5. supervise
6. evidence
7. proviso
8. visitation
9. evidential
10. visionary

EXERCISE 13.2

1. audible
2. audience
3. auditorium
4. audit
5. audio-visual
6. auditive
7. audiometer
8. audient

EXERCISE 13.3

1. tactless
2. intact
3. contact
4. tangible
5. intangible
6. contiguous
7. tactile
8. contingency
9. tangents
10. tangential

CHAPTER 14: LOOKING

EXERCISE 14.1

1. conspicuous
2. despicable
3. prospective
4. respective
5. auspicious
6. suspicious
7. spectacular
8. specious
9. circumspect
10. perspicacious

EXERCISE 14.2

1. specter
2. spectators
3. spectacle
4. suspicions
5. retrospect
6. specimen
7. perspicacity
8. auspices
9. perspective
10. aspect

CHAPTER 15: BEGINNINGS AND ENDINGS

EXERCISE 15.1

1. genial
2. indigenous
3. genuine
4. ingenuous
5. heterogeneous
6. ingenious
7. congenial

EXERCISE 15.2

1. genetics
2. genealogy
3. ingenuity
4. progenitor
5. progeny
6. homogeneous
7. generically
8. degenerate
9. congenital
10. generate

EXERCISE 15.3

1. natural
2. naive
3. native
4. nativity
5. naturalize
6. innate
7. prenatal
8. postnatal
9. neonatal
10. nascent

EXERCISE 15.4

1. confinement
2. refinement
3. finality
4. refinery
5. finally
6. definition
7. definable

EXERCISE 15.5

1. finite
2. final
3. infinitesimal
4. definite
5. indefinite
6. refine
7. refined
8. confine
9. affinity
10. definitive

CHAPTER 16: WORDS ABOUT LIFE

EXERCISE 16.1

1. revive
2. survive
3. devitalize
4. vitalize
5. vivid
6. convivial
7. vital
8. vivacious
9. viviparous
10. biodegradable

EXERCISE 16.2

1. vitality
2. biography
3. antibiotics
4. vivacity
5. biogenesis
6. vivisection
7. antivivisectionist
8. autobiography
9. biology

EXERCISE 16.3

1. g.
2. e.
3. f.
4. a.
5. b.
6. d.
7. c.

EXERCISE 16.4

1. magnanimous
2. pusillanimous
3. spiritualism
4. animosity
5. magnanimity
6. spirituality
7. spirituous
8. aspired
9. aspiration
10. equanimity

CHAPTER 17: WORDS ABOUT FEELINGS

EXERCISE 17.1

1. credulous
2. credentials
3. creed, credo
4. credence
5. discredit
6. creditors
7. credit
8. incredible
9. credible
10. incredulously

EXERCISE 17.2

1. infidel
2. infidelity
3. confident
4. diffident
5. confidential
6. fidelity
7. confidante
8. perfidious
9. perfidy
10. fiducial

EXERCISE 17.3

1. philology
2. bibliophile
3. philatelist
4. philanthropic
5. misanthrope
6. enamor
7. enamored
8. amorous
9. amicable
10. paramour

EXERCISE 17.4

1. T
2. F
3. F
4. T
5. F
6. T
7. T
8. F
9. F
10. F

CHAPTER 18: WORDS ABOUT WORDS

EXERCISE 18.1	**EXERCISE 18.2**	**EXERCISE 18.3**
1. circumlocution	1. evoke	1. scribes
2. soliloquy	2. verbal	2. illiterate
3. somniloquy	3. revoke	3. literate
4. colloquial	4. invoke	4. illiteracy
5. monologue	5. verbatim	5. literature
6. loquacious	6. vociferous	6. literary
7. circumlocution	7. advocate	7. alliteration
8. dialogue	8. vocal	8. literal
9. edict	9. vocation	9. inscribed
10. eulogy	10. verbalize	10. manuscripts

CHAPTER 19: EVERY WORD HAS A HISTORY

EXERCISE 19.1   **EXERCISE 19.2**

1. F
2. T
3. T
4. F
5. F
6. F
7. T
8. F
9. T
10. F

1. maudlin
2. bedlam
3. sadistic
4. boycott
5. chauvinism
6. cavalier;
   supercilious
7. supercilious;
   cavalier
8. vandalism
9. sabotage
10. dexterous

EXERCISE 19.3

1. Modern English—A; Old English—B; Middle English—C

2. Example A: "good-for-nothing"—hilding. Example B: haeleth under heofenum. Example C: "So the last shall be first, and the first last."

3. Woden—Wednesday; Frigga—Friday; Tiu—Tuesday; Thor—Thursday

4. English: A. baby; B. forever; C. shake; D. big; E. sweat; F. glad; G. hire; H. shiny; I. buy

5. *awful*—full of awe; full of wonder and reverence; *conceit*—vanity; an overly high opinion of oneself; *quick*—living persons

6. banana, chili, kayak, canoe, giraffe, kangaroo, telegram, submarine, plutonium, genetics

CHAPTER 20: WORDS FROM MYTHOLOGY

EXERCISE 20.1

1. F
2. F
3. T
4. F
5. T
6. F
7. T
8. F
9. F
10. F

EXERCISE 20.2

1. geometry
2. geology
3. chaos
4. chronology; chronicle
5. chronic
6. anachronism
7. terrestrial
8. extraterrestrial
9. subterranean
10. synchronize

EXERCISE 20.3

1. F
2. T
3. F
4. F
5. T
6. T
7. F
8. T
9. T
10. F

EXERCISE 20.4

1. psychosis
2. psychology
3. psychic
4. psychotic
5. psychiatry
6. narcissistic
7. narcissism
8. court-martial
9. martial law
10. martial

EXERCISE 20.5

1. T
2. F
3. T
4. T
5. F
6. T
7. F
8. T
9. T
10. F

EXERCISE 20.6

1. term
2. amnesia
3. amnesty
4. terminal
5. interminable
6. exterminate
7. terminate
8. fortunate
9. fortuitous

EXERCISE 20.7

1. T
2. T
3. F
4. F
5. T
6. F
7. T
8. T
9. F

EXERCISE 20.8

1. immortal
2. mortal
3. morticians
4. moribund
5. infuriates
6. furor
7. furious
8. aegis
9. fury
10. panic

CHAPTER 21: WORDS FROM ANCIENT PHILOSOPHY

EXERCISE 21.1

1. hedonist; 2. cynic; 3. agnostic; 4. skeptic; 5. stoic; 6. epicure

EXERCISE 21.2

1. stoical; 2. sophomoric; 3. skeptical; 4. cynical; 5. sophisticated;
   6. epicurean; 7. hedonistic 8. cognizant

EXERCISE 21.3

1. F
2. F
3. T
4. T
5. F
6. T
7. F
8. T
9. F
10. F

CHAPTER 22: ON YOUR OWN

EXERCISE 22.1	**EXERCISE 22.2**	**EXERCISE 22.3**
1. d.	1. j.	1. manual
2. f.	2. h.	2. pedal
3. c.	3. i.	3. pediatrician; podiatrist
4. n.	4. k.	4. pedestrian
5. r.	5. l.	5. manicure; pedicure
6. k.	6. m.	6. two; four; tripod
7. o.	7. n.	7. pedestal
8. m.	8. q.	8. manacle
9. e.	9. a.	9. emancipate
10. g.	10. b.	10. expedite

c

EXERCISE 22.4

1. s.
2. w.
3. t.
4. x.
5. v.
6. q.
7. r.
8. u.
9. p.
10. m.

EXERCISE 22.5

1. erect
2. pendant
3. rectangle
4. pendulous
5. director
6. rector
7. appendix
8. rectify
9. rectitude
10. interdependence

EXERCISE 22.6

1. docile
2. doctrine
3. indoctrinate
4. alter ego
5. alien
6. alienate
7. alibi
8. alteration
9. altercation
10. alternate

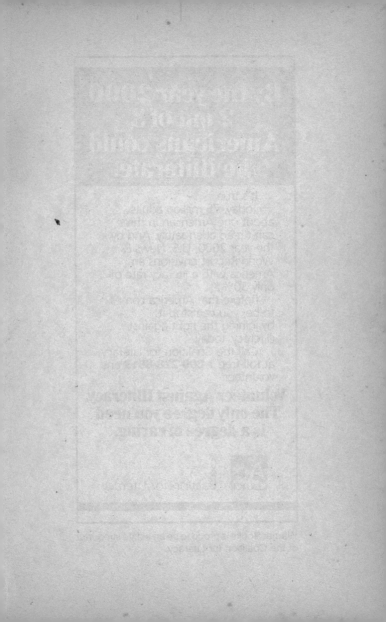

By the year 2000, 2 out of 3 Americans could be illiterate.

It's true.

Today, 75 million adults... about one American in three, can't read adequately. And by the year 2000, U.S. News & World Report envisions an America with a literacy rate of only 30%.

Before that America comes to be, you can stop it... by joining the fight against illiteracy today.

Call the Coalition for Literacy at toll-free **1-800-228-8813** and volunteer.

Volunteer Against Illiteracy. The only degree you need is a degree of caring.

Ad Council Coalition for Literacy

Warner Books is proud to be an active supporter of the Coalition for Literacy.